THE MACMILLAN COMPANY
NEW YORK · BOSTON · CHICAGO · DALLAS
ATLANTA · SAN FRANCISCO

MACMILLAN & CO., Limited
LONDON · BOMBAY · CALCUTTA
MELBOURNE

THE MACMILLAN COMPANY
OF CANADA, Limited
TORONTO

GOVERNOR WINTHROP CUP
London, 1610–11.   H. 11⅝ in.

# HISTORIC SILVER OF THE COLONIES AND ITS MAKERS

By FRANCIS HILL BIGELOW

THE MACMILLAN COMPANY

NEW YORK          PUBLISHERS          MCMXXXI

Norwood Press
J. S. Cushing Co. — Berwick & Smith Co.
Norwood, Mass., U.S.A.

TO

MY BROTHER-IN-LAW

CHARLES HENRY DAVIS, C.E.

IN RECOGNITION OF

HIS UNSELFISH EFFORTS TO ENCOURAGE

"NATIONAL HIGHWAYS"

IN ORDER TO

"BIND THE STATES TOGETHER IN A COMMON
BROTHERHOOD AND THUS PERPETUATE
AND PRESERVE THE UNION"

# ILLUSTRATIONS

## STANDING CUPS

vii

PAGE

## TANKARDS

## FLAGONS

## MUGS

## CANDLESTICKS

## SNUFFERS AND TRAYS

## SCONCES

## CANDLE BRACKETS

## PORRINGERS

## BAPTISMAL BASINS

## DISH CROSSES

## BAPTISMAL BASINS

## SPOONS

## LADLES

## FORKS

## CANDLESTICKS

## SNUFFERS AND TRAYS

## SCONCES

## CANDLE BRACKETS

## PORRINGERS

## CASTERS

## CHAFING DISHES

## DISH CROSSES

## TEAPOTS

## TEA KETTLES

## TEA SERVICES

## TEA URNS

## TEA CADDIES

## STRAINERS

## CHOCOLATE POTS

## COFFEE POTS

## SPOUT CUPS

## TOBACCO BOXES

## SNUFF BOXES

## NUTMEG BOXES

## SUGAR–BOXES BOWLS BASKETS

## SUGAR TONGS

## PITCHERS

## SAUCE BOATS

## PUNCH BOWLS

## JEWISH SYNAGOGUE SILVER

# BIBLIOGRAPHY

BUCK, J. H.   Old Plate.

BURLINGTON MAGAZINE, The   Various numbers.

BURNS, THOMAS   Old Scottish Communion Plate.

CHAFFERS, W.   Hall-marks on Gold and Silver Plate.

CONNOISSEUR, The   Various numbers.

CRIPPS, W. J.   Old English Plate.   Old French Plate.

CURTIS, GEORGE MUNSON   Early Silver of Connecticut and its Makers.

DAWSON, NELSON   Goldsmiths' and Silversmiths' Work.

ENCYCLOPÆDIA BRITANNICA   "Plate." (Comprehensive bibliography.)

FRENCH, HOLLIS   A List of Early American Silversmiths and their Marks.

GARDNER, JOHN STARKIE   Old Silver-Work, Chiefly English, from XVth to XVIIIth Centuries.

HUDSON-FULTON CELEBRATION   Catalogue of an Exhibition Held in the Metropolitan Museum of Art, 1909.

JACKSON, C. J.   History of English Plate.   English Goldsmiths and their Marks.

JAMESTOWN TER-CENTENNIAL EXPOSITION   Catalogue of the Massachusetts Colonial Loan Exhibit, 1907.

JONES, E. ALFRED   The Old Silver of American Churches. The Gold and Silver of Windsor Castle.   The Old English Plate of the Emperor of Russia.   The Old

Royal Plate in the Tower of London. The Old Plate of the Cambridge Colleges. Illustrated Catalogue of Mr. J. Pierpont Morgan's Collection of Plate. Also other works.

Metropolitan Museum of Art, New York   Catalogue of the Avery Collection of Spoons, 1909. Catalogue of Silver used in New York New Jersey and the South, 1911. Various Bulletins.

Museum of Fine Arts, Boston   American Silver, 1906. American Church Silver, 1911. Various Bulletins.

Pennsylvania Museum, Philadelphia   Various Bulletins.

ROSENBERG, M. Der Goldschmiede Merkzeichen.

WOOLSEY, THEODORE S. Old Silver.

Worcester Art Museum, Worcester   Exhibition of Old Silver Owned in Worcester County, 1913.

# HISTORIC SILVER OF THE COLONIES

# CHRONOLOGY

Reformation . . . . about 1540–1610
Elizabeth . . . . . . 1558–1603
James I . . . . . . 1603–1625
Charles I . . . . . . 1625–1649
Commonwealth . . . . . 1649–1660
Charles II . . . . . . 1660–1685
James II . . . . . . 1685–1689
William and Mary . . . . 1689–1694
William III . . . . . . 1694–1702
Anne . . . . . . . 1702–1714
George I . . . . . . 1714–1727
George II . . . . . . 1727–1760
George III . . . . . . 1760–1820

Louis XIV . . . . . . 1643–1715
Louis XV . . . . . . 1715–1774
Louis XVI . . . . . . 1774–1792

# Historic Silver of the Colonies

## FOREWORD

HAVING had so large a share in the making of "The Old Silver of American Churches" I feel somewhat justified in bringing out this smaller book in order to place before a larger number of readers some of the information imparted in Mr. E. Alfred Jones's masterful introduction to that volume and to illustrate and describe specifically some of the many important examples belonging to the churches, which he characterizes as "little monuments of American history." It also gives me the opportunity to include much of the silver designed for purely domestic purposes — many notable specimens discovered by me in the past ten years in private hands; and to add brief historical accounts of the craftsmen who made the vessels of both classes, as well as of the donors or original owners. Many of these bear the names or initials of men famous as governors and soldiers, Puritan leaders and prosperous merchants, leading citizens and eminent divines.

Rutgers College has conferred upon Mr. Jones the degree of Master of Arts, in appreciation of his valuable services in compiling an authentic catalogue of the early silver in the churches of the Colonies and in so ably describing the various vessels.

To my friend Mr. R. T. Haines Halsey must be accorded the credit of having inspired me to form the collection of American silver for the Museum of Fine Arts at Boston in 1906; and to his generosity is due the publication of the catalogue of that exhibition, which is one of the handsomest ever issued by any museum. His attributions to the silversmiths of the marks on these pieces has been invaluable in stimulating other investigations. Mr. Halsey characterizes it as "the finest exhibition of early plate, American or European, yet held in this country. To Americans it has a far deeper interest in that it represents the artistic conception and craftsmanship of the fathers by whose energy our country was developed and our Republic founded."

The news of this exhibition reached London and induced Mr. Jones, who had made a profound study of English and Continental plate, to come to Boston to see what the American craftsmen had produced. His high praise and great interest in the subject led me to begin a systematic search among the churches of Massachusetts, while my friend the late Mr. George M. Curtis of Meriden, Connecticut, undertook a similar search in that state. A wealth of communion silver little dreamed of was revealed. Many of the churches never realized that their pieces were of silver or of any great value. While some was in bank vaults, most of it was carelessly kept in wooden houses; and it is to be regretted that much of value has been destroyed by fire for lack of proper protection.

A very great deal of communion silver is not now in use. The Museum of Fine Arts at Boston having generously offered to store such relics, with the privilege of exhibiting them from time to time, many of the churches have wisely availed of this offer, as it insures safety; and some have presented their silver outright to the museum so that its preservation may be assured for future generations. By those who value church silver for its association, if for no other reason, some such precautions should be taken in order to prevent its future sale by those who may have no sentiment regarding it. The Museum will gladly lend to the churches from which derived, for special occasions, gifts so made.

A second exhibition of over eleven hundred pieces of silver from the New England churches, held at the Museum of Fine Arts in 1911, was the result of this research. To the catalogue of this collection Mr. Curtis contributed a most interesting introduction on the Connecticut silversmiths. His volume on "Early Silver of Connecticut and its Makers" is a valuable addition to the history of American silver.

I wish here to pay tribute to his warm friend-
ship, which is a pleasant memory.  His keen
interest in the pursuit of knowledge regarding
the silversmiths, not only of Connecticut but
of New England, has been most helpful and
inspiring to other investigators.

The necessity of permanently recording the
church silver of the Colonies seemed to me of
paramount importance; and Mr. Jones's offer
to do this gratuitously led the Colonial Dames
to get together the church silver in other states.

To Mrs. Elihu Chauncey, as chairman of
the Silver Committee of the Colonial Dames of
New York, is due the credit of the successful
exhibition held at the Metropolitan Museum
of Art at New York, also in 1911.  The labor of
gathering not only the church silver of that
state, but also much from states south of New
York, was an undertaking which merits the
highest praise.  To the catalogue of this exhibition Mr. Halsey contributed a valuable fore-
word on the New York silversmiths, which has
been freely quoted by me.

To the Colonial Dames of the other states
are due thanks for their efforts to locate the
church silver in order that the work might be
made complete.

To Mrs. Barrett Wendell, president of the
Massachusetts Society of the Colonial Dames,
cannot be accorded too high praise for her
efforts in carrying to a successful conclusion
the publication of the handsome volume com-

piled by Mr. Jones. Her kind permission to make use of the material in that book was readily granted and is greatly appreciated.

To my friend Mr. E. Alfred Jones of London I am under deep obligation for the very great privilege of making free use of the text of "The Old Silver of American Churches" as well as of his numerous and valuable publications on English plate; so I have availed myself to the fullest extent of this permission, and I have not changed his wording in my text.

To Mr. Charles James Jackson, F.S.A., etc., of London, I am equally indebted for his kind consent to make use of his important work entitled "History of English Plate." In tracing the development of the more purely domestic silver this has been of inestimable value to me.

To Miss Florence V. Paull of the Museum of Fine Arts I cannot adequately express my thanks. Her deep interest in the subject of American silver and her coöperation, alone made possible the exhibitions in 1906 and 1911. Her constant willingness to render assistance has encouraged me to undertake the writing of this book.

The photographs of the New England church silver used in the illustrations were taken under my supervision for "The Old Silver of American Churches" by my friend the late Mr. William Stone of Boston. Those of New York and the South were largely furnished by the Metropolitan Museum of Art,

New York; that these were supplied gratui-
tously for "The Old Silver of American
Churches" was not known until after the pub-
lication of that volume, which accounts for Mr.
Jones's failure to acknowledge the obligation.
To the museum and particularly to my friend
Mr. H. W. Kent I am indebted for other illus-
trations and much information.

To my friend the late Dr. Edwin A. Barber
of the Pennsylvania Museum of Philadelphia
I desire to record my thanks for photographs
supplied by that museum.

Many of the photographs used to illustrate
the purely domestic pieces in this volume have
been taken, under my supervision, by Mr.
Ralph C. Smith of Boston; some of these are
intended for Mr. E. Alfred Jones's volume "Old
American Domestic Silver" which will be issued
at a future date.

To the Museum of Fine Arts, Boston, I
wish to express my appreciation of their cour-
tesy in receiving the domestic silver on deposit
and in allowing me to have the photographs made
there.

To my many friends and acquaintances who
have allowed me to examine their silver and
to use pieces for illustration I am much indebted.

To the late Mr. John H. Buck of New York
acknowledgment is due for his pioneer work
in compiling, as early as 1888, a volume entitled "Old Plate," published by the Gorham

Manufacturing Company, which contains a vast accumulation of knowledge regarding American church silver.

Also to my friend Dr. Theodore S. Woolsey of New Haven should be accorded mention for his article "Old Silver" contributed to *Harper's Magazine* and reprinted in 1896 in pamphlet form by John Wells esquire, of New York.

I am also indebted for much information to the works of Samuel Adams Drake, Savage's "Genealogical Dictionary" and Francis S. Drake's "Dictionary of American Biography."

The late Mr. John Ware Willard deserves recognition for much historical and genealogical data on the Massachusetts silversmiths — a labor undertaken for my special benefit.

To my friend the late Mr. Theodore F. Dwight of Boston for his aid in revising and for many helpful suggestions I am sincerely grateful.

FRANCIS HILL BIGELOW.

Cambridge, Massachusetts,
No. 4 Channing Street,
May 4, 1917.

# INTRODUCTION

THE scope of this work must necessarily be very limited, as the subject is almost inexhaustible, and for a comprehensive study of English plate the reader is referred particularly to the various important works of Mr. E. Alfred Jones and of Mr. Charles James Jackson, in which may be seen prototypes of the Colonial examples. In the bibliography are other works which will be found valuable to the interested reader. A more complete list will be found in the last edition of the "Encyclopædia Britannica" under the article "Plate" written by Mr. Jones.

"Plate" is the word most generally used in England and on the Continent when referring to articles made of the precious metals; and during the first hundred years or more in the Colonies "plate" was naturally used in wills and inventories. Some confusion seems to exist in our country regarding the word "plate," which perhaps arose from the invention of "Sheffield plate." About the middle of the eighteenth century it was discovered in Sheffield, England, that a very thin plate of silver, laid either side of a heavier plate of copper, could be fused. By pressure between rollers the combination was so strengthened and hardened that it could be wrought as solid silver was wrought. Much genuine old Sheffield plate is now in existence in our country, and it is often difficult to decide, upon a casual examination, whether it is silver or plated. Usually the rims, the edges of the bases, or the bottoms of the feet show traces of the copper where the silver has been rubbed off by constant cleaning or wear. Sheffield plate was produced to a considerable extent in New England, but undoubtedly a great deal was imported from England.

The word "silver" therefore has come to be commonly used in our country; and the museums in general have sanctioned such use of the word. The customary term applied in England to the craftsman who worked in the precious metals was "goldsmith"; and in our country for a century or more the same designation was used. By the middle of the eighteenth century "silversmith" was used to some extent, and it is now invariably applied in the United States to workers in the white metal.

Dr. Theodore S. Woolsey in his article on the subject says: "Old silver has a color, a touch, a feeling, peculiar to itself. The genuineness of a piece must be determined by a study of these points, as well as of the style, the marks of wear, and the history. It is only by the examination, the handling if possible, of a large number of specimens that one can gain accurate knowledge of these qualities."

The silver which first came to the Colonies was naturally of English workmanship; and many of these vessels were copied by the silver-smiths who came to New England in the early days of its settlement. The first of whom we have knowledge was John Mansfield (1601–74) who came to Boston from London in 1634; Robert Sanderson (1608–93) came to Hampton in 1638, and his daughter Lydia is said to have been the first white child baptized there; he had practised his trade in England and settled at Boston in 1652, becoming the partner of John Hull (1624–83) who had come to Boston in 1635 but who learned his trade in New England.

The American silversmiths not only pursued their craft with success but were also prominent citizens and discharged many public duties. Just as the silversmiths in the Old World were versed in the other crafts so too were the silver-smiths in the Colonies. Many were notable engravers of prints, book-plates and paper money; others seem to have discontinued their craft and become merchants of distinction; a number of the Boston silversmiths were members of the Ancient and Honorable Ar-tillery Company. There were silversmiths who settled in Virginia as early as 1608, but for the purpose of discovering gold and not to practise their craft, as related by Captain John Smith.

Mr. R. T. Haines Halsey, in his introduction to the catalogue of "American Silver," Museum

of Fine Arts, Boston, 1906, pays tribute to the
ability and craftsmanship of these men thus:
"The silver is of the period when the ancient
geometrical shapes held sway among craftsmen:
when purity of form, sense of proportion and
perfection of line were preferred to elaborateness of design; when dignity and solidity were
considered superior to bulk, and when the beautiful white metal was allowed to take its colors
from its surroundings rather than be made the
medium for the display of skill by workers in
metal. The early American silver, as in the
case of our early architecture and furniture, is
thoroughly characteristic of the taste and life
of the period in America. Simple in design
and substantial in weight, it reflects the classic
mental attitude of the people. Social condi-
tions here warranted no attempt to imitate the
magnificent baronial silver made in England,
illustrations of which are to be found in all
English books on plate."

Much English silver came to the Colonies
as gifts, or to fill orders sent from our country.
It should be borne in mind that there were many
merchants in New England as well as in Virginia whose principal trade was with the mother
country, and it was but natural to order goods
in return for those sent. Furthermore many
persons in those days were pro-English as they
are to-day, and undoubtedly preferred the imported article to anything that could be made
in the Colonies. Unfortunately this preference

has been prevalent since the settlement of the country, and doubtless if the opportunity offered to purchase as cheaply and conveniently, most persons would have been prone to secure the English article. For art lovers it is fortunate that the people as a whole were obliged to patronize home talent, otherwise we should not now possess the examples of silver, furniture, glass, miniatures and portraits which are just beginning to be appreciated by our museums and collectors.

Neither must it be forgotten that much silver made by the Colonial craftsmen has gone to England : some as gifts, but doubtless the larger part was taken by the two thousand loyalists when they left the country at the time of the Revolution. The silver of King's Chapel in Boston was carried off by Dr. Henry Caner, the last royalist rector of this church. To be sure this was largely the work of English goldsmiths and the gifts of the English sovereigns, William and Mary, George II and George III ; but doubtless there were also amongst it pieces made by the Colonial silversmiths. The pieces known to have been taken by Dr. Caner consisted of "six flagons, six cups, four large basins, six dishes, two christening basins, six salvers and four tankards, etc." As the estimated weight of the silver carried off was 2800 ounces, the pieces enumerated could have accounted for only half this weight! Of what the "etc." consisted we shall never know. In the records

of King's Chapel in June, 1695, is this item:
"pd Cross for makeing 2 p$^s$ plate £3.0.0";
he was without doubt a Colonial silversmith.

The destruction in Europe of vast quantities
of priceless silver vessels of the earliest times,
on account of the intrinsic value of the metal,
was mostly for conversion into money in times
of war. At the Reformation the destruction
of ecclesiastical vessels of great historic and
artistic value was due to excessive Protestant
zeal. But in England, in the eighteenth and
nineteenth centuries, the remodelling of older
plate, domestic as well as ecclesiastical, was
incredibly large. As each new fashion was
introduced in domestic plate the cost was largely
met by melting and transforming older vessels.
It would be impossible to picture the havoc
wrought by this unhappy custom to mediæval,
Tudor, Elizabethan and Stuart plate, in the
eighteenth century. In a lesser degree the
same unfortunate custom prevailed in the Colonies, especially as to church vessels. A long
list could be compiled of old silver which has
been destroyed to make way for new vessels
of a more "convenient" form or of a newer
fashion.

The loss of many early vessels listed as belonging to the Second Church, Boston, in 1730
is to be deplored and leads one to infer that the
loss sustained by other early churches may
have been as great. Much to be regretted is
the disappearance from this list of four cups

given in 1620, 1624, 1639 and 1680; three
bowls in 1675, 1680 and 1681; and a flagon
given by Sir William Phips in 1689. In any
case they must have been of great interest;
but if made by Colonial silversmiths they would
have added very materially to the relics of
New England art of the seventeenth century.
The temperance agitation of the nineteenth
century "brought cups and tankards into dis-
repute; silver forks became the fashion and the
housewife seizing the opportunity turned the
one into the other — a conversion afterwards
bitterly regretted." (T. S. W.)

France at two periods of her history suffered
almost more grievous losses in domestic plate
than any other country. First, towards the
close of the reign of Louis XIV, when the royal
treasure was converted into coin to meet the
financial embarrassments of the king, caused by
his personal extravagance and by the wars
against the Netherlands and England. Again,
at the time of the Revolution, the magnificent
services and ornaments of silver, wrought only
a few years before for the royal palaces of Louis
XV and Louis XVI by the noted silversmiths of
the times, were ruthlessly destroyed. The finest
examples of French plate of the eighteenth
century are in the royal collections of the Emperor of Russia and of the kings of Portugal.

It is quite an easy matter to determine the
age of any piece of English silver, as the custom prevailed after 1478 of using a date-letter

to represent the year when made; to prevent confusion, different types of letters were substituted every twenty years, on the 29th May. Each article also bore the stamp of the silversmith, usually his initials in some device: Britannia or the lion passant denoting nationality; the leopard's head showing the approval of the London goldsmith companies authorized to pass on the quality; and, after 1784, the sovereign's head. If the silver was not up to the required standard, the articles were liable to forfeiture; when silver was brought by the owner to be remade into other vessels the goldsmith escaped the obligation of having them assayed and hall-marked, as there was no penalty. Consequently some genuine English plate is without hall-marks.

Other cities had, instead of the leopard's head, some other device. Mr. Charles J. Jackson's "English Goldsmiths and their Marks," by which the marks in this book have been identified, is the only complete work of the kind.

In our country it is only possible to give an approximate date to a piece of silver; and the guiding factors must be the working period of the silversmith, the form of the vessel, and perhaps the date of gift. In the early days the arrival of a "new fashion" in England, while probably adopted in New England in due course, did not apparently deter the silversmiths from continuing to supply the older and perhaps

better design and one which may have been
more pleasing to their customers. The length
of time that intervened between the rise of a
fashion in England and its adoption in New
England is impossible to tell : in some cases it
may have so happened that it was almost contemporary ; while in others doubtless some years
elapsed, perhaps ten or even twenty, before the
new fashion was copied to any extent in our
country.

The disinclination to adopt the newer fashions
is especially noticeable in the churches when
additional pieces were required. While there
was little uniformity in the vessels which they
received by gift, when ordering new silver the
preference always seemed to be to reproduce
some piece the church already possessed. A
notable instance is that of the old Barnstable
Church, which before the separation into the
East and West parishes in 1719 possessed several
of the early flat-bottomed beakers made by
Edward Winslow (1669–1753) and by his
nephew Moody Russell (1694–1761). A divi-
sion of the silver was made; and as late as
April 8, 1815, an exact copy of these beakers
was made for the East Parish by Jesse Churchill (1773–1819). Fortunately, in this case the
church records would have furnished the proof
had the maker's mark been missing; never-
theless this shows the difficulty that may be
met in determining the date from the form
alone.

Reference is constantly made to a Colonial silversmith becoming a "freeman" at a certain date. "Before a member of society could exercise the right of suffrage or hold any public office he must be made a freeman by the general or quarterly court. To become such he was required to produce evidence that he was a respectable member of some Congregational church. 'This regulation was so far modified by Royal order in 1664 as to allow individuals to be made freemen who could obtain certificates of their being correct in doctrine and conduct from clergymen acquainted with them.' In 1631 a test was invented which required all freemen to be church members. This was upon the first appearance of a dissent in regard to religious opinions. But even this test, in the public opinion, required great caution, as in 1632 it was agreed that a civil magistrate should not be an elder of the church." — New England Historical and Genealogical Register, Vol. III.

The most complete list of the American silversmiths yet published is that in the catalogue of "American Church Silver," Museum of Fine Arts, Boston, 1911; the dates of the birth and death of many silversmiths are there noted.

The makers' marks on Colonial silver of the seventeenth and eighteenth centuries is an interesting study. The earliest adopted naturally followed the contemporary English custom

c

consisting of initials enclosed in a device, like the following:

In the first quarter of the eighteenth century some silversmiths placed a crown above their initials — perhaps to make it appear that they had enjoyed royal patronage — and a device below, all being enclosed in a shaped shield; John Coney placed below his initials a coney, as a rebus on his name. With the prosperity of the Colonies came an ever increasing number of silversmiths; and probably, largely as an advertisement, many adopted the fashion of using a stamp with the surname often preceded by the initial of the Christian name which was usually enclosed in a plain rectangle or in one of irregular outline: at the same time a stamp with initials only was often used for articles like teaspoons, too small for the larger stamp; both are frequently found on the larger pieces:

It was not customary to use separate devices in conjunction with the makers' stamps, but Cesar Ghiselin of Philadelphia, who died in 1733, stamped a star either side of his initials. Early in the nineteenth century some of the silversmiths, chiefly in New York and vicinity, added marks

resembling those of the assay office in Birmingham, England, which would appear to
have been done with the intention of making their wares pass for English.
These stamps depressed the surface of the silver, leaving the
letters raised. They were, as a rule, placed to
the left of the handle near the lip or on the
bottom of the piece and sometimes in both
places on the same piece; but there are, of
course, exceptions. In the last quarter of
the eighteenth century some of the silversmiths
adopted a stamp which left the impression
incised : **MOULTON**
It must not be inferred, however, that any
particular form of mark can be fixed as of any
specific date; some silversmiths appear never
to have had but one form of mark, while their
contemporaries may have had several different
devices.

To attribute the marks, consisting of initials
only, is a comparatively easy matter for the
seventeenth century, as there were few silversmiths with the same initials ; and these attributions have been made with satisfactory ac-
curacy. But in the early eighteenth century
the difficulty begins and vastly increases, after
the middle of the century, with the growing
number of silversmiths. The positive proof
of identification is where these initials are
found in conjunction with the full name. The
mark, IN with a cross below in a shield, for

John Noyes (1674–1749), on the flagon in
the Brattle Street Church, Boston, seems to
need no further proof, as he was a member
of that church and would have been likely
to be commissioned to make it; and the same
initials in an oval, on a set of six beakers in
the Congregational Church, Newbury, Massachusetts, may be safely attributed to John
Noyes, for his grandfather the Rev. James
Noyes was the pastor of the church when
the beakers were ordered. Another instance
where sufficient proof exists is the mark IG
crowned, with a fleur-de-lis below, in a shield
for Joseph Goldthwaite (1706–80), on the
two-handled beakers in the Second Church,
Boston, and in the First Church, Lynnfield,
Massachusetts, as he was connected by marriage with both of the donors. The initials,
SG in a rectangle, attributed to Samuel Gilbert who advertised in 1798 at Hebron in
Connecticut, is undoubtedly correct, for considerable silver with these initials was found
among the old families of that town by Mr.
Curtis. Where sets of spoons are in the same
family the stamp with initials on the small
spoons will usually be found to correspond to
the full name on the large ones. This appears
to be another satisfactory proof of identity.
These instances show the necessity of using
great care in the attributions of initials, as
some proof—other than simply fitting the initials
to the name of a silversmith which corresponds

— is certainly required to convince the seeker
after truth.

A very important factor in determining the
maker, when other proofs are lacking, must
necessarily be the locality in which the original
owners lived. This is particularly difficult to
ascertain when once these pieces have passed
out of the family into hands not interested in
the identification of the marks. Doubtless
much silver still remains in the possession of
the descendants of the original owners, and it
is hoped that they will see fit to take these
heirlooms, for identification, to some of the
museums in the country now interested in this
subject.

Reproduced in "The Old Silver of American
Churches" will be found facsimiles of the marks
of those American silversmiths whose craftsmanship is represented in that important volume. Most of these marks were furnished by
my friend Mr. Hollis French of Boston, who
has in preparation a small volume containing
additional identifications with facsimiles of
marks, which will be issued under the auspices
of the Walpole Society.

One should not be too credulous in ac-
cepting every piece of silver as American which
is stamped with initials in a rectangle, a form
so generally used in the eighteenth century,
unless these initials can be identified. Many
Dutch and Irish pieces are marked much like
the American. Spurious marks are also being

put upon old unmarked pieces by unscrupulous
vendors ; and even modern pieces made of inferior metal have appeared with forged marks
which may easily deceive the unknowing.
Pieces of silver, so English in design as to deceive no one, appear from time to time with
all the marks erased except the stamp of the
maker. Some English hall-marked silver also
bears the stamp of the Colonial silversmith
through whose hands the pieces passed, like
the English candlestick of 1741–42 with the
mark of Thomas Dane (1724–96) of Boston.
The erasure of the English marks is not difficult
and judgment must be exercised in distinguishing between English and Colonial designs.

The Colonists followed the English custom
in placing upon silver their initials to denote
ownership. RH, in block letters, on the standing cup in the First Church, Boston, was for
Robert Hull. Where the piece was jointly
owned by husband and wife it was customary
to place the first letter of the surname above
the first letters of the Christian names of husband and wife, as $\frac{H}{A\ E}$ for Atherton and Elizabeth
Hough, on the standing cup in the First Church,
Boston. Towards the end of the eighteenth
century the marking was in script, with the
initials entwined, in the same order. These
would then appear *AEH* and both styles
should be mentioned in this order. At this later
time, however, it was not uncommon to have a

middle name, and the three initials may be those of an individual and not of husband and wife.

This marking is by no means infallible however. Jonathan Merritt by his will dated June 19, 1738, left a legacy to the church at Scituate, Massachusetts, to purchase a cup to be marked $\frac{S}{I\ M}$: the S for Scituate and the IM for Jonathan Merritt. In Christ Church, Philadelphia, a beaker presented to John Kearsley by that church was probably originally marked IK for John Kearsley. His wife was named Margaret, and the beaker which was presented by her, after her husband's death, to the same church is marked $\frac{M}{I\ K}$. The letter M may have been added during his life in order that his wife might share in its ownership, or she may have had this letter added before presenting it.

The initials $\frac{T}{B\ C}$ are on five vessels in the First Church, Boston: the English standing cup of 1626–27 given by Atherton Hough; the English cup of 1639–40 given by Jeremy Houchin; the cup made by Sanderson and Hull, given by Thomas Clarke junior; and on the two beakers, with granulated bands, made by Sanderson and Hull, which are dated 1659 and were probably purchased by the church. It is incredible to conceive of any common ancestor who could have owned these five vessels, and the initials

are without doubt for "The Boston Church,"
which was ordinarily the designation applied
to this — the earliest church at Boston. This
theory is further borne out by the fact that the
First Church possesses three tall beakers and
a pair of spoons, made early in the eighteenth
century by John Edwards (1670–1746), marked
$\frac{T}{O\ C}$ doubtless for "The Old Church," the name
by which the church is designated in the will
of James Everell, dated December 11, 1682,
and by which it was commonly distinguished
after the founding of the Second and Old South
churches.

While the original initials on early silver
should always be identified when possible, as
the date of marriage is an important clew to
the date of the piece, still it does not always
furnish conclusive proof; but usually it may be
relied upon. The two examples made by
Timothy Dwight (1654–91) of Boston bear the
initials of a later generation than that to which
these pieces originally belonged, and the probability is that they were not marked with other
initials when made. An instance of their initials
being placed on silver after the death of both
husband and wife may be noted on the pair of
beakers made by Sanderson and Hull which
bear the initials of Thomas and Alice Lake; in
his will dated October 25, 1678, Thomas Lake
directs "£5 to be laid out in plate with mine and
my wife's name engraved thereon" and given to

the First Church, Dorchester.    In the First
Church of Christ at New Haven a caudle cup
bears the initials $\frac{R}{H\ S}$ for Henry and Sarah Ruther-
ford who died respectively in 1668 and 1674.  The
cup was made by John Dixwell, who was not born
until 1680 and doubtless did not make it before
1705.  The probability is that their daughter
Mary Prout, who bequeathed it to the church
in 1724, had the cup made from earlier silver
belonging to her parents and wished to perpetuate their memory by marking it with their
initials.  But these exceptions only prove the
rule, and it is to the church silver and the pro-
bate court records that we are indebted for
the discovery of such discrepancies ; it seems
quite safe to rely upon the marking in most cases.
    Neither can the dates found on early silver
be relied upon with impunity.  A noticeable
instance is the date 1654 upon two tankards
made by John Coney belonging to the First
Parish (Unitarian) at Cambridge.    William
Wilcocks died in 1654 leaving lands to that
church upon the death of his wife, which did
not come into its possession until many years
later.  The church records show that it was
not until March 1705 that the sale of these
lands was authorized by the church, and that
the tankards were bought June 7, 1705, for the
sum of £22.8.2.  Of course 1654 was a perfectly proper date to put on the tankards inas-
much as the gift was made in that year.

It is unfortunate that many owners of old silver think it necessary to have dates added to their heirlooms without first ascertaining when the silversmith could have made them. Reference is made to this vagary because so many instances have been noted when the date and recent inscriptions (even in the churches) show such glaring discrepancies. Perhaps one of the most flagrant inconsistencies is shown in the marking of a tankard which belongs to Harvard University. It was made by Ephraim Cobb (1708–75) of Plymouth, Massachusetts, a descendant of Henry Cobb, an early settler of Barnstable; he was undoubtedly apprenticed to Moody Russell (1694–1761) of Barnstable; his wife was Margaret Gardner of Yarmouth. Upon the end of the handle is a Queen Anne shilling struck at the Edinburgh mint in 1707–08 : the date 1638 has been engraved, probably by the donor's instructions, upon the handle; and below it, in succession, are the initials
E   E   M   M
HD  ID  HD  ID.   Further, it seems incredible that four generations of males should have had wives whose Christian names began with the letter D. In all probability the D is intended for the surname ; while no record exists as to the donor, the initials are thought to be those of the Dunster family.

Genealogists should find a new field in our ancestral silver when pursuing their investigations for missing ancestors. Rev. Theophilus

Cotton bequeathed in 1726 a beaker to the church at Hampton Falls, New Hampshire. He married in 1708 Elizabeth Elliott of Marblehead, widow of Andrew Diamond a prosperous merchant of Ipswich in Massachusetts, after whom the "Diamond Stage," a well-known wharf at the mouth of the Ipswich River, was named. The beaker came into the possession of Theophilus Cotton upon the death of his wife in 1710; that it had belonged to Andrew Diamond and a former wife is proved by the initials $\begin{smallmatrix} & D & \\ A & & I \end{smallmatrix}$. Who was she? As he was born in 1641 it is only reasonable to suppose that he had been married prior to 1705, the date of his marriage to Elizabeth (Elliott) Diamond. Many clews may be found in the initials on vessels described in "The Old Silver of American Churches."

The Colonists in having silver engraved with their arms followed a custom comparatively common in the mother country in the seventeenth century, which affords a further interesting clew in proving many marriages. The baptismal basin in the Old South Church at Boston given by Madam Mary Saltonstall, who had formerly been the wife of William Clarke, is engraved with the Clarke arms. The same arms are engraved upon a tankard given to the North Church, Salem, Massachusetts, by Mrs. Elizabeth Cabot in 1784. She was the daughter of William Clarke,

nephew of William Clarke the former owner of
the basin and tankard. The nephew inherited
the tankard from his uncle; and at his death it
passed to his daughter Elizabeth who married
Francis Cabot.

The arms engraved upon the Richard Sprague
tankard in the Charlestown Church are those
of Chester, proving the marriage of Richard
Sprague to the daughter of Leonard Chester.
A tankard given to the First Church, Dorchester, by Hopestill Clap is engraved with
the arms of Rogers, which confirms the marriage of his maternal grandmother to Captain
Rogers. The flagon given by Rev. William
Welsteed to the Second Church at Boston, is
engraved with the arms of Steer. Many apparent inconsistencies are noted in "The Old
Silver of American Churches," where all these
arms have been reproduced; doubtless there
was some family relationship which justified
the use of the arms.

A few words of warning should be given to
the owners of old family silver. Never take it
to a jeweller to be cleaned without explicit
instructions not to "buff" it. These male-
factors — for such they are — have no regard
for the beautiful blue color that only comes
with age; and by buffing rare old pieces they
are practically ruined by the removal of the
surface and the obliteration of the makers'
marks which destroys the commercial value
at least one half. But they do succeed won-

derfully in their ambition of making them look like tin! Silver that has been badly tarnished can be cleaned by one or two applications of some polish such as is used for harsher metals (such as brass or copper) which will, with a little patience, remove the worst of the discoloration; afterwards a silver polish should be used. Camphor put with silver when packed away will prevent tarnish, but care should be taken to procure tissue-paper wrapping which contains no sulphur; rubber bands also contain sulphur and should never be used.

The height noted below the illustrations is that of the body of the vessel including the finial; but it does not take into account the thumb-piece, or the handle which often projects above the body.

The order of insertion of the illustrations is not particularly satisfactory; it was hoped that the English prototype might be shown with every Colonial example, but this was soon found to be an impossibility, as such apparently do not exist even in England; and if by chance they exist in our country, to find them would be hopeless. Many of the English types shown are considerably later in date than the Colonial; and, with the great difficulty of placing even an approximate date on the latter, any attempt at chronological order as to the period when wrought has been abandoned. It is hoped, however, that the illustrations will convey an idea of the sequence of the various types that prevailed at different periods, even if the Colonial examples were not made within that period. This work has been extended beyond the Colonial period up to the beginning of the nineteenth century, after which date little worthy of mention was produced by the silversmiths.

Blacksmiths often wrought the white metal quite as skilfully as those who had been apprenticed to the craft. John Bridge, a blacksmith, made the flagon given to the New North Church, Boston, by Mrs. Mary Hunnewell; also that given to the Second Church by Rev. William Welsteed. That their competition was most objectionable to the silversmiths of Waterbury and Farmington appears in an article in the *Connecticut Courant* of August 31, 1767, which ends : "it is to be wished that the Legislative Body would pass an act that no man should set himself up at any trade without having served a regular Apprenticeship of seven years, and have a Certificate from his master. Then we should not see every Blacksmith and Tinker turn Goldsmith." (G. M. C.)

# STANDING CUPS

THE earliest English communion vessels in the Boston churches and in a few other early New England churches were not originally designed for such purposes, but in many cases, if not in all, had been previously in domestic use. It is probable that the owners of these cups were in the habit of taking them to the churches for use in the communion service and that gradually they came to be looked upon with veneration and as something sacred. "By gift or bequest they came straight from secular to sacramental use — from the table of the giver to the table of the Lord." (T. S. W.)

This hypothesis would seem to be borne out by the will of Hezekiah Usher, dated May 11, 1676, in which he leaves to the Old South Church "1 peece of plate commonly called a Church Cup." Some of these cups were doubtless given during the lives of the donors; but unfortunately the church records as a rule have been very carelessly kept, so that no proof is now available.

The Governor Winthrop cup, shown as the frontispiece, is as characteristically English as the contemporary pineapple cup (*Ananaspokal*) is German. It doubtless had a cover sur-

mounted by an obelisk, called a steeple, which
was derived from Elizabethan and Jacobean
architecture.   These steeples are perforated or
solid ; when solid they are plain or engraved with
chevrons and plain lines.   Many of them are
surmounted with figures of warriors, usually in
classical dress.   The embossed or engraved decoration on these cups usually consists of acanthus
foliage and large fruit, roses and scrolls, plain
strap-work, trefoils, scallops and fleurs-de-lis,
bunches of grapes, pears, tulips and flutings, and
more rarely, as on the John Winthrop cup, of
panels of sea monsters.   These panels of sea
monsters were chiefly employed in the decoration of Elizabethan and Jacobean plate between
the years 1580 and 1620, and have no counter-
part in plate of any other European country.
The short baluster stems are invariably supported by animal or scrolled brackets ; while
the high bases are bell-shaped, considerably
depressed in the middle.   Three standing cups
with covers, by the unknown maker of the Winthrop cup, are illustrated in "Old English Plate
of the Emperor of Russia," by Mr. E. Alfred
Jones, 1909.

This variety of cup first made its appearance
in England at the end of the sixteenth century.
The earliest recorded example is dated 1599–
1600, in Charing Church, Kent, though not given
to that church until 1765 ; and another historical specimen of the year 1604–05, made from
Queen Elizabeth's great seal of Ireland, is in the

collection of the late Mr. J. Pierpont Morgan. This is illustrated in Mr. Jones's catalogue of that important collection. Of great interest is a similar cup, dated 1618–19, at Emmanuel College, Cambridge, for it was there that the founder of Harvard College and other Puritans were educated — a college which gave to New England twenty-one Puritans, including Thomas Hooker, John Cotton, Simon Bradstreet, Nathaniel Rogers, Samuel Whiting, Zechariah Symmes, Samuel Stone, Francis Higginson and Thomas Shepard.

The Winthrop cup belongs to the First Church, the mother church of Boston, and bears the London date-letter for 1610–11 and the well-known mark of a maker of this type of cup. The baluster stem had originally three scrolled brackets, two of which are missing; the high bell-shaped base is engraved with acanthus leaves and fruit, the edge being stamped with ovolo work. Around the lip is inscribed: "The gift of Governor Jn° Winthrop to y$^e$ i$^t$ Church in Boston." The donor was one of the founders of that church in 1630, with Governor Thomas Dudley, Isaac Johnson and its first pastor, John Wilson. He was the son of Adam Winthrop of Groton Manor in Suffolk, and his name may still be seen in the old register as having been baptized January 16, 1587. He entered Trinity College, Cambridge, in 1602 and embarked at Southampton on the *Arbella*, March 22, 1629–30. One thousand persons came in the fleet,

D

consisting of eleven ships, to Salem, Massachusetts; they shortly moved to Charlestown and
then to Shawmut which they named Boston.
John Winthrop was "the real founder of the
Massachusetts Bay Colony." He married four
times, his last wife being Martha Rainsborough,
the widow of Thomas Coytmore who commanded the *Trial*, the first ship built at Boston,
which was completed in 1642. Adam Winthrop,
a great-grandson of Governor Winthrop, was
the donor, in 1706, of a baptismal basin, engraved
with the Winthrop arms, to the Second Church,
Boston, which was made by Edward Winslow
(1669–1753). A portrait of Governor Winthrop
is in the Massachusetts senate chamber at
Boston.

A second variety of steeple cup has a tall
slender baluster stem without the bracket supports, and also a low splayed base, similar to
those of the Jacobean cup of 1607–08 in the
Old South Church. A specimen of this variety,
with a steeple cover, dated 1611–12, is in the
church of Barford St. Martin, Wiltshire, which
has historical connection with New England in
that its incumbent was John Woodbridge. He
was the father of Timothy Woodbridge whose
wife, Abigail, was the donor of a mug to the
First Church of Christ at Hartford, Connecticut.

A third and much rarer variety of steeple cup
has a globular body, such as the two of 1605–06
and 1608–09 which are in the collection of the
Emperor of Russia, in the treasury of the Kremlin

at Moscow. A plain cup of this variety without its cover (which has been lost) is in John Winthrop's own college — Trinity College, Cambridge. It was made in 1615–16, and was given by Thomas Neville, sometime master of that college.

The earliest English vessel in any American church is the silver-gilt standing cup (Illus. 1) of the time of James I, in the Old South Church, Boston, with the London date-letter for 1607–08, by an unknown maker. The oviform body is appropriately decorated with grapes on a granulated ground; the lower part having flat flutings. It is supported by a tall baluster stem on a splayed — flat and spreading — base which is fluted like the body, the edge being stamped with an ovolo. The decoration is done in flat chasing which Mr. Jackson describes thus : "it consists of surface decoration, composed of flat lines incised, or rather depressed, with a mallet and chisel without a cutting edge; and differs from engraving, in that the latter is executed with a sharp-edged graver which, in being used, actually cuts away a part of the metal surface worked upon." It was in the Old South Church that Benjamin Franklin was baptized. His printing press is in the collection of the Bostonian Society in the old State House. He was born on Milk Street opposite the spot where the second meeting-house of that church, erected in 1729, still stands at the corner of Washington Street; in this church it was that the British troops were

1. London, 1607–08.  H. 7¾ in.

quartered in 1775 at the instance of General John Burgoyne.

A cup of the same shape, almost identically decorated and made in 1614–15, is in the picturesque and historical little church of Llanrhychwyn in Carnarvonshire. Cups of the same form were made entirely plain or with an ovolo decoration on the edge of the base. It was from a plain cup of this variety made in 1629–30, now owned by the Duke of Portland, that Charles I received the last sacrament on the scaffold. An illustration of this cup may be seen in Mr. Jackson's "History of English Plate." The inscription on the foot is: "King Charles the first received the Communion in this Bowle on tuesday the 30th of January 1648 being the day in which he was Murthered." This sacred rite was administered by William Juxon, Bishop of London, and later Archbishop of Canterbury, who was the uncle of Nathaniel Byfield — principal settler of the town of Bristol in Rhode Island. Nathaniel Byfield was the donor of a baptismal basin made by Jacob Hurd (1702–58), engraved with the Byfield arms, to the First Church of Boston; and also in 1693 of a pair of beakers made by John Coney (1655–1722) to the church at Bristol.

Another type of standing cup (Illus. 2) with the London date-letter for 1626–27 was made by Fred Terry, the maker of four historical cups illustrated in "Old Eng-

2. LONDON, 1626–27. H. 9 in.

lish Plate of the Emperor of Russia." It has a
plain inverted bell-shaped body on a tall slender
baluster stem, which rests on a splayed base
with a moulded edge. It is pounced, or pricked
in dots, with the initials $\begin{smallmatrix}T\\B\,C\end{smallmatrix}$ for The Boston
Church; and $\begin{smallmatrix}H\\A\,E\end{smallmatrix}$ for Atherton and Elizabeth
Hough, who came to Boston with Rev. John
Cotton and in 1633 joined the First Church
to which the cup belongs. Atherton Hough had
been mayor of Boston in Lincolnshire, in 1628.
This class of cup would seem to have first come
into vogue in England early in the seventeenth
century. Although occasionally found in use
as a communion cup in English churches, it is
purely a domestic cup for wine. One of the
earliest examples in ecclesiastical use, dated
1610–11, is in St. Cybi's Church at Holyhead in
North Wales.

Another variety of standing cup, which first
appeared in England in the reign of Charles I,
was popular during the Commonwealth and continued in vogue in a less degree for some few
years after the restoration of Charles II. A
specimen of this type (Illus. 3) with the London
date-letter for 1631–32, by an unknown maker,
has a plain bell-shaped body on a baluster stem
and a splayed base. It had undoubtedly belonged to Rev. Samuel Newman, the compiler of
a Concordance of the Bible and the first pastor
of the Rebohoth Church. It is engraved with

the initials N N for Noah Newman, his son, and is inscribed : "The Gift of our Rev^d Pastor Mr. Noah New-man who went to the Church Triumphant Ap^r 16. 1678." This church is now known as the Newman Congregational Church, East Providence, Rhode Island. A set of six similar cups of the same date as the New-man cup belongs to the French Huguenot congregation which has worshipped in Canterbury Cathedral for over three hundred and fifty years, first in Ernulf's large

3. LONDON, 1631–32. H. 7½ in.

crypt and now in the smaller chantry of the Black Prince; these cups bear the initials of Jean Bulteel, who was pastor when they were given, and of his wife Marie Gabry. Two others, dated 1638–39, are in the Rijks Museum at Amsterdam.

4. LONDON, 1639–40.  H. 9⅜ in.

The standing cup (Illus. 4) with the London date-letter for 1639–40, by an unknown maker, does not differ, save in decoration, from the cup previously described. A wide granulated or matted band surrounds the bell-shaped body, leaving the lip and base plain. The splayed base has the same granulated work as well as the upper part of the baluster stem; while the lower part, separated by a beading, is chased with rough foliage. This granulated ornamentation originated in the reign of Charles I and would seem to have passed out of fashion with the death of Charles II in 1685. One of the earliest specimens with this decoration dates from the year 1636–37 and was given to Queens' College, Cambridge,

by Lord Compton who was commander under
the royal banner in the Civil War. Some of
the later cups of this variety have high pointed
covers with various finials. The plain oval
panel on the bowl is pricked, in a scrolled
ornament, with the initials $_{B\ C}^{\quad T}$ for The Boston
Church; the ornament and initials (Illus. 5)
were copied by Sanderson and Hull on a plain
cup of similar form given to the church by
Thomas Clarke, called
junior. Engraved on the
lip are the initials I H
for Jeremy Houchin a tan-
ner, whose gift it was to
the First Church which he
joined in 1640. His daughter Elizabeth married first
the second John Endicott,
and after his death she
married Rev. James Allen

5. PRICKED ORNAMENT.

— one of the ejected ministers, the father of
John Allen the silversmith (1671–1760).

Without doubt these English standing cups
in the First Church served as models for our
earliest Boston silversmiths, Deacon Robert
Sanderson (1608–93) and John Hull (1624–83),
both members of that church when they formed
their partnership, in 1652, to coin the first silver
money of the Colonies in defiance of the royal
prerogative. These coins (Illus. 6) were known
as pine-tree shillings; and the dies were made by

our first iron founder, Joseph Jenks of **Lynn,**
who had his works at Saugus.   There the Leon-
ards, also iron founders, built about 1645 their
house, which recently has been acquired by Mr.
Wallace Nutting and restored under the supervision of Mr. Charles Henry Dean.   Jenks was
a pioneer inventor, and in 1654 he contracted with
the selectmen of Boston " for an engine to carry
water in case of fire " ; his grandson Joseph Jenks,
governor of Rhode Island, was the tallest man in
the state, standing seven feet two in his stockings.

When John Hull's daughter Hannah married Samuel Sewall, tradition says that she was
placed in one side of the scales and balanced by
a dower of pine-tree shillings.   Five hundred

6.  Pine-tree Shillings and Pence.

pounds was the amount which John Hull promised his daughter upon her marriage, so her weight in pine-tree shillings would have been only one hundred and twenty-five pounds! She is said to have been a very buxom lass and her weight was considered something of a joke among the inhabitants. The story is interestingly told in Nathaniel Hawthorne's "Grandfather's Chair."

7. SANDERSON AND HULL. H. 7¼ in.

The standing cup (Illus. 7) was made by these silversmiths, Sanderson and Hull. Except for a difference in the baluster stem it is similar to the English cup given to the same church by Noah Newman and which undoubtedly served as a model. It belongs to the Newman Congregational Church and was purchased in 1674 from the legacy of £5 of Captain Thomas Willet, one of the last of the Leyden Company to cross the

Atlantic.   His  tombstone  is  inscribed :  "1674
Here lyes ye body of wor. The Thomas Willett Esq,
who died August 4 in 64th yr of his age, who was
the first Mayor of New York and twice did
sustain ye place." His daughter Esther married Rev. Josiah Flint of Dorchester.

Another Boston silversmith who made a similar plain cup was Jeremiah Dummer (1645–1718).
who was apprenticed to John Hull in 1659 for a
period of eight years.   He became an important
man in the Colony, serving in the Artillery Company, as selectman, treasurer of the county,
justice of the peace, judge of one of the inferior
courts, and, in 1689, one of the Council of Safety.
He was the son of Richard Dummer of Newbury
and the father of William Dummer, lieutenant-
governor of Massachusetts, and of Jeremiah
Dummer, political writer and agent from 1710–
21 in London for Massachusetts. Jeremiah
Dummer was a deacon of the First Church of
Boston and married Hannah the daughter of
Joshua Atwater, whose daughter Mary married
John Coney : he printed the first paper money
for Connecticut in 1709–13, and presumably engraved the plate for it.

The cup is engraved: "C C 1712" for Chebacco
Church — now the Congregational Church at
Essex, Massachusetts, and has historical associations with the Rev. John Wise, the first pastor
of the church from its foundation in 1683 until
his death in 1725.  He was imprisoned by
Andros in 1688 for remonstrating against the

grievance of taxes imposed without authority from the Assembly, and was one of the very few ministers who favored inoculation for smallpox in 1721.

A different variety of this type of standing cup (Illus. 8) made by Jeremiah Dummer, has the lower part of the body spirally fluted; the baluster stem has a beading and cast foliage at the lower part; and the base has a fluted or gadrooned border. These terms are synonymous, but gadroon is usually

8. JEREMIAH DUMMER. H. 8⅝ in.

applied to the narrow borders or edges rather than to the deeper fluting of the bodies. This form of decoration was fashionable in England toward the end of the reign of Charles II. The cup was bought in 1701 from a legacy of £6 to the First Church of Milton, Massachusetts, —

9. I. Clark.   H. 8¾ in.

now the First Congregational Parish, — from William Stoughton, the presiding justice in the Salem witchcraft trials and lieutenant-governor of Massachusetts. His portrait hangs in Memorial Hall, Cambridge. William Stoughton also bequeathed two similar cups, engraved with the Stoughton arms, to the First Church, Dorchester.

In the First Parish Church, Universalist, Saugus, Massachusetts, is a plain standing cup (Illus. 9) with a bell-shaped body on a very tall slender baluster stem. It bears the maker's mark, I. Clark. In a panel decorated with acanthus leaves is inscribed: "The Gift of the

Honourable Theophilus Burrill Esq:. To the
third Church of Christ In Lynn." Colonel
Theophilus Burrill (1699–1737) also bequeathed
money, for the purchase of plate, to the Second
Church as well as to the First Church of Christ
at Lynn. In the latter is a tankard, a pair
of beakers and a baptismal basin, all made
by Jacob Hurd (1702–58), and engraved with the
Burrill arms. Colonel Burrill was a brother of the
distinguished John Burrill, also a donor of silver
to the First Church at Lynn, who fought in the
Indian wars, served the town as clerk, selectman,
treasurer, assessor, judge, as member of the house
of representatives for twenty-one years, during
ten of which he was speaker, and as member of the
governor's council under the Province charter.

A Colonial cup (Illus. 10) without a maker's
mark, in the Second Presbyterian Church at
Philadelphia, has a "bellied" or bulbous form of
body which first made its appearance in England about the middle of the eighteenth century.
It is inscribed: "Donum G: Tennent Eclesiæ
Sub cura ejus Anno D. 1752." Rev. Gilbert
Tennent, the donor, was born in 1703 in the
county of Armagh in Ireland; at an early age
he emigrated to America and in 1743 founded
the church of which he became the first pastor.
He was a powerful preacher and one of the
most conspicuous ministers of his day, accom-
panying Whitefield on some of his tours. In
1753 he went to England to solicit funds for
Princeton College, of which he was made head.

10. COLONIAL, 1752.   H. 8 in.

In Bluff Presbyterian Church in Cumberland County, North Carolina, is a pair of plain standing cups with bell-shaped bodies on baluster stems with splayed bases, made by an unknown Colonial silversmith. They are inscribed; "For The Presbyterian Congregations In Cumberland County North Carolina Under the Care of The Rev^{ed} John MacLeod Ap^{r} 21^{st} 1775." They belonged to the three churches of Bluff, Barbacue and Long Street in North Carolina, all founded in 1758, and served by Rev. John MacLeod, who came from the Island of Skye, Scotland, in 1770. This pastor was accompanied by a large number of families from the Highlands, who took up their residence upon the upper and lower Little Rivers in Cumberland County in that state. Flora Macdonald, the celebrated

Jacobite heroine, who aided the escape of Charles
Edward the Young Pretender, was a member of
the church of Barbacue and also worshipped in
Long Street Church. Rev. John MacLeod
espoused the cause of the loyalists, as did Flora
Macdonald, and, imprisoned after the battle of
Moore's Creek, he
was liberated by
order of the Pro-
vincial Congress
in 1777.

A cup (Illus. 11)
with a perfectly
plain stem is en-
graved in a circu-
lar panel deco-
rated with foliage:
"The Gift of Mrs.
Lydia Hancock to
the first Church
of Christ in Bos-
ton Sept. 4, 1773."
The donor was the
daughter of Daniel
Henchman — the
enterprising but
dishonest book-
seller who caused
the first edition in
America of the
English Bible to
be printed with a

11. Daniel Henchman. H. 8⅜ in.

E

false titlepage to evade the right of the King's
printer; she became the wife of Thomas Hancock whose large estate was bequeathed to his
nephew John Hancock, the first signer of the
Declaration of Independence. The arms of
Hancock impaling those of Henchman are engraved on the other side of the cup. The
maker of the cup was Daniel Henchman (1730–
75) of Boston, the son of Rev. Nathaniel Henchman of Lynn, who married Elizabeth the
daughter of Jacob Hurd (1702–58) to whom
he was probably apprenticed; he was second
cousin to Lydia Hancock. The competition
existing between the English and Colonial
silversmiths is shown in his advertisement in
the *Boston Evening Post* of January 18, 1773 :

### Daniel Henchman

Takes this Method to inform his Customers
in Town & Country, That he still continues to
carry on the Gold and Silversmiths Business
at his shop opposite the Old Brick Meeting House
in Cornhill, where he makes with his own Hands
all Kinds of large and small Plate Work, in the
genteelest Taste and newest Fashion, and of the
purest Silver; and as his work has hitherto met
with the Approbation of the most Curious, he
flatters himself that he shall have the Preference
by those who are Judges of Work, to those
Strangers among us who import and sell English
Plate, to the great Hurt and Prejudice of the

Townsmen who have been bred to the Business
— Said HENCHMAN therefore will engage to those
Gentlemen and Ladies who shall please to employ him, that he will make any kind of Plate
they may want equal in goodness and cheaper
than any they can import from London, with
the greatest Dispatch.

A cup (Illus. 12) made by Andrew Fogelberg
and Stephen Gil-
bert, with the Lon-
don date-letter for
1781–82, has an
oviform body em-
bossed with large
acanthus leaves.
The slender stem
has a beaded
moulding around
the middle, and the
edge of the base is
also beaded — a
form of decoration
popular in England
between the years
1775 and 1815. It
was the gift in 1825
to the First Parish,
Watertown, Mas-
sachusetts, of Mrs.
Nathaniel Amory,
the daughter of

12. LONDON, 1781–82.  H. 6¼ in.

13. AMERICAN, 1796.  H. 6¼ in.

Ebenezer Preble and a niece of Commodore Edward Preble. A plain cup with beaded decoration, made by Silas Sawin, was given to the First Church, Boston, by Mrs. Joshua Davis in 1811.

Belonging to the Congregational Church at Shrewsbury, Massachusetts, is a plain American cup (Illus. 13) without a maker's mark, inscribed: " The Gift of the Hon^{ble} Artemas Ward, Esq^r to the Church of Christ in Shrewsbury, 1796." The donor was the first major-general in the Revolutionary army and one of the "glorious 92." He took an active part in affairs at the time preceding the Revolution, became commander-in-chief of the army, and commanded at the siege of Boston until the arrival of General Washington in July, 1776. His son Artemas Ward, an eminent lawyer, presented in 1834 a circular dish to the Church in Federal Street, Boston, — now the Arlington Street Church.

With the exception of the steeple cup of Governor Winthrop, such cups as have been described were often designated as goblets, a term commonly applied in our country to glass vessels of similar form. The inventory of plate belonging to Hezekiah Usher junior, in 1689 speaks of "a cover for a goblet." In England, hanap was the earliest word applied to the standing cup.

# BEAKERS

THE beaker was the next purely domestic drinking vessel that appeared in the New England churches. Thomas Nelson of Rowley, Massachusetts, by his will of December 24, 1645, leaves to his wife "a silver beaker." It is the earliest form of drinking vessel known, having been made of glass and doubtless of silver by the Egyptians, Greeks and Romans. Glass beakers of the thirteenth and fourteenth centuries are in the British Museum and specimens of the Venetian of the sixteenth century are in many museums. Cylindrical beakers of the precious metals were used at the banquet in 1352 when the *Ordre de l'Etoile* was instituted and at the banquet given by Charles V of France to the Emperor Charles IV in 1378. Beakers of gold and silver are depicted in Flemish paintings of the late fourteenth and early fifteenth centuries.

In Holland at the Reformation the mediæval chalice was superseded by the beaker, which was adopted as a communion cup throughout the country. Most of the sixteenth century examples have disappeared, but one dated 1592 is in St. Bavo's Church at Haarlem. In shape these beakers are cylindrical with the bases moulded;

and the lips usually engraved with a double
interlacing strap-band, enclosing conventional
flowers and leaves, from which depend sprays
of flowers. Some
are engraved with
symbolic figures.
The beaker be-
came known in
Holland as the
"Lady's Cup."

Of this type is
the Dutch beaker
(Illus. 14) with the
mark of Amster-
dam and the date-
letter for 1637. It
was a legacy in
1652 to the First
Church of Boston,
from the Rev.
John Cotton, the
most distinguished
divine who came
from England in

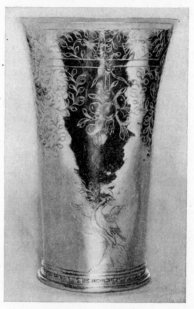

14. AMSTERDAM, 1637. H. 6⅞ in.

the early period
and a teacher of that church which he joined
in 1633. In his will he calls it "a silver tunn."

Engraved on the bottom are the initials $\begin{smallmatrix} & S & \\ R & & E \end{smallmatrix}$
probably those of some of the Story family, as
John Cotton's second wife was Sarah Story, a
widow of Boston in Lincolnshire. His portrait

is in the possession of Miss Adèle Thayer of Boston, a descendant.

Of much interest is a similar beaker (Illus. 15) with the mark of Haarlem and the date-letter for 1643. In the three oval medallions are finely engraved figures of Justice, Prudence and Temperance. Engraved on one side is: "Memento Martha Saffin obijt:11:Dec:78." Martha Saffin was the daughter of Captain Thomas Willett who gave the standing cup to the Rehoboth Church, and the wife of John Saffin who was speaker of the house, councillor and judge. The initials of the original owners are engraved on the bottom, $\frac{V}{I\,H}$. It

15. HAARLEM, 1643.  H. 7⅝ in.

seems not improbable that these may stand for John and Helena Underhill; he had served under the great Dutch prince in the war of the Netherlands and came in the fleet with Winthrop to

serve as captain of any military force that might
be employed. He with Captain John Mason and
seventy-seven Englishmen exterminated, in May
1637, the Pequot Indians who were in the stock-
aded fort by the
Mystic River
near the pres-
ent site of Ston-
ington in Con-
necticut. Upon
the death of
Martha Saffin
this beaker ev-
idently passed
into the hands
of Mrs. Re-
becca Farr, as
her grandson
Farr Tollman,
a bookbinder,
bequeathed it
in 1751 to the
Third or Old
South Church
at Boston.

The fine and
massive Dutch
or Flemish
beaker (Illus.
16) is an un-
usual specimen
of about 1700.

16. DUTCH OR FLEMISH, 1700. H. 11 in.

It has a low cover surmounted by a large open crown composed of six beaded scrolls and acanthus leaves, which is fixed on six plain wire scrolls. The centre of the cover is spirally fluted and the top is finely engraved with a huntsman and three hounds hunting a stag : these animals are running among scrolled foliage, on one part of which a bird is sitting. The border is spirally fluted and the edge is engraved with a narrow band of foliage. The lip is engraved with a double interlacing strap-band, enclosing foliage and three birds ; the straight body is engraved with cherubs' faces, large sprays of foliage, clusters of fruit suspended from large knots, a stork, a peacock, and an eagle attacking a serpent. Just above the moulded base is an applied band of acanthus leaves. Engraved in one of the intersections on the lip is a double monogram T B R which has not been identified ; the same monogram engraved at a later date in a different style is on the body. The beaker was the gift in 1711 to St. Mary's Church, Burlington, New Jersey, of Colonel Robert Quary, the donor of vessels to Christ Church at Philadelphia, an ardent and conspicuous churchman and surveyor general of the customs for the American Colonies ; he succeeded Edward Randolph in that important position in 1704. Among his public offices were secretary and receiver, in 1685, of the Province of South Carolina, and admiralty judge in New York and Pennsylvania.

In Germany this variety of drinking vessel

became popular in the sixteenth, seventeenth
and eighteenth centuries, a fact not surprising
in a beer-drinking country. One of the earliest
illustrations of a covered beaker is a design by
Albrecht Altdorfer, early in the sixteenth century. A beaker of pottery with a golden mount
is shown on the table in the German triptych
painted in 1511
by the master of
St. Severin, in the
Museum of Fine
Arts at Boston.
Beakers of glass
and precious metals
are also displayed
in other pictures of
the early German
school.

The cylindrical
beaker (Illus. 17)
made about 1610,
with the mark of
Cologne in Ger-
many, is one of the
earliest examples
of old silver in an
American church.
Beakers of this va-
riety were some-

17. COLOGNE, 1610.  H. 7¼ in.

what popular among the Cologne silversmiths
of that period, a fact which is doubtless due to
the proximity of that city to Holland, where

beakers were highly common at that time. The
moulded base is decorated with diamond work.
Engraved on the body are the figures of the six
apostles, inscribed: "S. Matthevs, S. Thomas,
S. Petrvs, S. Pavlvs, S. Ioannes, S. Iacobvs."
The beaker belongs to the historic Christ
Church at Philadelphia which, with its peal
of bells, is mentioned by Longfellow in the
closing scene of "Evangeline"; it was in use
when George and Martha Washington worshipped there between the years 1790 and 1796
and was doubtless a familiar object to Benjamin Franklin. It belonged to Dr. John Kearsley
a prominent layman of the Episcopal church in
America who was instrumental in the recon-
struction of the present edifice of Christ Church.
In recognition of their indebtedness the beaker
was purchased at a cost of forty pounds and
presented to him on May 11, 1747, in the name
of the vestry and congregation. Dr. Kearsley
also had a part in the erection of Independence
Hall and bequeathed most of his property to
the united parishes of Christ Church and St.
Peter's, to be used to erect a building to be
called Christ Church Hospital, for the relief of
poor women of the Church of England. Engraved upon the beaker are the initials $\frac{M}{I\ K}$
for Dr. Kearsley and his wife Margaret who
probably gave it to the church after the death
of her husband, which occurred in 1772. Rev.
William White, rector of Christ Church in 1779,

was the first bishop of Pennsylvania. The
"Book of Common Prayer" was revised by him
and Bishop Seabury for the use of the Episcopal
church in this country.

A beaker (Illus. 18) wrought about 1700,
with the mark of Hamburg, is boldly embossed
with tulips. The
embossed decora-
tion of flowers is
as typical of Ger-
man plate of that
period as the en-
graved decoration
is of the Dutch.
It is inscribed in
one line: "The
Gift of the Rev.ᵈ
Joseph Sewall,
D.D. to the South
Church in Boston
who was Ordained
Pastor of said
church Sepᵗ. 16.
1713 & Decᵈ June
27, 1769 Ætat 81."
Rev. Joseph Sewall

18. HAMBURG, 1700. H. 5⅝ in.

"was a man of great benevolence, a friend of
learning and a donor to Harvard College of a
fund to be appropriated to indigent scholars."
His portrait by John Smibert has been inherited
by Dr. Theodore S. Woolsey of New Haven.
Joseph Sewall's wife Elizabeth was the daughter

of the Hon. John Walley one of the principal
founders of the town and church of Bristol.
He was the son of Judge Samuel Sewall and his
first wife Hannah, the only child of John Hull.
A tankard made by John Edwards (1670–1746),
believed to have been given to commemorate
the membership of Samuel Sewall in the Old
South Church, is engraved with the Sewall
arms.   Samuel Sewall was one of those who
shared in the general belief in witchcraft in
1692.

In France, early beakers are rare.   What is
perhaps the only French mediæval covered silver
beaker extant today is the celebrated piece with
the Paris mark for the year 1462–63, which is at
Oriel College, Oxford.   Early in the eighteenth
century a fashion arose in France for small
silver beakers.   In shape they are like inverted
bells and the decoration followed that of contemporary plate.   A French beaker of that kind,
dating from about 1750, is in use as a communion cup in Kirk Barown Church in the Isle
of Man.

In England the beaker never became a popular communion vessel in Post-Reformation
times, as it did in Holland and Scotland, although
it is occasionally found in country churches.   It
is very similar in shape and decoration to the
Dutch beaker except that the symbolical figures
of Faith, Hope and Charity, and other sacred
subjects have not been copied.   The earliest
English beaker known is the historical specimen

of the fourteenth century at Trinity Hall, Cambridge, where Rev. Robert Hunt, chaplain of the expedition to Virginia in 1607, was educated. Another early English beaker of great historical interest is one at Christ's College, Cambridge, the *alma mater* of Milton, of many English Puritans and of Ezekiel Rogers the first pastor and founder of the town of Rowley in Massachusetts, and the donor of vessels to that church. A set of six plain English beakers of great historical interest was made in the year 1654–55 for the Congregational church of the seaboard town of Great Yarmouth, a church which is closely associated with Puritan history. Ironsides and regicides were members of that congregation and these beakers bear the initials of prominent Puritans. A member of the community was Daniel Bradford, a kinsman of Governor Bradford. In the oldest Congregational church in England, namely, the "Pilgrim Fathers' Church" in the south-east of London — so called because it furnished the London contingent of the Pilgrim Fathers in 1620 — are four English beakers. It was there that John Lathrop was pastor before his departure for New England where he became pastor of the Scituate and Barnstable churches. As is the case with the communion vessels of the churches of St. Peter and St. Pancras at Leyden, where the Pilgrim Fathers worshipped during their exile in Holland, these vessels postdate that period.

The beaker (Illus. 19) made in the reign of
Charles II, probably in the year 1671–72, is
somewhat unusual in decoration for an English
beaker.   It belongs to the First Congregational
Church at Marblehead, Massachusetts, the first

19. LONDON, 1671–72.  H. 5½ in.

pastor of which was
Rev. Samuel Chee-
ver  (1639–1724),
the son of Ezekiel
Cheever  (1616–
1708) the famous
schoolmaster who
was  one  of  the
founders  of  New
Haven and who had
charge of the Bos-
ton  Latin  School
after 1670.  A copy
of this beaker was
made  in  1772  by
a  Colonial  silver-
smith,  (possibly
Joseph  Smith  of
Boston) by order of
the church, from the earlier gifts of 1730 of William Jones (1694–1730) a silversmith of Marblehead, and of Ruth Wadlons the daughter of Rev.
Samuel Cheever, and the wife of Moses Wadlon.
There  are  but  two  other  English  beakers  in
the  American  churches.   Both  are  plain  with
moulded  bases.   That  made  by  Timothy  Lee
in 1704–05 belongs to All Hallows' Parish (All

Hallows' Church, South River) Anne Arundel County, Maryland; the other with the London date-letter for 1773-74 was the gift of Tacitus Gaillard to the Parish of St. Matthew's, Orangeburg, South Carolina.

In the New England churches there are over five hundred beakers of American workmanship, and more than half of them were made after 1750. This large number of beakers, as well as of cups and other vessels, is accounted for by the fact that, as in the Nonconformist bodies in England, the intervention of a priest or minister in the administration of the sacrament was deemed unnecessary. Several cups were handed around at the communion service. An English Nonconformist minute book of the eighteenth century clearly explains the distinction: "The administration of the ordinance of the Lord's Supper did not exclusively belong to the pastor of a church, but might and should be attended to by a society of Christians, though deprived of that office-bearer."

The earliest type of the New England beaker (Illus. 20) has a straight body slightly curved at the lip and a flat bottom; a broad granulated band encircles the body, leaving the lip and base plain, as in the English standing cup of 1639-40. It was undoubtedly that very cup which inspired Robert Sanderson (1608-93) and John Hull (1624-83) of Boston, to copy this form of decoration — as both were members, at that time, of the First Church for which they

F

20. SANDERSON AND HULL.  H. 3⅞ in.

made this beaker. In a plain shield upon the matted ground is engraved the date 1659 and also the initials T over B C for The Boston Church. A straight-sided beaker with the same decoration, wrought by John Hull, is in that church; and a pair made by Sanderson and Hull in the First Church, Dorchester, engraved with the initials L over T A for Thomas and Alice Lake, was delivered to the Deacons on January 6, 1679, by the donor's executor, Henry Leadbetter — referred to as "two silver cups or small beakers." English beakers with this same band were made in small numbers in the Stuart period between 1660 and 1690. Such form of decoration was used in Scandinavia and Germany in the seventeenth century on tankards, cups and other vessels and to a less degree in Holland.

Jeremiah Dummer (1645–1718) of Boston, made a beaker, with the granulated band, to which two solid flat handles were fitted at a later date. It is inscribed: "The Gift of Francis Skerry to the Church in Salem," now the First Congregational Society. The donor was a planter and died in 1684. Governor John Endicott was sent in 1628 as the agent of the Massachusetts Colony to make a settlement at Naumkeag and there he laid the foundation of the first permanent town in Massachusetts. This he called by the Bible name of Salem — "Peace." The Rev. Francis Higginson was the first pastor of the church. Roger Williams, who succeeded him in 1633, was one of the noblest men of the time; on account of his opinions he was banished and in 1636 made his way through the wilderness, in the winter time, and founded Providence — so called because God's mercy had provided for him. His first son, born there, was named Providence and his daughter, Mercy.

Another type of beaker made in New England in small numbers is of the same shape, with the flat bottom, but the body is plain. The earliest example was without doubt made by Sanderson and Hull and is in

21. EDWARD WINSLOW. H. 3⅞ in.

the Old South Church, Boston, where there is also a similar beaker made by John Coney (1655–1722); but neither is dated. A beaker (Illus. 21) of this description was a legacy in 1693 to the church in Barnstable, Massachusetts — now the West Parish—from Mary Haughton the daughter of Thomas Hinckley the last governor of Plymouth. It was made by Edward Winslow (1669–1753) of Boston — the grandson of John Winslow, who came in the *Fortune* in 1621, and of his wife Mary Chilton. He was a great-grandson, on his mother's side, of the famous Anne Hutchinson — "a well-educated, bright and intelligent lady" who had come from Lincolnshire in 1634. Her teachings caused a violent theological discussion in Boston called the "Antinomian Controversy," and in 1636 she and her sympathizers were driven from Massachusetts. Some became the settlers of Exeter in New Hampshire, but Anne Hutchinson with other friends settled Rhode Island and founded the town of Portsmouth. Edward Winslow held many important offices and was judge of the inferior court of common pleas at the time of his death; he was colonel of the Boston Regiment and captain of the Artillery Company. His first wife was Hannah the daughter of Rev. Joshua Moody, pastor of the church at Portsmouth, and later assistant pastor of the First Church, Boston. Two of Edward Winslow's sons lost their lives at Louisburg. The inventory of his estate amounted to £1083.18.5. no inconsiderable sum at that time.

Another type of beaker, with a decorated
body and a moulded base, is less common in
New England than in New York where the
silversmiths were
inspired by the
greater number of
Dutch examples
before their eyes.
In the First Con-
gregational Church
at Marblehead,
Massachusetts, is
one of the finest
New England
beakers of this va-
riety (Illus. 22)
which was acquired
in 1728. The base
is stamped with
conventional ovolo
work. The early
Dutch beakers in
the First and Old
South churches
probably inspired
Robert Sanderson (1608–93) and John Hull
(1624–83) of Boston to make this beaker.

22. SANDERSON AND HULL.   H. 6 in.

In the Newman Congregational Church in
East Providence, Rhode Island, is a beautifully
engraved beaker (Illus. 23) made by John Hull
(1624–83) of Boston. The decoration is much
more conventional than that on similar beakers.

The donor was Daniel Perren who married Abigail Carpenter in 1706. It is one of the few
objects which bear the mark of John Hull
(1624–83) without that of his partner Robert
Sanderson (1608–93). John Hull came to Boston in 1635 with
his father Robert
Hull who was a
blacksmith, and it
is probable that he
learned the rudi-
mentsofhisfather's
trade which would
amply qualify him
to become a silver-
smith. If he had
needed any special
instruction he very
probably acquired
it from John Mans-
field (1601–74), a
brother-in-law of
Rev. John Wilson
and of Captain
Robert Keayne,
who was the only

23. JOHN HULL.  H. 6⅜ in.

silversmith known to have been in Boston before
John Hull entered into partnership, in 1652, with
Robert Sanderson, a practical silversmith, who
then came to Boston from Watertown in Massachusetts. With the coining of the pine-tree
shillings, upon which he received a large royalty,

John Hull acquired wealth and became a shrewd
and prosperous merchant; and it is as a merchant and never as a silversmith that he refers to
himself.   The fact that it was to John Hull that
Jeremiah Dummer (1645–1718), Daniel Quincy
(1651–90) and others were apprenticed is quite
natural, for Hull was doubtless the moving spirit
in the partnership; it is, however, more than
probable that the instruction was given by
Robert Sanderson.   Daniel Quincy was the son
of John Hull's step-brother Edmund Quincy
junior and was sent to England in Hull's em-
ployment, which may account for the fact that
no silver with Quincy's mark has been found.
John Hull's father married the widow of Edmund Quincy senior and John Hull married
Judith Quincy his step-sister! John Hull was
active in public life, serving as town treasurer in
1660; representative from Wenham in 1668;
and treasurer of the Colony in 1676; he was
captain of the Artillery Company in 1675; a
member of the First Church and one of the
founders of the Third or Old South Church in
1669.

In the First Reformed Church at Albany,
New York, is a tall cylindrical beaker (Illus. 24)
which is an exact copy of one in the same church
with the mark of Haarlem and the date-letter
for 1660.   Below the intersections are three oval
panels engraved with figures of Faith, Hope and
Charity; between the panels are large clusters
of fruit suspended from the interlacing band;

three birds on branches are engraved above the moulded base.    It was made in 1678 by Ahasuerus Hendricks the earliest local silversmith in New York.    "He was an old-world silversmith, who sought to better himself by coming to New

24. AHASUERUS HENDRICKS.  H. 7⅜ in.

York, where he supplied the local demand for jewelry, rings, funeral spoons, and beakers, and, as well, fashioned the silver spears, pikes, and sword hilts affected by the militant burghers. We first find his name in New York on the list of those who swore allegiance to the King in 1675. His house, in Smith Street, appears on the tax list in 1677. He was one of those appointed in 1686 to assist in giving the inhabitants of the city better drinking water, and was, in that year, ordered to take care of the public well near his house.    The position was one of honor and responsibility."    (R. T. H. H.)

Another example of the decorated type (Illus. 25) is engraved with a band of scrolled foliage from which depend acanthus leaves alternating with Vandyke ornaments. It is engraved with the initials $\frac{W}{P\ T}$ for Philip and Thankful Withington who were married in 1682. It was made by that short-lived silversmith David Jesse (1670–1705) of Boston and was a legacy in 1711 to the First Church, Dorchester, Massachusetts. David Jesse was born at Hartford, Connecticut, and married Mary, the daughter of Phineas Wilson a prosperous merchant who had come from Dublin in

25. DAVID JESSE. H. 4¼ in.

1675 and settled at Hartford. Mary Wilson's step-sister Abigail Warren married Rev. Timothy Woodbridge. David Jesse was a member of the Brattle Street Church, Boston, and in 1704 was chosen constable in place of Mr. John Noyes who declined to serve; he became a member of the Artillery Company in 1700.

By far the largest class of the Colonial beaker

is plain with a cylindrical body, curved at the
lip which is sometimes moulded, and supported
on a moulded base, similar in shape to those
made in Holland and England in the sixteenth
and seventeenth centuries.   Such were made for
a century for use in the churches of New Eng-

26. JOHN ALLEN.   H. 5⅜ in.

land.   One of the
earliest dated ex-
amples of this plain
type (Illus. 26) be-
longs to the First
Church — now the
Congregational —
at Ipswich, Mas-
sachusetts, whose
first   pastor   was
Rev.   Nathaniel
Rogers.   It was a
gift in 1693 from
Captain John Ap-
pleton of the ex-
clusive   Ipswich
horse troop, to
which none could
belong who did not pay a tax on £100 of estate.
John Appleton was one of the signers of the
loyalist petition of 1666.   Judge Sewall in his
diary describes John Appleton as an "Israelite
indeed, a great Ornament of that Church and
Town."   He married Priscilla, the daughter of
Rev. Jose Glover whose initials with those of his
wife are on the salt belonging to Harvard Uni-

versity. This beaker was made by John Allen
(1671–1760) of Boston—doubtless an apprentice
of Jeremiah Dummer (1645–1718) to whom he was
related. John Allen's father Rev. James Allen
married Hannah the sister of Jeremiah Dummer;
and, as his second wife — the mother of John
Allen — he married Elizabeth Houchin the widow
of the second John Endicott. This marriage
brought about a family connection with John
Edwards (1670–1746) which turned into a relationship by the marriage of John Edwards's
sister Elizabeth to John Allen.

In the United Congregational Church, Little
Compton, Rhode Island, is a similar beaker
wrought by Arnold Collins of Newport, who
made the Rhode Island seal "Anchor and Hope"
in 1690. In 1729 he was one of the building
committee of the Seventh Day Baptist Society
whose meeting-house is now occupied by the
Newport Historical Society. Arnold Collins
died in 1735. The beaker was the legacy in
1711 of Joseph Church, a carpenter of Hingham,
Massachusetts, the son of Richard Church who
came in the fleet with Winthrop and who built
the earliest church edifice in Plymouth. Colonel
Benjamin Church, a brother of Joseph Church,
distinguished himself in the Indian wars: he
was commander in August, 1676, of the party
which stormed the palisaded fortress in South
Kingston, Rhode Island, slaughtered the Indians and killed King Philip and Canonchet.
The sword worn by Benjamin Church in that

attack has been presented to the Massachusetts
Historical Society of Boston, by his great-
granddaughter Mrs. Anne Atwood of Taunton,
Massachusetts. From the minutes of Benja-
min Church and under his supervision, his son
Thomas wrote a "History of Philip's War."

27. ANDREW TYLER.   H. 4⅝ in.

A plain beaker
(Illus. 27) was the
legacy in 1723 to
the First Parish at
Groton, Massachu-
setts, of Jonas Pres-
cott, the grand-
father of Colonel
William Prescott
who was command-
er of the Provincial
forces at the battle
of Bunker Hill.
Belonging to the
Massachusetts
Historical Society
of Boston are the
swords of Colonel
William Prescott; and of Captain John Linzee,
R. N., who commanded the British sloop-of-war
*Falcon*, while acting against the Americans at the
battle of Bunker Hill.   Colonel William Prescott
was the grandfather of the historian William
Hickling Prescott, whose wife's grandfather was
Captain John Linzee.   In the opening chapter of
"The Virginians" Thackeray thus speaks of these

swords which he noticed when he visited Prescott
in 1852 at his house on Beacon Street in Boston :
— "On the library wall of one of the most famous
writers of America, there hang two crossed
swords, which his relatives wore in the great
war of Independence. The one sword was gallantly drawn in the service of the king, the other
was the weapon of a brave and honourable re-
publican soldier. The possessor of the harmless
trophy has earned for himself a name alike
honoured in his ancestors' country and in his
own, where genius such as his has always a
peaceful welcome." The maker of the Prescott
beaker was Andrew Tyler (1692–1741) of Boston,
prominent in public affairs and having important
family connections. He married Miriam Pepperell, sister of Sir William Pepperell. Their
daughter Catherine married Sir Isaac Heard
and moved to London; she had previously
married Captain David Ochterlony, and their
son was the distinguished baronet Sir David
Ochterlony, who was prominent as a British
general in the wars in India. Andrew Tyler's
house was situated on North Street, and after
the death of his widow it passed into the hands
of the Ochterlonys. There is a tradition connected with this house to the effect that when
Paul Revere was starting on his midnight ride,
an emergency arose for mufflers for his oars ;
upon calling at the house for some substitute he
was handed a "yet warm petticoat." *

* Mrs. Emma Elizabeth Brigham.

In the First Congregational Society of the
historic town of Lexington, where the first battle
of the Revolution was fought, is a similar beaker
made in 1738 from the combined legacies of
Matthew Bridge, the first of that line born in
America; and of Thomas Meriam whose mother
was a daughter of Gregory Stone of Cambridge.
John Cooper, the step-son of Gregory Stone,
built in 1657 in Cambridge the house now known
as the Cooper-Austin house, recently restored to
its original condition by the Society for the Preservation of New England Antiquities, under
the supervision of Mr. Joseph Everett Chandler.
The Rev. John Hancock, styled "Bishop," the
first pastor of the church, was the grandfather of
John Hancock and the father of Thomas Hancock. The maker of the Lexington beaker was
John Burt (1691–1745), son of William and
Elizabeth Burt, who was born in Boston January 5, 1691–92, and married Abigail Cheever
in 1714. He was constable, tithingman and
clerk of the market and left an estate valued at
£6460.4.9. Three of his sons, William (1726–
52), Samuel (1724–54) and Benjamin (1729–
1805) followed in their father's footsteps and
became silversmiths.

One of the few pieces of silver wrought by
William Burt is the plain cylindrical flagon bequeathed to the Old South Church, Boston, in
1748 by Nathaniel Cunningham, a prosperous
merchant and the holder of many public offices
in Boston, including a captaincy in the Artillery

Company. He married Ann Boucher daughter
of Louis and Sarah Boucher, the possessors
of silver described elsewhere. Ruth Cunningham, the donor's daughter, married James Otis
the patriot.

The plain beaker (Illus. 28) with a straight
body, a moulded base and lip, is engraved with
the initial W. It
is one of a set of
twelve camp cups
made for General
Washington by
Edmund Milne of
Philadelphia, as is
shown by the bill
dated 1777 (Illus.
29). It belongs to
Mr. W. Lanier
Washington the
great-great-grand-
son of Colonel Wil-
liam Augustine
Washington, the
only son of Wash-
ington's eldest half-

28. Edmund Milne.  H. 3¼ in.

brother Augustine Washington and one of the executors of General Washington's will, the first of
his nephews mentioned. The battle-sword which
Washington wore during the Revolution is in
the State Department at Washington. Another
sword, in the State Library at Albany, New
York, is said to have been presented to Wash-

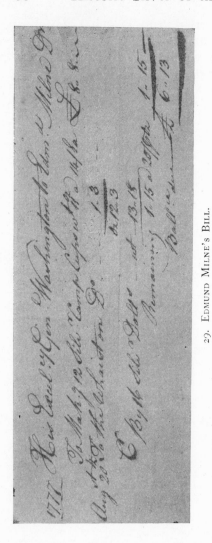

29. EDMUND MILNE'S BILL.

ington by Frederick the Great with a message "from the oldest to the greatest general in the world."

Washington's will makes reference to the four swords which he willed to his four nephews: "These swords are accompanied by an injunction not to unsheath them for the purpose of shedding blood, except it be for self-defence or in defence of their country and its rights; and in the latter case, to keep them unsheathed, and prefer falling with them in their hands to the relinquishment thereof."

In the rooms of the Massachusetts Historical
Society at Boston may be seen the gorget which
Washington wore at the defeat of Braddock's
army by the French and Indians in 1755. It
is of copper-gilt and it is engraved with the

30. SAMUEL VERNON. H. 4⅛ in.

arms of Virginia. It is depicted in the portrait of Washington by Charles Wilson Peale
(1741–1827) of Philadelphia, who was at one
time a silversmith.

Hollow handles have been added at a later
date to the plain beaker (Illus. 30) belonging to
the First Congregational Church, Groton, Connecticut — where important events occurred

G

during the Revolution, which are recorded on the monument there: "This Monument was erected under the patronage of the State of Connecticut, A.D. 1830, and in the 55th year of the Independence of the U. S. A., In Memory of the Brave Patriots who fell in the massacre of Fort Griswold, near this spot, on the 6th of September A.D. 1781, When the British, under command of the Traitor, Benedict Arnold, burnt the towns of New London and Groton, and spread desolation and woe throughout this region." The beaker was purchased with the sum of £6 presented in 1707 to the Church of Christ at Groton, by Sir John Davie fifth baronet, upon his departure for England where he died in 1727. He was recorder or town clerk upon the incorporation of Groton; his stock and lands were purchased by John Gardiner of the Isle of Wight, now called Gardiner's Island. He was a cousin of Sir William Davie of Creedy in Devon, England, who died in 1707 without male issue. Tradition says that John Davie, barefooted and in his shirtsleeves, was hoeing corn on his farm when the messenger arrived to tell him of his good fortune and to salute him as Sir John Davie. The maker of the cup was Samuel Vernon (1683–1737) of Newport, Rhode Island, — great-grandson of Anne Hutchinson and second cousin of Edward Winslow (1669–1753). He was a merchant and "in 1730 was one of a commission to have the care and oversight of the people and goods that should be suspected to have come from Boston where smallpox prevailed."

A beaker, fitted with two thin solid handles, engraved on the shoulders, has a moulded base surmounted with flat scalloped work. Similar decoration was frequently used on tankards made by the New York silversmiths at that time. It was a gift in 1729 to the First Congregational Church of Milford, Connecticut, from Mrs. Abigail Beech the wife of Samuel Beach, who married for her second husband the Rev. Samuel Andrew second rector of Yale College. The maker of the beaker was Cornelius Kierstead (1674–1753) whose "grandfather Hans was the famous surgeon, and a very important personage. He married Sarah Roelofse, the daughter of Anneke Jans by her first husband. Sarah was well acquainted with the Indian language and acted as interpreter for Peter Stuyvesant. It was at their wedding that Governor Kieft, taking advantage of the condition of the guests 'after the fourth or fifth drink,' induced them to subscribe very liberally toward a new church in the Fort. Rum and religion went hand in hand in New Amsterdam. After working in New York for a quarter of a century Cornelius Kierstead migrated in 1772 to New Haven." (R. T. H. H.)

The class of beaker with an inverted bell-shaped body on a moulded base, came into fashion later than those previously described. The earliest is in the Old South Church, Boston,

31. JOHN CONEY. H. 5¾ in.

(Illus. 31) : it is engraved with the date 1715 and the initials $\frac{M}{W\ P}$ for William and Phebe Manley who were admitted to that church in 1689. William Manley was in King Philip's War in 1675. The beaker was made by John Coney (1655–1722) of Boston who engraved the plate for the first paper money for the Colonies (Illus. 32). This bill belongs to the Massachusetts Historical Society. The irregular outline at the top exemplifies the term "indenture" — commonly used in legal documents when it was the custom to fold the paper or parchment upon which they were engrossed. It was then cut or indented as a sure means of identification — the two parts fitting together and furnishing the proof of the integrity of the two copies. John Coney married in 1694, for his second wife, Mary Atwater the widow of John Clark and the sister of Jeremiah Dummer's wife. He was a member of the Second Church,

Boston, and among the pieces in the possession
of that church in 1730 was a tankard, given by
John Coney's heirs in 1725, which has disappeared; he was a subscriber to the fund for

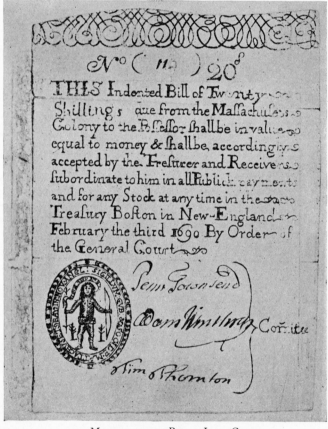

32. MASSACHUSETTS BILL. JOHN CONEY.

the erection of King's Chapel in 1689. John
Coney's mother was Elizabeth Nash, the daughter of Robert Nash a butcher whose slaughter-
house caused considerable trouble in Boston on
account of the careless disposition of his gar-
bage. In 1647 "he was warned not to kill
beasts in the streets."

Formerly belonging to St. James's Church at
New London, Connecticut, on the Thames River
— names which the settlers in New England
adopted out of love for Old London and Father
Thames — is a beaker (Illus. 33) with a wide
splayed base. It was partially the gift in 1773

of Doctor Anthony
Yeldall, a loyalist
of Philadelphia
who advertised his
medicines in a New
London paper in
1775, and was used
in the celebration
of the sacrament by
the first Protestant-
Episcopal bishop
in America, Samuel
Seabury, whose
ashes repose in the
chancel of that
church. The beak-
er was wrought
by John Gardner
(1734-76) of New

33. JOHN GARDNER. H. 5¼ in.

London, son of Jonathan and Mary (Adams)
Gardiner and a descendant of the Gardiners of
Gardiner's Island.

It now belongs to
St. Luke's Chapel,
Berkeley Divinity
School at Middle-
town, Connecticut.

A plain beaker
(Illus. 34) on a trun-
cated base belongs
to the First Pres-
byterian Church at
Southold on Long
Island. "Southold
was settled in Sep-
tember, 1640, by a
party of thirteen
under the leader-
ship of the Rev.
John Youngs, who
crossed from New
Haven. The for-
mation of the

34. SIMEON SOUMAINE. H. 6 in.

church was coincident with the settlement of
the town. Very strict was the government in
this primitive community; the laws of the
Bible were followed as a civil code and communion with the church was made a necessary
qualification for admission to the privileges of a
Freeman." The beaker is believed to have been
given by Hon. Ezra l'Hommedieu, who was a

member of that church ; a delegate to the New
York Provincial Congress 1775–78 ; assisted in
forming the first state Constitution.   He married
a sister of General William Floyd signer of the
Declaration of Independence and commander
of the Long Island militia at the Revolution.
His ancestor Benjamin l'Hommedieu was a
Huguenot who came from Rochelle, France, to
New York in 1687 and settled in Southold in
1690.   The beaker was made about 1720 by
Simeon Soumaine of New York.   *The American
Weekly Mercury* of March 23, 1727, contains the
following : "This is to give Notice to all Gentle-
men and others, That a Lottery is to be drawn
at Mr. *John Stevens* in *Perth Amboy*, for £501 of
Silver and Gold work, wrought by *Simeon Sou-
main* of *New York*, Gold-Smith, all of the newest
Fashion.   The highest Prize consists of an Eight
square Tea-Pot, six Tea-Spoons, Skimmer and
Tongues, Valued at £18 3*s.* 6*d.*   The lowest
Prize consists of Twelve Shillings Value.   There
is 278 Prizes in all, and their is only five Blank
to each Prize.   Tickets are given out at Six
Shillings York money, or Seven Shillings Jersey
Money for each Ticket at the House of Mr.
*John Stevens* in *Amboy*, at Mr. *Lewis Carrees* in
*Allens Town*, at Mr. *Jolines*, in *Elizabeth Town*,
at Mr. *Cortlandts* at *Second River*, by Mr. *An-
drew Bradford* in *Philadelphia*, at Mr. *Samuel
Clowse* in *Jamaica* in *Long Island*, and by *Simeon
Soumain* in the City of *New York*, at which last
Place, the Goods so to be drawn are to be seen,

and the said Goods are to be valued and apprised
by Mr. *Peter Van Dyke*, and Mr. *Charles Leroux*,
two GoldSmiths in the city of *New York*. And
said Lottery is to be drawn the 22nd day of May
next, anno. 1727.
If said Lottery be
full sooner, it will
be drawn before
the 22nd of May
next." (R. T. H. H.)

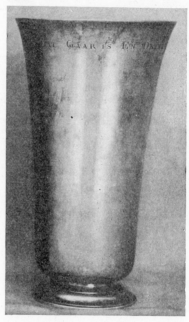

35. NICHOLAS ROOSEVELT. H. 7⅝ in.

Belonging to the
Reformed Church
at Flatbush on
Long Island is a
beaker (Illus. 35)
of this descrip-
tion with a much
taller body and the
upper part curv-
ing outward to a
greater degree,
made by Nicholas
Roosevelt of New
York. This is in-
scribed : " Spreek
Dat Waar is Eet
Dat Gaar is Em Drink Dat Klaar is. Boswyck.
Novʳ 1763."

The bell-shaped beaker, on account of its
form, seemed to lend itself with special suit-
ability to the solid flat scrolled handles with
which many of them are fitted : they undoubtedly

were inspired by those on the caudle cup which
came into fashion at an earlier date; having
two handles they were much more conveniently
passed by the communicants. Such a beaker
(Illus. 36) was a gift in 1722 to the Church of

36. JOHN DIXWELL.   H. 5¼ in.

Christ at Norwich in Connecticut, from Sarah
Knight noted for her now famous journey on
horseback from Boston to New York and return
in 1704. She was the wife of Richard Knight
of Boston where she kept a shop and also taught
school, having among her scholars Benjamin
Franklin and Samuel Mather. She was buried

in New London where her only child Elizabeth,
the wife of Colonel John Livingston, resided.
Her father was Thomas Kemble who received
in 1651 a shipload of Scotch prisoners who
were some of the captives of Dunbar sold into
slavery by Cromwell. These so-called white
slaves were generally sold for a specific term of
service and were used chiefly as farm laborers:
many were sent to North Carolina, and indeed
but few of the Colonies were without them.
The maker of the beaker was John Dixwell
(1680–1725), son of Colonel John Dixwell, the
regicide so closely associated with those other
regicides Goffe and Whalley, whose adventures,
pursuits and escapes form such interesting in-
cidents in New England history. Colonel John
Dixwell fled to this country and settled in New
Haven where, as the "mysterious stranger,"
under the name of "James Davids," he lived in
retirement until his death. John Dixwell was
born at New Haven and married Mary Prout,
donor of the caudle cup, mentioned in the introduction, to the New Haven church: in 1698
he moved to Boston where he died from
inoculation of smallpox. He was a deacon
of the New North Church formed in 1714 by
"seventeen substantial mechanics unassisted
by the more wealthy part of the community
except by their prayers and good wishes."
John Dixwell was the donor to that church in
1717 of a similar beaker made by him, now belonging to King's Chapel. Lieutenant Basil

Dixwell (1711–46) his son, a silversmith, died at Louisburg.

The handles on the New England beakers of this type vary somewhat in the scrolling.

A beaker (Illus. 37) with two solid flat handles, on which are notched rat-tails, originally had but one handle, the other being added about the

37. PETER VAN DYCK. H. 5 in.

year 1879 by Ford, a jeweller of New Haven, Connecticut. It belongs to the Presbyterian Church at Setauket on Long Island, of which Nathaniel Brewster (Harvard College, 1642) was at one time pastor. The maker of the beaker, Peter Van Dyck (1684–1750) of New York, was the father of Richard Van Dyck a silversmith, and probably an apprentice of Bartholomew Le

Roux who died in 1713, as he married Rachel
Le Roux the daughter.

"Peter Van Dyck was an active participant
in the factious strife which kept the city in a
state of political unrest during the administration of Governor Cosby, and, along with his
fellow-silversmiths, Charles Le-Roux, Tobias
Stoutenburgh, and Philip Goelet, affixed his
name to the petition herewith; which was
made in protest against the illegal election of
Adolph Phillipse in 1737, an election with the
same issues at stake, and as exciting as that of
the famous election at East Chester, in 1733.
To the Honour^ble GEORGE CLARKE Esq.
Leiv^t Governour & Command^r in Chief of New-
Yorke & Territorys thereon Depending in
America. The Petition of the Subscribers Most
Humbly Sheweth That wee have this day seen or
heard of the most Barefaced Villany Committed
by Will^m Cosby Esq^r present high Sheriff of this
Citty & County of New York in the Face of
the world in Declareing Adolphe Philipse to be
chosen Representative for this Citty and County
Contrary to the Duty of his Oath and office.

Wee therefore most Humbly pray that our
Lives Libertys and properties may no Longer
Remain Committed to the Said William Cosby;
but that he may be forthwith removed from his
said Office and the S^d Adolph Philipse may not
be qualified to Sit as an Assembly man untill a
fair Hearing of the matter and y^r Petitioners
shall Ever pray."   (R. T. H. H.)

A beaker (Illus. 38) with the same type of
body, supported by a short thick stem, belongs
to the Congregational Church at North Haven,
Connecticut.  It was made in 1797 by Abel
Buel (1742–1825) of New Haven, an apprentice of
Ebenezer Chittenden (1726–1812) of East Guilford, Connecticut, whose daughter he married.
Abel Buel is believed to have constructed the
first lapidary machine used in this country; at
the age of twenty he was convicted of counter-
feiting but released on account of his youth; to
the day of his death he bore the scars of cropped
ears and branded forehead.   (G. M. C.)

38. ABEL BUEL.  H. 4¾ in.

The remaining class of New England beaker, has a fluted surbase, similar to that of the Stoughton standing cup, and was made in small numbers by the Boston silversmiths who derived this fluting from English plate of the last quarter of the seventeenth century. Of this type is the beaker (Illus. 39) with

39. JOHN DIXWELL. H. 4⅞ in.

vertical flutings made by John Dixwell (1680–1725) and belonging to the First Congregational Church, Exeter, New Hampshire. It was bought in 1710 with a legacy of £5 from David Lawrence "to be layed out by them for a silver cupp to be used at the Sacrament." He was one of the early settlers of Exeter.

An interesting example (Illus. 40) with two handles belongs to the First Congregational Church, of Hatfield, Massachusetts. It was bought in 1713 with a legacy of £4 from Lieutenant Daniel White who came to Boston in the *Lion* in 1632 and settled at Hatfield in 1662. Just above the fluted surbase is a row of punched acorns with pellets between them. The beaker

was made by John Edwards (1670–1746) who
came to Boston from Limehouse, now a part
of London, as did his father John Edwards a
chirurgeon and taxpayer of Boston in 1688 who
is mentioned in Sewall's diary in 1689.  John

40. JOHN EDWARDS.  H. 5¼ in.

Edwards married in 1694 Sybil daughter of Rev.
Antipas Newman ; she was the granddaughter
of the second John Endicott, as well as the
step-daughter of Zerubbabel Endicott son of
Governor Endicott.  John Edwards's sister
Anna married John Endicott son of Zerubbabel

Endicott. This relationship explains why John
Edwards applied for the privilege to make use
of the late Governor Endicott's tomb in the
South Burying place (Granary) for his family.
The Boston Selectmen's minutes of March 5,
1722: "Granted that the Said John Edwards
has Liberty to Improve the Said Tomb until a
person of Better Right to it appears to claim it."
That John Edwards was a man of education is
shown by his appointment on a committee to
visit "the Wrighting School at the Southerly End
of Boston" and to examine the scholars under
the teaching of Mr. Ames Angier. He was
prominent in town affairs, holding many public
offices, and became 4th sergeant of the Artillery
Company in 1704. He married in 1740 Abigail Fowle widow of William Smith of Charlestown; his step-son Rev. William Smith married
Elizabeth daughter of Colonel John Quincy,
and their daughter Abigail Smith was the wife
of President John Adams. John Edwards's son
Samuel Edwards (1705–62), a silversmith, had
previously married the daughter of the widow
Smith; another son Thomas Edwards (1701–55)
and a grandson Joseph Edwards junior (1737–
83) were also silversmiths. The estate of John
Edwards amounted to £4840.

The beaker (Illus. 41) is one of a set of four
made in 1705 by Jeremiah Dummer (1645–1718)
of Boston for the North Church, Portsmouth,
New Hampshire. It has a spirally fluted surbase above which is a rosette and scalloped orna-

H

41. JEREMIAH DUMMER.   H. 5¾ in.

ment.  The upper part of the body is encircled with an embossed or gadrooned band which came into fashion in England at the end of the seventeenth century.

From the absence of any great number of beakers in the early inventories and from the fact that so few made prior to the Revolution are found amongst old family plate it may be inferred that as a domestic vessel its popularity was not comparable to its use as a communion cup.   In the last quarter of the eighteenth and early in the nineteenth century the fashion was revived to some extent. They were frequently barrel-shaped but more often cylindrical.

Belonging to Mrs. John Campbell Robinson is a cylindrical beaker (Illus. 42) with straight sides divided into twenty-one sections.  In a wreath are the initials BSR for Benjamin Russell and his wife Sarah Guest, widow of John Campbell of New York.  Colonel Benjamin Russell, a mechanic born in Boston September

13, 1761, learned the trade of a printer with Isaiah Thomas and in 1784 began the publication of the *Columbian Centinel;* he served in the Revolutionary army; was representative to the general court many years and held other positions of importance. The beaker is one of a set of six presented to Benjamin Russell as a wedding gift in 1803 by the maker, Paul Revere (1735–1818) the best known of any of the Boston silversmiths, for his name has been immortalized by Longfellow in "The Midnight Ride of Paul Revere." He was the son of Apollos Rivoire (1702–54) a silversmith who died when Paul Revere was nineteen years of age but amply qualified to carry on his father's business. Not only did he become proficient in the art of fashioning silver vessels of all sorts and descriptions but as an engraver of crests, arms, panels and inscriptions upon such vessels he was unequalled: he also engraved book-plates and prints; he made many of the carved wood frames for Copley's portraits;

42. PAUL REVERE. H. 3⅜ in.

cast bells and cannon at his foundry and was the dentist who repaired Washington's teeth when he was in Boston! The following advertisement appeared in *The Boston Gazette and Country Journal*, August 20, 1770.

## "ARTIFICIAL–TEETH"

"Paul Revere, Takes this Method of returning his most sincere Thanks to the Gentlemen and Ladies who have employed him in the care of their Teeth, he would now inform them and all others, who are so unfortunate as to lose their Teeth by accident or otherways, that he still continues the Business of a Dentist, and flatters himself that from the Experience he has had these Two Years (in which Time he has fixt some Hundreds of Teeth) that he can fix them as well as any Surgeon-Dentist who ever came from London, he fixes them in such a Manner that they are not only an Ornament, but of real Use in Speaking and Eating: He cleanses the Teeth and will wait on any Gentleman or Lady at their Lodgings, he may be spoke with at his Shop opposite Dr. Clark's at the North End, where the Gold and Silversmith's Business is carried on in all its Branches."

# TUMBLERS

THE small silver cup which came into vogue in England towards the end of the seventeenth century was called a tumbler. This was the only drinking vessel without handles which was made to any considerable extent at that time. The rounded bottom of these cups was what gave to them the designation of "tumbler." Mr. Jackson says: "because the extra thickness and weight of silver in the base makes them roll or tumble from side to side when tilted until they finally rest in an upright position. The term 'tumbler' applied to the modern glass vessel is a misnomer and was probably derived from the silver vessel because both were used for the same purpose." In form, the straight or tapering beakers bear greater resemblance to the glass tumblers of to-day.

Belonging to Mr. R. T. Haines Halsey is a tumbler (Illus. 43) made by Adrian Bancker (1703–61) of New York, son of Evert Bancker mayor of Albany, the maker in 1744 of a plain baptismal basin engraved with the seal of the Collegiate Church, New York, to which the basin belongs. An inscription on the rim of this basin in Dutch, translated is:

# CAUDLE CUPS

CAUDLE was a warm drink, consisting of thin gruel mixed with wine or ale and sweetened and spiced. Pepys in his diary in 1659–60 says that he "went to bed and got a caudle made for me and slept upon it very well." An earlier instance of the drinking of caudle at Merton, the most ancient of the Oxford Colleges, is given by Antony à Wood, the antiquary, who states that the freshmen of that college entertained the other undergraduates to a brass pot "full of cawdel" on Shrove Tuesday in 1648. He describes how "every freshman according to seniority, was to pluck off his gowne and band and if possible to make himself look like a scoundrell. This done, they conducted each other to the high table, and there made to stand on a forme placed thereon; from whence they were to speak their speech with an audible voice to the company; which if well done, the person that spoke it was to have a cup of cawdle and no salted drink; if indifferently, some cawdle and some salted drink; but if dull, nothing was given to him but salted drink or salt put in college beere, with tucks to boot."

The caudle cup is of purely English origin and was frequently called a porringer in England. A gourd-shaped cup with two handles can be traced to the reign of Henry VIII. An elaborately decorated cup of this shape, dated 1533–34, is at Corpus Christi College, Oxford, having been given by Robert Morwent who secreted and saved the priceless plate of that college from destruction in the troublous times of Edward VI. An illustration of this, the earliest known English cup of that shape, is in Mr. H. C. Moffatt's "Oxford Plate," 1906.

The great popularity of the caudle cup came in the reign of Charles II when it was considered, next to the tankard, an indispensable possession of every English household. Most of the early cups of that period were gourd-shaped, fitted with two scrolled solid cast handles which often have human heads on the shoulders to serve as thumb-pieces. The embossed (or repoussé) decoration consists of tulips and other flowers frequently interspersed with animals — lions and unicorns, stags and boars and hounds. Another popular scheme of decoration for about twenty-five years consisted of Chinese figures and trees, as on the mug of 1688–89 in St. Michael's Parish, Maryland.

Belonging to the Scroll and Key Society of Yale College is a caudle cup (Illus. 44) with the date-letter for 1667–68 and the maker's mark E G in a rectangle. The lower part of the gourd-shaped body is embossed with four large tulips; on the shoulders of the solid cast

town.    The lower part of the body is decorated
with six varieties of flowers in scrolled compartments;  the base has a twisted moulding;  the
two short cast handles are scrolled and notched.
Pricked on one of the flowers are the initials
$\begin{smallmatrix} C \\ A\ E \end{smallmatrix}$ for Augustin and Elizabeth Clement who
settled at Dorchester as early as 1635.   By his

46. John Coney.    H. 3⅜ in.

will of January 30, 1671, Augustin Clement
left his wife his "plate to dispose of as she
shall see most meet after her death."    He died
October 1, 1674, and his inventory shows "6 silver spoons and drinking cup £4.10.0."    This is
doubtless the cup which the records of the First
Church of Dorchester show as having been received from his widow November 17, 1678.

Belonging to the Congregational Church, Strat-
ford, Connecticut, is a caudle cup (Illus. 46)
with a gourd-shaped body decorated with

square panels of punched ornaments between two punched lines. The decoration suggests that the maker, John Coney (1655–1722) of Boston, had seen an English saucer dish with similar work, which originated in the reign of Charles I and went out of fashion shortly after the restoration of Charles II.

Because of the difficulty of obtaining the metal in the disturbed period of Charles I, the English goldsmiths devised a scheme of making vessels much thinner than theretofore. "These were ornamented, and at the same time strengthened, by being embossed with some-what crude designs composed of lobes and dots struck with a hammer and round-ended punches on the outside of the object, forming a series of depressions, which appeared as raised dots on the inside. These dots were arranged in patterns of various kinds, such as lobes, leaves, flowers, scrolls and concentric circles." (c. j. j.)

A caudle cup (Illus. 47) decorated with six flat flowers on a matted ground, enclosed in compartments separated by plain flat vertical bands, has above and below the flowers a row of punched dots; the restored base is ribbed. The initials $\frac{\text{IF}}{\text{SB}}$ engraved on the bottom are those of John Foster and of his niece Silence Baker. The date "19th Sept$^r$ 81" engraved upon it is that of the death of John Foster, the ingenious printer and mathematician who de-signed the arms for the Colony of Massachusetts

Adams and his son John Quincy Adams —two
of the presidents of the United States — worshipped and are buried.

The decoration on these Colonial cups only
remotely resembles the ornament on English
plate of the second half of the seventeenth century. The flat flowers have been derived from
the English caudle cups of the early years of
the reign of Charles II.

In England such caudle cups were often fitted
with covers having a single reel-shaped handle
which also acts as a foot, evidently derived from
the paten-cover of the contemporary communion
cup. A plain caudle cup of this description
with the London date-letter for 1662–63 is at
Queen's College, Oxford, having been presented
by Thomas Smith bishop of Carlisle and chaplain to Charles II. The Rev. John Oxenbridge,
pastor of the First Church, Boston, to which he
bequeathed three standing cups wrought by
Sanderson and Hull, mentions in his will in
1674 a "caudle cup and cover."

John Coney (1655–1722) of Boston made a
covered cup (Illus. 48) with a reel-shaped
handle-foot, and scrolled beaded handles with
female heads. It is engraved with the arms of
Addington and on the bottom : "Ex dono I. L."
These initials are for Sir John Leverett (1616–
79), "among the most illustrious of the fathers
of New England," who was created knight and
baronet by Charles II in 1676. His father had
been alderman of Boston in Lincolnshire in

1633.   He was the grandfather of John Leverett,
president of Harvard College, and great-grandfather of Knight Leverett the silversmith (1703–
53).   It is through the marriage of Sir John
Leverett's daughter Mary to Paul Dudley, the

48. JOHN COEEY.   H. 6⅞ in.

son of Governor Dudley, that the caudle cup has
descended to the present owner Mrs. Dudley H.
Bradlee.

Plain cups with gourd-shaped bodies were very
popular in England between the years 1660
and 1730.   The earliest plain Colonial cup with
a gourd-shaped body, made by John Coney, is
engraved with the date 1676 and was the gift
of Margaret Bridges of Finglas, Ireland, to the
First Parish, Concord, Massachusetts.   It was
in that historic town that Henry David Thoreau,
the naturalist, lived; where Nathaniel Haw-

I

Of unusual shape is the plain caudle cup
(Illus. 51) with a deep neck and a reeded lip,
belonging to the First Congregational Church,

50. SAUNDERS PITMAN.   H. 4¼ in.

Milford, Connecticut.   It was made by Edward
Winslow (1669–1753) of Boston, who evidently
derived its form from some English mug such

51. EDWARD WINSLOW.   H. 4⅝ in.

as that of 1688–89 in St. Michael's Parish,
Maryland, which has a globular body decorated
with Chinese subjects.

In the reign of Charles I a small caudle cup
with a straight body was introduced. A rare
example, dated 1641–42, decorated with flat
burnished foliage, is in Pitt Chapel at Rusholme,
Lancashire. Caudle cups of both shapes were
made during the Commonwealth — necessarily
in small numbers in that disturbed period of
English history when the progress of the Arts
was virtually at a standstill. Among the earliest
examples of caudle cups with straight bodies
is the covered pair of 1659–60 at Gonville
and Caius College, Cambridge, illustrated in
"Old Plate of the Cambridge Colleges" by
Mr. E. Alfred Jones. They were the gift of a
member of the college, Francis Glisson the
great English physiologist of the seventeenth
century.

Between 1670 and 1695, a popular decoration
in England consisted of embossed vertical acanthus and palm leaves along the base, as on the
caudle cup (Illus. 52) from the Betts collection
belonging to the Scroll and Key Society of Yale
College. It bears the London date-letter for
1686–87 and the maker's mark WA in a monogram.

A decoration found on English plate between
the years 1660 and 1690 and in isolated examples
as late as 1720 frequently consists of appliqué
foliage or "cut-card" work, resembling in effect

52. LONDON, 1686–87.  H. 3¾ in.

that of a pattern cut out of cardboard and
applied.  Cut foliage of this kind may be seen
on New England Colonial furniture of the last
quarter of the seventeenth century, especially in
Connecticut.

Of the same shape and with "cut-card" decoration is the silver-gilt caudle cup with cover

53. LONDON, 1686–87.  H. 4¼ in.

(Illus. 53) in Christ Church, Bruton Parish, Williamsburg, Virginia. It was made in London in 1686–87 by Pierre Harache, a Huguenot refugee silversmith, who wrought one of the few pieces of English gold plate extant — namely a "tazza" dated 1691–92, bearing the cipher of William III, which forms part of the great treasure of the kings of Hanover, now the property of the Duke of Cumberland. The arms engraved on this cup are those of William Stanton and his wife Margaret Gavell. Their daughter Rebecca married William Gooch, created a baronet in 1746, who saw much active service in the British army during the wars of Queen Anne's reign. He became colonel of an American regiment in 1740 and in 1742 served in Admiral Vernon's unsuccessful attack on Carthagena, where he was wounded; in honor of Admiral Vernon, Lawrence Washington named his estate Mount Vernon. In memory of her son Lady Gooch in her will of August 12, 1773, bequeathed to William and Mary College, Williamsburg: "as a small token of my Remembrance to the place of his education my Gilt Sacrament Cup." The cup was in use as a sacramental vessel in the chapel of William and Mary College, the burial place of Sir John Randolph and Norborne, Lord Botetourt. The historic church of Bruton Parish is a fitting repository for so priceless a relic of Virginian history, for it was there that the donor's husband, Sir William Gooch, worshipped during his governorship of

Virginia, to which office he had been appointed in 1727 by George I.

In the First Congregational Church at Woburn, Massachusetts, is a plain caudle cup (Illus. 54) with a bell-shaped body and two solid scrolled handles which are notched on the shoulders.   It was a legacy in 1726 from Colonel

54. George Hanners.   H. 5 in.

Eleazer Flegg, the son of Lieutenant Gershom Flagg, who was born in Woburn August 1, 1670. He was selectman and held various military positions from 1708 until his death.   The maker of the cup was George Hanners (1696–1740) of Boston, the son of Robert and Hannah (Matson) Hanners, who married Rebecca Peirson and left an estate valued at £2667.11.11.   George Hanners (1721–60), his son, was also a silversmith.

In England, toward the end of the reign of

Charles II, a straight-sided caudle cup appeared
with a spirally fluted surbase, a style followed
up to the accession of Queen Anne.  In St.
Saviourgate Presbyterian Chapel at York are
two specimens dated 1680–81.

In the First Congregational Society, Chelms-
ford, Massachusetts, is a Colonial caudle cup
(Illus. 55) of this description, with vertical flut-

55. JEREMIAH DUMMER.   H. 3¼ in.

ings, which is fitted with scrolled handles
foliated and beaded.   It was made by Jeremiah
Dummer (1645–1718) of Boston.   The body
and its fluting are similar to that of the standing cup by the same maker and exactly like
three cups on tall baluster stems wrought by
him, and the gift of James Everell in 1705 to the
First Church, Boston.   The diameter of each
is the same, 4¼ inches, which would suggest that
Dummer had made up bowls of this kind and
fitted handles to some as caudle cups and stems

to others as standing cups, according to the
requirements of his customers. Engraved on
the bottom are the initials $_{I}^{F}$ $_{L}$ for John and
Lydia (Fletcher) Fisk who were married in 1666.
He was the son of Rev. John Fisk first pastor of
the church. Rev. Sampson Stoddard, its third
pastor, grandson of Anthony Stoddard called
by Sewall "the ancientest shopkeeper in Town,"
bequeathed to the church in 1740 a plain flat-
topped tankard made by Thomas Millner (1690–
1745) of Boston.

A little later an embossed fluted or corded
band was added just below the lip, to the same
kind of English fluted cup which also became

56. LONDON, 1718–19. H. 3⅝ in.

somewhat taller. An example of this type
(Illus. 56), belonging to Dr. Denman W. Ross,
has the London date-letter for 1718–19.

A very fine Colonial example (Illus. 57) of
this type was the gift of Ebenezer Withington
May 22, 1721 to the First Church, Dorchester,

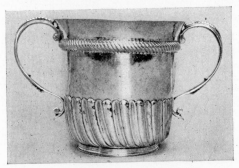

57. WILLIAM COWELL. H. 4¾ in.

which has presented it to the Church of the
Unity, Neponset, Massachusetts.   It was made
by William Cowell (1682–1736) of Boston, the
son of John Cowell a blacksmith of Boston,
who married Elizabeth Kilby.   William Cowell
held various town offices; constable, overseer of
shingles, scavenger, and clerk of the market.
His estate amounted to £3309.19.4.   Sewall, in
his diary, under the date of June 21, 1707 notes :
"Billy Cowell's shop is entered by the Chimney,
and a considerable quantity of Plate stolen.   I
give him a Warrant to the Constable, they find
James Hews hid in the Hay in Cabal's Barn on
the Back side of the Comon; while they was
seising of him under the Hay, he strip'd
off his Pocket which was quickly after found,

and Cowell's silver in it." His son, William
Cowell junior (1713–61), was also a silversmith.

The next stage in the progress of the caudle
cup is that which shows the same fluted body
and band, with the embellishment of a large oval
panel surrounded by scrolls and acanthus foliage. Its introduction in England would seem
to coincide with the accession of Queen Anne
during whose reign and that of George I it
was exceedingly popular. An historical cup of
this kind, dated 1721–22, was given by Josiah
Wedgwood, the famous potter, to the Old Meeting
House at Newcastle-under-Lyme, of which he was
a trustee and member. Hogarth shows a similar
cup in the picture, "Death of the Countess," in
his celebrated series, "Marriage à la Mode."

58. London, 1702–03. H. 4 in.

Belonging to the Scroll and Key Society of
Yale College is a caudle cup (Illus. 58) from the
Betts collection, with the London date-letter for

1702–03, which exemplifies the type. It was
made by Robert Peake who wrought the service
in St. Philip's Church, Charleston, South Caro-

59. LONDON, 1775–76. H. 4½ in.

lina, that was presented by Colonel William
Rhett, churchwarden. The donor was captain
of the merchant ship *Providence*, and there is a
tradition that he had captured the silver in 1718
from the privateer Stede Bonnet, who was
hanged at Charleston.

This variety of cup was revived towards the
end of the third quarter of the eighteenth century in England. It, however, had a higher
base and the decoration was apt to be even
more ornate. Of this period is a caudle cup
(Illus. 59) also from the Betts collection, with
the London date-letter for 1775–76, probably
made by Thomas Wynne. Neither of these
varieties seems ever to have been copied by the

Colonial silversmiths as doubtless the ornateness did not appeal to them.

The caudle cup was rarely made on the continent of Europe. A Portuguese cup (Illus. 60) belonging to Dr. Theodore S. Woolsey, dates from the early part of the eighteenth century. It shows a very marked difference from the English and Colonial cups. The upper part of the body is plain but scalloped in octofoil shape; the lower part is embossed in a diaper pattern; the small scrolled handles extend above the lip and the base is low and plain.

60. PORTUGUESE, 1700. H. 3½ in.

That so comparatively few caudle cups are found in the old families may be accounted for perhaps by the fact that most of the earliest made were given to the churches upon the decease of the owners; they were more convenient to pass at the communion service than the standing cup or beaker : consequently when the churches required more vessels they ordered cups with handles. Probably the caudle cup thus came to be looked upon more conventionally as a communion cup rather than as a cup for secular use. During the corresponding period the tank-

ard was being made in New England more generally than theretofore; and for domestic use
this superseded the caudle cup, as the caudle
cup had superseded the beaker and the beaker
the standing cup.

# TANKARDS

THE tankard enjoyed great popularity as a drinking vessel in the beer drinking countries of Northern Europe during the sixteenth, seventeenth and eighteenth centuries. Its unsuitability for a wine vessel was against its adoption among the Latin nations of Europe. The earliest form of the tankard was globular, usually heavily embossed, while the shape had been derived from the pottery jugs so often mounted by the Elizabethan silversmiths. One of these silver mounted German jugs (Illus. 61) dated 1590 was

61. STONEWARE, 1590. H. 5⅝ in.

given to Governor John Winthrop's father in
1607 by his sister Lady Mildmay. It came
into the possession of the American Antiquarian
Society of Worcester in 1825, upon the death of
William Winthrop, "the seventh proprietor in
direct lineal descent," who also gave a tankard,
made by Josiah Austin (1719–80), to St. Mary's
Church, Newton Lower Falls, Massachusetts.

A very rare variety of English tankard was
small in size with a plain tapering body from
which the moulded lip and base, inseparable
in later tankards, is absent; the cover is quite
flat and the wide scrolled thumb-piece has been
copied from those on the Jacobean flagons.
One dated 1635–36 is at Trinity Hall, Cambridge. This type of Charles I tankard was
succeeded in the Commonwealth by a larger
tankard also devoid of decoration. The low
flat-topped cover is in two stages, while the base
is wide and splayed like those of the tall flagons
of the reign of Charles I. With the restoration
of the monarchy in 1660, and the more settled
condition of the country, the English silversmiths
were busily engaged in making tankards in that
luxurious period.

An example (Illus. 62) has the London date
letter for 1674–75 and the maker's mark W C.
It has a plain cylindrical body with a narrow
moulded lip and base; a flat-topped cover
pointed in front; a large scrolled handle and a
thumb-piece, or purchase as it is often called,
formed of two semi-globular or cupped discs,

K

62. LONDON, 1674–75.  H. 5¼ in.

flanking a pear-shaped hollow. Pounced on the handle is the date 1674 below which are the initials F I E undoubtedly those of some of the Frost family. It was bequeathed in 1724 to the Church at Berwick, Maine, by Major Charles Frost; he was a son of Major Charles Frost who was killed by the Indians on his way home from that church July 14, 1697. His second wife was Jane Eliot widow of Andrew Pepperell, a brother of Sir William Pepperell.

A very rare type of tankard made in England in the last quarter of the seventeenth century is the "peg" tankard, which was introduced from Denmark, of which not more than eight English examples are known. It was so called from the row of eight pegs fixed vertically inside, where the handle is attached; it was from this drinking vessel that the expression "taking down a peg" was derived. A very fine peg tankard made by John Plummer of York in 1684–85 is in the collection of the late Mr. J. Pierpont Morgan: and an illustration of one by the same

maker, dated 1681–82, presented to William IV
by Lord Ducie, is shown in "Gold and Silver
of Windsor Castle," 1911. This tankard is
cylindrical, delicately engraved with sprays of
tulips and other flowers, and stands on three
pomegranate feet. The plain scrolled handle
terminates in a shield and the thumb-piece is
formed of two pomegranates. The slightly
domed cover is engraved with tulips and fruit.

Of similar decoration to the English caudle
cup of 1686–87 is the tankard (Illus. 63) with a
surbase of acanthus leaves, a variety of ornament popular on English plate between 1670
and 1695. The flat cover engraved with tulips

63. TIMOTHY DWIGHT. H. 6 in.

is in two stages; a long V-shaped support,
pierced with a trefoil, is on the body where the

handle is affixed; the spout was added at a later date.  Engraved on the front is a full-rigged ship and the initials $\frac{C}{WD\&E}$ for William Downes and Elizabeth (Edwards) Cheever who were married in 1749.  It belongs to Dr. Frederick C. Shattuck, a descendant.  This fine tankard was made by one of the earliest of the second generation of Boston silversmiths, Timothy Dwight (1654–91), whose father Captain Timothy Dwight of Dedham married for his third wife Anne Flynt the niece of Edmund Quincy: he was apprenticed to John Hull without doubt.  Timothy Dwight's half-brother Nathaniel was the great-grandfather of Timothy Dwight president of Yale College.  There is no record of this tankard prior to the date 1749, but it is supposed to have come into the Cheever family through Elizabeth Edwards — daughter of Thomas Edwards (1701–55), the silversmith, whose first wife was Sarah Burr of Charlestown. John Stedman came to Cambridge in 1638 as steward or general superintendent in the affairs of Rev. Jose Glover who left "his faythful servant, John Stedman, the sum of fifty pounds." John Stedman, the son, to whom was granted the monopoly of the fur trade for Cambridge in 1658, was treasurer of the county for twenty-six years and was prominent in military affairs. He died December 16, 1693, at the age of 92. His eldest daughter Elizabeth married, as her second husband, Henry Thompson a merchant of Boston; their daughter Dorothy Thompson married Nov. 16, 1692 Samuel Shove of Boston, by whom she had a daughter Sarah who took the name of Burr upon her mother's second marriage to Samuel Burr. The latter's will, probated in 1719, contains the following clause: "to my daughter Sarah my silver tankard w$^{ch}$ was her Great G$^d$ fathers Stedman." This is without doubt the Dwight tankard.

64. Jeremiah Drummer. H. 5$\frac{3}{8}$ in.

A tankard (Illus. 64), wrought by Jeremiah Dummer (1645–1718), has a flat cover serrated in front, with a fluted shoulder and applied on the top is a flat cut tulip. A similar flower is applied on the body where the lower part of the handle is affixed; the thumb-piece is a double scroll. The applied foliage, or "cut-card" work, is a familiar decoration on English plate between the years 1660 and 1690, as has been noted on the caudle cup of 1686–87. The tip of the handle is missing, but undoubtedly it was either a cherub's face or a plain shield. It was the gift to the South Parish, Portsmouth, New Hampshire, of Mrs. Mary Shurtleff, widow of Rev. William Shurtleff

second pastor of that parish, and sister of Theodore Atkinson.   Engraved on the bottom are
the initials $_W^S{}_S$ for William and Susanna Shurtleff, the parents of Rev. William Shurtleff, who
were married in 1683.

An unusually fine tankard (Illus. 65) with a
fluted shoulder, has a cover which is serrated
on either side of the hinge as well as in front.
The flat top is encircled with an engraved border
of leaves and flowers ;  the handle is embossed
with fruit, terminating in a leaf;  a cherub's
head, cast and chased, is on the tip, and the
thumb-piece is a
mask between two
dolphins.   It was
made by Henry
Hurst (1665–1717)
of Boston.   The
original initials en-
graved on the bot-
tom $_T{}_K$ cannot be
identified, but the
initials AL are for
Abigail Lindall who
married on October
26, 1704, Benjamin
Pickman of Salem,
the great-great-

65. HENRY HURST. H. 5⅞ in.

grandfather of the present owner, Mr. Dudley
L. Pickman.

In the First Parish (Unitarian) Cambridge, Massachusetts, where the Rev. Thomas Shepard was pastor, is a pair of plain tankards wrought by John Coney (1655–1722) of Boston. They are similar to the Hurst tankard except in the twisted thumb-piece, and have been referred to in the introduction as the gift of William Wilcocks in 1654. They are additionally interesting from the fact that presidents of Harvard College

66. PETER VAN DYCK. H. 6¼ in.

and other distinguished men of past generations have received the sacrament from them. These flat-topped tankards appear to have been made in New England from about 1690 to 1730.

Belonging to the First Congregational Church, (Old Stratfield) Bridgeport, Connecticut, is a tankard (Illus. 66) made by Peter Van Dyck (1684–1750) of New York. The moulded base has a border of cut acanthus leaves and a zigzag wire applied — forms of decoration frequently found upon objects wrought by the silversmiths of New York. The flat-topped cover has an elaborate serrated front and the thumb-piece is a horizontal twist. The handle has an applied cherub's face surrounded by ornamentation from which depends fruit; and upon the flat serrated disc on the end of the handle a cherub's face is also applied. Lieutenant Richard Hubbel of Stratfield, a wealthy and influential planter, by his will dated November 12, 1734, gives: "my Silver Tankard to the Church of Christ in Stratfield for ye use of ye Lords Tabell." This tankard, it will be observed, does not differ in form from the flat-topped tankards made by the New England silversmiths. It is purely English in origin and not Dutch; and is typical of the tankards wrought by the New York silversmiths, who were not influenced by the changing fashions in England.

A tankard with a domed cover came into fashion in England a few years after the accession of Queen Anne, but it had made its appearance as early as 1695 and was popular from 1710 to 1735. The style was not abandoned until about 1765. This type seems to have made its appearance in New England about 1715.

67. George Hanners. H. 7¼ in.

A plain tankard (Illus. 67) of this description, made by George Hanners (1696–1740) of Boston, belongs to Mr. Dwight M. Prouty. It is engraved on the bottom with the date 1738 and the initials $\begin{smallmatrix} P \\ P\,M \end{smallmatrix}$ for Philip and Mehitable Pollard of Nantucket. The tip of the handle

68. JOSEPH KNEELAND. H. 6¾ in.

is a Queen Anne shilling. George Hanners also made five tall beakers for the Congregational Church at Greenland, New Hampshire, one of which has been generously given to the Museum of Fine Arts at Boston.

A moulded band encircles the body of the plain tankard (Illus. 68) made by Joseph Kneeland (1698–1760) of Boston, which is one of a pair given to Harvard College in 1729 by John and William Vassall who were graduated there in 1732 and 1733 respectively. This tankard was the gift of John Vassall, who was born in the West Indies in 1713, and who married Elizabeth the daughter of Lieutenant-Governor Spencer Phipps. He built the house on Brattle Street in

Cambridge now known as the residence of the poet Longfellow. At the time of the Revolution he fled with his family to England and his estate was confiscated; the house then became the headquarters of General Washington. The father of John and William Vassall was Leonard Vassall, a conspicuous churchman, who gave to Christ Church, Boston, in 1730 a plain paten engraved with the Vassall arms enclosed in a panel similar to that on the tankards. The paten bears the London date-letter for 1715–16 and was made by John Read the maker of the service of 1710–11 in St. Michael's Parish, Talbot County, Maryland.

Towards the end of the seventeenth century, the lower part of the English tankard was occasionally spirally fluted, like the contemporary caudle cup. The type with the domed cover was so made and also had a fluted border on the cover. Tankards with this decoration do not appear to have been made by the Colonial silversmiths. Of the latter variety is the tankard (Illus. 69) with the London date-letter for 1716–17, made by Seth Lofthouse, and engraved with the Lowell arms. It belongs to Mrs. Stanley Cunningham — a granddaughter of James Russell Lowell, who had previously owned it during his life at "Elmwood." This fine house was the residence in Revolutionary times of Thomas Oliver, the last of the lieutenant-governors appointed by the king: his wife was the daughter of John Vassall. In September,

1774, in compliance with the commands of four thousand people who surrounded the house, he signed his resignation and took refuge with the British soldiers in Boston. Benedict Arnold and his Connecticut company were quartered at Elmwood upon their arrival in Cambridge just after the battle of Lexington, and after the battle of Bunker Hill the house became a hospital.

Comparatively few tankards with domed covers are found without finials, which seem to have been a product of the New England silversmiths, as were too the cherubs' heads and masks so frequently found on the terminations of the handles. Such finials and tips are rarely found on English tankards. Some of these finials are similar to those found on New England furniture.

69. LONDON, 1716–17.   H. 7½ in.

In the First Parish, Plymouth, Massachusetts, founded in 1620, is a plain tankard (Illus. 70) that has a domed and moulded cover with a turned finial, a scrolled thumb-piece and a plain boss on the end of the handle. It was made by John Edwards (1670–1746) of Boston,

70. JOHN EDWARDS. H. 7 in.

and was a gift from Priscilla Faunce; she was the daughter of Elder Thomas Faunce (1647–1746) who, by his long life of ninety-nine years, served as a connecting link between the Pilgrims — many of whom he had known in boyhood — and later generations. The traditions with relation to Plymouth Rock were derived from him.

The only English tankard (Illus. 71) of this description in an American church has a plain moulding encircling the body, a heart termination on the end of the handle, and a finial which on an English tankard is very unusual. It was a bequest to the Baptist Church of Warren, Rhode Island, from Nicholas Campbell, whose monument in the North cemetery bears the following inscription: "Sacred to the memory of Mr Nicholas Campbell who was born on the Island of Malta Dec. 24, 173. and came to this country previous to the American Revolution and died in this town July 21, 1829 in the 97th year of his age. He was one of the ever memorable Boston Tea Party who performed one of the first acts of Resistance to the British oppression by the destruction of a Cargo of Tea in the Harbour of Boston; and commenced that glorious struggle which terminated in our National Independence. He faithfully discharged all the duties of a good citizen and has ever been highly respected for his industry benevolence and integrity of character." The tankard bears the Birmingham date-letter for 1779–80 and the makers' marks for James Fothergill and Matthew Boulton. The latter was a manufacturer of plated goods and steel in Birmingham and became the partner of James Watt, through whose wise and vigorous management the steam-engine was made a success. To his father James Watt wrote from Birmingham in December, 1774: "The business I am here about has turned out rather successful; that is to say, that the fire-engine I have invented is now going, and answers much better than any other that has yet been made, and I expect that the invention will be very beneficial to me." Such was

71. BIRMINGHAM, 1779–80. H. 8¾ in.

Watt's modest announcement of the practical
success of the greatest invention of the eighteenth century!  When Boswell visited him in
1776 Boulton remarked: "I sell here, sir, what
all the world desires to have — Power."  Boulton
and Watt were employed by the British government to recoin the
copper specie of the
kingdom.   These
massive large cop-
per pennies with
their raised rims
and incised letter-
ing weighed fully
an ounce and effec-
tively checked the
great outburst of
tokens at that time
appearing.

72. LONDON, 1775–76.   H. 8 in.

In the middle of
the eighteenth cen-
tury the tankard
with a "bellied"
or bulbous body, a
domed cover and a high moulded foot, with and
without a moulding encircling the body, came
into vogue in England, and its popularity was
greatest in the third quarter of that century.

Of this type is the tankard (Illus. 72) with
the London date-letter for 1775–76, made by
Charles Wright.  It belongs to Mrs. James A.
Garland and was given to Martin Hern by the

two London parishes of St. Giles-in-the-Fields
and St. George, Bloomsbury, for "having laud-
ably assisted in bringing forward a number of
volunteers which
these parishes had
to raise for His
Majesty's army in
December 1796."

A massive tank-
ard of this descrip-
tion (Illus. 73) has
gadrooned borders
on the base and lip.
The maker's ini-
tials J A in script,
are perhaps those
of some Boston
silversmith, al-
though the Co-
lonial silversmiths
seldom made this
variety of tankard.
The borders are
derived from such
a piece of English

73. Colonial? H. 9 in.

plate as the covered caudle cup at Williamsburg. The scrolled thumb-piece has a fluted top.
Engraved in front are the entwined initials
B M D for Barnt and Mary De Klyn; he was
born in Boston and moved to a farm near Trenton in 1784. It was presented in 1857 to the
First Presbyterian Church of Trenton in New

Jersey, by their daughter Catherine Beatty widow of General John Beatty who was taken prisoner at Fort Washington. In 1780 John Beatty settled at Princeton as a physician; he was a member of the convention that adopted the Federal Constitution and from 1795 to 1805 was secretary of state for New Jersey.

74. Samuel Williamson.    H. 8¼ in.

Tankards, both barrel-shaped and cylindrical, and hooped like a barrel, were made in large numbers in England at the end of the eighteenth and at the beginning of the nineteenth century. Of the latter type is the tankard (Illus. 74) presented in 1832 to the First Congregational Church, Deerfield, Massachusetts, by John Williams a prominent tory at the time of the Revolution. The domed cover is surmounted by an eagle and the thumb-piece is pierced. It was made by Samuel Williamson of Philadelphia. Inscribed on one side is: "Presented by the Directors of the Banks of the United States, North-America & Pennsylvania To John Wil-

liams Esquire, of Deerfield in the State of Massachusetts Justice of the Peace, in consideration of
Services rendered their Institutions A.D. 1801."
The National Bank of North America, Philadelphia, was the first bank to take a charter
under the National Banking Act. The donor's
grandfather Rev. John Williams, first pastor of
Deerfield, was among the inhabitants carried
into captivity when the Indians burned the
town in 1704; his wife was murdered on the
way to Montreal where he was held for two
years; upon his return he wrote a narrative of
his adventures in "The Redeemed Captive."

In the churches are more than one hundred
and thirty tankards that have been used, not as
flagons to hold the wine, but as sacramental cups.
Flagons were used in England for "Church
Ales" and for serving hot spiced drinks at
funerals. In New England similar hospitable
customs prevailed and liquor was supplied at
the cost of the parish. At the funeral of Mary
Norton, widow of Rev. John Norton minister of
the First Church, Boston, over fifty-one gallons
of best Malaga wine were consumed by the
mourners. In 1742 the General Court of Massachusetts forbade the use of wine and rum at
funerals.

A long-cherished delusion is that the ends of
most of the handles of the tankards after 1660
are fitted with "whistles," for the purpose of
whistling for a further supply of liquor. But
these are in reality "blow-holes," which insure

L

equality between the internal and external pressure of the air and, therefore, prevent any deformations of the metal which may be softened as the result of the changes of temperature occurring during the process of soldering.

Many an early tankard was saved from the · melting pot by adding a spout, at the time of the temperance movement. In a way, this enabled the possessor to eat his cake and have it too! A spout in no way interfered with its customary use; nor, for that matter, was anything gained — the early flagons pour readily; but the tankard assumed a more respectable appearance in the eyes of the envious neighbor who did not possess one and the fortunate owner eased his conscience by the reflection that "things are not what they seem."

# FLAGONS

THE development of the flagon was the same as that of the tankard and both were used for the same purpose. The earliest type was of globular form, but the tall cylindrical flagons were first wrought in England towards the close of Queen Elizabeth's reign. Examples of both the globular and cylindrical forms made in 1594–95 are illustrated in Mr. E. Alfred Jones's book on the old English plate of the Emperor of Russia, whose collection of early cylindrical flagons is unrivalled.

In the church of St. Mary Woolnoth in London — the burial place of Sir William Phipps, governor of Massachusetts — is a pair of cylindrical flagons dated 1587–88; and in St. Mary's Church, Great Brington, in Northamptonshire, the burial place of Robert Washington and his wife Elizabeth, is a plain flagon dated 1605–06. The shape of these flagons was retained throughout the seventeenth century, while the Jacobean decoration was abandoned about 1620. The flagons of Charles I and of the Commonwealth tend to become less in height and greater in width, while the short moulded bases of the earlier flagons are superseded by wide splayed

75. LONDON, 1649–50.  H. 10 in.

bases. These plain cylindrical flagons with their bright surfaces reflecting light and shade are unsurpassed in dignity and in purity of form.

The cylindrical flagon (Illus. 75) of the Commonwealth period, with the London date-letter for 1649–50 and the maker's mark TG, with the thumb-piece broken, is inscribed: "Hampton parrish in Yorke County in Verginia." It belongs to Grace Church, York-Hampton Parish, York County, at Yorktown, Virginia, where the surrender of Lord Cornwallis occurred in 1781.

This shape of flagon was generally adopted by the churches in England, at the restoration of Charles II, to take the place of the vessels destroyed during the Civil War a few years previously. A pair of plain flagons of the year 1660–61 in the private chapel of the Archbishops of Canterbury at Lambeth Palace is of great historic interest; these were in use at the consecration services in 1787 of the bishops of the American Episcopal church — William White rector of Christ Church, Philadelphia, and Samuel Provoost rector of Trinity church at New York. They also figured in 1790, in the consecration of James Madison as bishop of Virginia, the last of the American bishops to be consecrated in England.

The tall plain cylindrical flagons, with flat-topped covers, remained the conventional type throughout the reigns of William and Mary and of Queen Anne. One of the finest cylin-drical flagons of the reign of William and Mary is that of 1691–92 in the Tower of London; it is decorated with cherubs' faces and festoons of flowers and fruit in a man-ner suggestive of the influence of the carvings of Grin-ling Gibbons, and of the sculptured work of Sir Chris-topher Wren.

In Christ Church, at Cambridge, Massachusetts, is a flagon (Illus. 76) with an X-shaped thumb-piece, and

76. LONDON, 1694–95. H. 12½ in.

the London date-letter for 1694–95. It is inscribed :— "The gift of K William & Q Mary to
y$^e$ Reve$^d$ Sam$^{ll}$ Myles for y$^e$ use of their Maj$^{ties}$
Chappell in N : England : 1694." Rev. Samuel
Myles, son of Rev. John Myles first pastor of the
Baptist Church at Swansea in Massachusetts,
was rector and the virtual founder of King's
Chapel in Boston, to which this flagon and a
chalice with a paten-cover were originally given
by William and Mary, whose cipher and royal
arms are engraved upon them. It was in Christ
Church that Washington worshipped when he
came to Cambridge to take command of the
American army in July, 1775 ; he lived in the
Craigie house, later the residence of the poet
Longfellow. The flagon was wrought by Francis
Garthorne the maker of the large service presented by Queen Anne to Trinity Church, New
York, and of the flagon given by William III
to St. Anne's Parish, Annapolis, Maryland. He
was also the maker of vessels dated 1711–12 at
St. Paul's Church, Halifax, Nova Scotia, which
are of historical and sentimental interest, for they
were used by the American loyalists and by
Charles Inglis, the first English Colonial bishop
of Nova Scotia and the last British rector of
Trinity Church, New York.

In the Presbyterian Church at Hyattsville,
Prince George's County, Maryland, is a plain
cylindrical flagon (Illus. 77), made by Matthew
Lofthouse, with a domed cover and a scrolled
thumb-piece, bearing the London date-letter for

1707–08. It was the gift of Colonel Ninian
Beall originally to the old Presbyterian Church
at Patuxent, or Upper Marlborough, for which
he had given the site. He was born in 1625 in
Scotland and fought against Cromwell in the
battle of Dunbar
in 1650; there he
was taken prisoner
and transported to
Barbados and
thence to Mary-
land. In 1692 he
was made "colonel
and commander-
in-chief of all their
Majesty's forces or
militia of horse and
foot in Calvert
County." He was
elected in 1696 one
of the first two
Burgesses; in 1703
he received from
Lord Baltimore a
grant of 795 acres

77. LONDON, 1707–08. H. 11 in.

called the "Rock of Dumbarton," which includes
much of the ground on which Georgetown in the
District of Columbia now stands. A similar
flagon in Hungars Parish, Northampton County,
Virginia, with the London date-letter for 1736–
37 and an unknown maker's mark, HL, was the
gift in 1741 of John Custis Esq. of Williamsburg.

He married in 1706 Frances daughter of Colonel
Daniel Parke secretary of the Colonial council; their son Daniel Parke Custis married in
1749 the beautiful Martha Dandridge, afterwards the wife of George Washington. In his
will of 1749 John Custis leaves explicit instructions about his tombstone and the inscription
to be placed upon it, which ends: "Aged —
years and yet lived but seven years which was
the space of time he kept a Batchelors House at
Arlington on the Eastern Shoar of Virginia."

In St. George's Parish, formerly Baltimore
(now Harford) County in Maryland, is a tall
flagon (Illus. 78)
with a turned finial
which is unusual on
an English flagon;
it bears the Lon-
don date-letter for
1717–18 and was
made by Thomas
Langford.

A plain English
flagon with a
domed cover, dated
1763–64, is in St.
George's German
Lutheran Church
in Goodman's
Fields, London, E.,
whose first pastor,
Gustave Anthony

78. London, 1717–18.  H. 13 in.

Wachsel, will be remembered for the part he played in 1764, when the incident of the six hundred Wurtzburgers and Palatines took place. These unfortunate Germans had been induced, by an adventurer named Stumple, to leave their homes in Germany under the promise that they would be permitted to settle in the islands of St. John and St. Croix, in America; but as soon as they had been shipped for England, their so-called benefactor deserted them and they reached London in a destitute condition. This worthy pastor, however, with much energy and benevo-lence, succeeded in interesting King George III and the people of London in their unhappy con-dition, and, mainly owing to his efforts, their immediate wants were alleviated by public sub-scription and other material support, while their future was assured by means of the King's grant of land in South Carolina. It is believed that the flagon was used when the communion was administered to many of these unhappy Ger-mans, just before their departure for America.

The introduction of silver flagons into the Puritan churches of New England is not only a sign of the growing material prosperity of the people, but also marks the gradual decline in the repugnance to vessels which were common in the Church of England, and which would have been regarded by the early emigrants as osten-tatious if not ritualistic. The use of such costly accessories of the communion table confirms in some degree Daniel Neal's remark in 1720 that the Colonists "affect to be as English as possible."

One of the earliest Colonial flagons (Illus. 79) belongs to the Second Church of Boston. It

has the tall cylindrical body with mouldings encircling the body below the moulded lip and above the moulded base; the moulded cover has a flat top with a turned finial, and the thumb-piece is formed of two cupped discs. Within the large foliated panel is inscribed: "Mrs. Elizabeth Wensley to the Second Church of Christ In Boston

79. PETER OLIVER.  H. 12¼ in.

1711." She was the daughter of William Paddy who went to Plymouth in 1635 and later moved to Boston, where she married John Wensley a mariner. The flagon was made by Peter Oliver (1682–1712) of Boston who married March 1, 1712 the donor's daughter Hopestill Wensley. Peter Oliver had previously married Jerusha, daughter of Increase Mather, who died December 30, 1710. He was the son of John Oliver,

a merchant of Boston, and of his wife Susanna
Sweet. His mother's sister Mary Sweet married
David Edwards, and they were the parents of
Susanna Edwards who married John Noyes
(1674–1749) the maker in 1711 of a similar
flagon for the Brattle Street Church. Three
other similar flagons are in the same church;
one dated 1711, made by Nathaniel Morse
(1685–1748) of
Boston ; one 1712,
by John Edwards
(1670–1746), and
one 1713 made
by Edward Win-
slow (1669–1753).
They are now the
property of the
Museum of Fine
Arts at Boston.

The earliest flag-
on (Illus. 80) made
south of New
York is in Christ
Church, Philadel-
phia, and is a copy
of the Queen Anne
flagon of 1708 in
that church. This
was the gift in
1712 of Colonel
Robert Quary, do-
nor to St. Mary's

80. PHILIP SYNG. H. 11 in.

Church at Burlington, New Jersey, of the covered beaker. The maker was Philip Syng (1676–1739) of Philadelphia; he was the probable maker and joint donor of a silver paten in Holy Trinity Church at Oxford, Pennsylvania, whose son Philip Syng (1703–89) made the

silver inkstand used at the signing of the Declaration of Independence.

Belonging to Immanuel Church at New Castle, Delaware, is a small plain flagon (Illus. 81) with a low flat cover, a scrolled thumb-piece and a moulded band encircling the body. It was made by Simeon Soumaine of New York.

81. SIMEON SOUMAINE. H. 7 in.

There is a tradition, which still survives, that it was the gift of Queen Anne.

A flagon (Illus. 82) with a domed and moulded cover and a cherub in relief upon an oval disc on the end of the handle, made by William Cowell junior (1713–61) of Boston, is dated 1753. It is engraved with the Dummer arms and inscribed: "Presented to the Church of Christ in Hollis-Street under the Pastoral care of the Rev<sup>d</sup> Mather Byles, D.D. By the Honorable William Dummer, Esq<sup>r</sup> Late Lieu<sup>t</sup> Governor and Commander in Cheif of the Massachusetts." A portrait of the donor, painted by Sir Godfrey Kneller, and also a gold snuff box that belonged to William Dummer, are in the possession of the Misses Loring. The Rev. Mather Byles had decidedly pronounced tory proclivities and the church records under date of August 9, 1776 state that Rev. Dr. Byles had joined the British after the siege of Boston "against the liberties of the country." He was a noted wit and of him a contemporary wrote these lines:

82. WILLIAM COWELL, JUNIOR.
H. 13¼ in.

"There's punning Byles provokes our smiles,
    A man of stately parts;
Who visits folks to crack his jokes,
    That never mend their hearts.

With strutting gait and wig so great,
  He walks along the streets,
And throws out wit, or what's liké it,
  To every one he meets."

Governor Belcher gave the land upon which
the church was built; but the street was
named for Thomas Hollis, the benefactor of
Harvard College, whose nephew gave the bell
to that church.

A flagon similar to that in the Hollis Street
Church, belonging to the Old South Church,
was made by Joseph Moulton 2d (1740–1818)
of Newburyport, Massachusetts, whose father
William Moulton and grandfather Joseph Moulton (1680–1756) were silversmiths. It was the
gift in 1804 of Hon. William Phillips a deacon
of the church. He was a son of Rev. Samuel
Phillips, first pastor of the South Church at
Andover, Massachusetts, and married Abigail
daughter of Edward and Abigail (Coney) Bromfield. Engraved upon it are the arms of Phillips
impaling those of Bromfield. Lieutenant-Governor William Phillips was his son. He and his
brothers Samuel and John and his nephew Lieutenant-Governor Samuel Phillips (the donor of a
silver flagon to the South Church at Andover)
were the founders of Phillips Academy. Samuel
Phillips (1658–1722), a silversmith of Salem and
Boston, was the grandfather of the donor, and
also the great-grandfather of John Phillips, who
was the first mayor of Boston and the father
of Wendell Phillips the orator and abolitionist.

A flagon of the ewer-shape (Illus. 83) with the London date-letter for 1767–68, made by W. & J. Priest, has a bulbous or "bellied" body. It was bought with a legacy of £70 to the First Congregational Society, Salem, Massachusetts, in 1731 from Colonel Samuel Browne who was the most prominent merchant of his time in Essex County. He was representa-

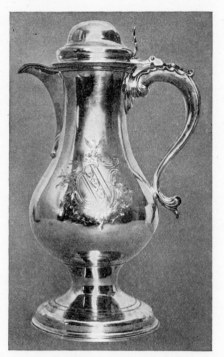

83. LONDON, 1767–68. H. 13 in.

tive at the general court; first town treasurer of Salem; judge of the superior court; colonel of the regiment, and a councillor. The flagon was not purchased until thirty-six years after his death, when a committee of the church was appointed to apply for a fulfilment of the legacy. A shield of arms is engraved upon it. In 1769 a duplicate of this flagon was made for the same church by John Andrew (1747–91) a silversmith of Salem, at the sign of the "Golden Cup." He was the grandfather of John A. Andrew known as the "war governor" of Massachusetts.

The old house at Salem in which Nathaniel Hawthorne was born is still standing; and the "House of the Seven Gables," restored to its former condition by Miss Emmerton, is of much historic interest. The desk which Hawthorne used in the Custom House and upon which he began to write the "Scarlet Letter" is in the Essex Institute at Salem.

84. John David.   H. 10 in.

Belonging to St. Peter's Church at Lewes, Delaware, is a flagon (Illus. 84) with a cone-shaped body, and a domed cover which has an arched thumb-piece. It was made by John David (1736–98) of Philadelphia, whose father Peter David was also a silversmith. It is inscribed as the gift in 1773 of the Hon. John Penn who was the grandson of William Penn the founder of Pennsylvania; but it was in reality purchased with funds received by him, as governor of the Three lower counties, from the estate of Henrietta Sims "who died without any relations or known kindred." A tankard engraved with the Penn arms, made by Joseph Anthony of Philadelphia and belonging to Captain W. L. Willey, is inscribed: "Presented by John Penn Jun$^{r.}$ & John Penn Esq$^{r.}$ to Mr. Charles Jarvis as a Respectful acknowledgment of his Services 1788." Charles Jarvis, a distinguished physician of Boston, was the son of Colonel Leonard Jarvis whose wife was a granddaughter of Colonel Benjamin Church; he was a patriot at the time of the Revolution and was appointed by Thomas Jefferson surgeon of the Marine Hospital, Chelsea.

In the First Congregational Church, Derby, Connecticut, is a flagon (Illus. 85) with a long pear-shaped body on a high moulded base, and a domed cover with a vase-shaped finial. The inscription within double branches is: "A Gift to the first Church of Christ in Derby by N$^{l.}$ French 1781." The donor Nathaniel French was the son of Francis French junior and was born at Derby in 1717. He took the oath of freeman and loyalty to the Colony in 1777 and 1778 and died in 1781. His will contains the following legacy: "I give one hundred pounds lawful money unto the First Ecclesiastical Society in Derby Forty pounds of which to be put into the Bank for the support of the Gospel in sd Society & Forty pounds of

M

which sd sum to purchase a silver Flaggon for the Church in sd Society & the remaining Twenty pounds to purchase small Bibles for the poor in sd Society sd Bibles to be purchased & distributed at the discretion of my Executors." This flagon was not ordered until later. The church records state: "April 5th 1800. The business was completed according to the appointment and a silver Flagon procured of the value of 40 Pounds L Money — which was made by Mr. Ebenezer Chittenden of New haven who was upwards of 70 years of age." Ebenezer Chittenden (1726–1812) was born at Madison in Connecticut, and worked at his trade in that place;

85. Ebenezer Chittenden.   H. 17¼ in.

he moved to New Haven about 1770.

In the second half of the eighteenth century the classical revival in Europe exerted a great influence and manifested itself in various ways. A change took place, in England, in the shapes and decoration of the goldsmiths' work in the third quarter of the century when "consequent upon the discoveries made in the course of excavations at Herculaneum and Pompeii, classical forms were adopted in place of the rococo designs of the preceding period."

86. JESSE CHURCHILL. H. 15¾ in.

Jesse Churchill (1773–1819) of Boston made a pair of flagons for the West Church at Boston. The son of their first pastor, Rev. William Hooper, was a signer of the Declaration of Independence.

These are of the quasi-classical shape with reeded edges and an engraved border of leaves and flowers. It was probably from some such cup as the English one of 1781–82 in the First Parish, Watertown, that the shape of the body of the flagons was derived. The handles are square-shaped and the domed covers have pineapple finials. The inscription : "The Property of the Church at West Boston" is engraved within an oak wreath. That church was discontinued in 1892 and the building is now used as a branch of the Boston Public Library. Most of its silver was presented at that time to the Museum of Fine Arts. John Smibert, who came to Boston in 1728 with Dean Berkeley, attended that church with his wife Mary Williams whom he married at Boston ; he painted most of the contemporary worthies of New England and the only known portrait of Jonathan Edwards the greatest of American metaphysicians. In 1806 Rev. Charles Lowell, the father of James Russell Lowell, became minister of the church.

A flagon of similar shape with a handle formed of two flat wires joined together by an oval ring, was made by Rufus and Henry Farnam of Boston. The bill dated Oct. 15, 1805, is in the possession of the First Baptist Church, Salem, Massachusetts, which has generously presented the flagon to the Museum of Fine Arts, Boston.

In the First Reformed Church, Fishkill, New York, is a flagon (Illus. 87) made by I. W. Forbes of New York, decorated with bands of

classical honeysuckle. It is inscribed: "Presented by Samuel Verplanck Esq[r.] To the
First Reformed Church in the Town of Fishkill
To commemorate Mr. Eglebert Huff by birth
a Norwegian, in
his life-time at-
tached to the Life
Guards of the
Prince of Orange
(afterwards King
William III of
England), he re-
sided for a number
of years in this
country, and died
with unblemished
reputation at Fish-
kill, 21, March,
1765, aged 128
years Fishkill Jan-
uary 1820." In
his "Pictorial Field
Book of the Revo-
lution," Benson
John Lossing, who

87. I. W. FORBES. H. 12½ in.

was at one time a silversmith, says: "it is related of Huff that when 120 years old he made
love to a pretty girl of twenty. She already
had an accepted lover of her own age, and of
course rejected the suit of the Nestor. The old
suitor was indignant at the refusal. He thought
he had the best right to claim the heart and

hand of the maiden, for he had a hundred years more experience than 'the foolish boy,' and knew better how to treat a wife than the interfering stripling." Fishkill has great historic associations connected with the Revolution: a place chosen as a depository for military stores and for the confinement of tory and other prisoners; and there the "Constitution of the State of New York" was printed in 1777 by

88. WELLES AND COMPANY.  H. 12 in.

Samuel Loudon. That vicinity is the scene of many of the most thrilling events portrayed by Cooper in "The Spy: a Tale of the Neutral Ground."

In Grace Church, Providence, Rhode Island, is a complete communion service of six pieces which was made by Welles and Company of Boston, of which firm George Welles (1784–1827) had been a partner. The flagon is here reproduced (Illus. 88). These pieces are decorated with a band of classical ornament applied in relief, a fashion prevailing in England and derived from the designs of John

Flaxman "a gifted English artist who was deeply influenced by this classical revival, the sculptor of many notable monuments." He was engaged by Wedgwood at the age of twenty-two to copy a head of Medusa after an antique gem and later entered his employ. How far-reaching was his influence in effecting a change in the design of English silver is apparent from the "old-fashioned" vessels that were cast aside to make way for the new passion for classical design. The "Shield of Achilles," with subjects from the eighteenth book of the Iliad, at Windsor Castle, was designed by him. An illustration of this shield, as well as of other objects designed by Flaxman, is in Mr. E. Alfred Jones's "Gold and Silver of Windsor Castle," 1911. The Elgin marbles, brought to England in 1801–03, had much effect in directing the public taste into classical channels.

# MUGS

WHILE mugs followed the forms of the tankard and flagon, it will be seen that the caudle cup and beaker influenced the silversmiths as well.

A mug (Illus. 89) made by Alexander Forbes, with the Edinburgh date-letter for 1682–83, belongs to Mr. Guy Warren Walker. The shape of the body, and the notched handle also, has been derived from the earlier made English caudle cups. The vertical strap-work on the lower part of the body would seem to be a glorified form in relief of the flat sort of fluted ornamentation such as that on the English standing cup of 1607–08 in the Old South Church, Boston. The decoration is similar to the applied flutings and leaves with which the Huguenot silversmiths, who fled to England after the revocation of the

89. EDINBURGH, 1682–83. H. 3 in.

Edict of Nantes in
1685, embellished
their work, as on
the English two-
handled cup with
cover of 1726–27.

In St. Michael's
Parish, Talbot
County in Mary-
land, is a mug
(Illus. 90), the gift
in 1728 of Mary
Peck, that bears
the London date-

90. LONDON, 1688–89.  H. 4 in.

letter for 1688–89.  It was made by John Jackson
and is of a rare class which originated in England
towards the end of the reign of Charles II and
derived its globular body and reeded neck from
the German stoneware jugs of the sixteenth
century, so extensively mounted by the English
silversmiths.  The handle is reeded.  The mug
is decorated with Chinese subjects such as were
popular on English plate from about 1670 until
1695.  It was doubtless this shape that was
referred to by Colonel William Byrd of Virginia
when ordering the "new-fashioned silver mug"
from his merchant in London in 1684.  Mugs
of this kind were copied in Chinese porcelain
for the English market in the eighteenth century and were also made in England early in
that century of Elers ware and Nottingham
stoneware.

91. JOHN CONEY.  H. 3½ in.

Of this variety is the Colonial mug (Illus. 91) made by John Coney (1655–1722) of Boston, engraved with the initials MW for Mary Willoughby, who was born in 1676 at Salem, a granddaughter of Francis Willoughby who was the deputy governor from 1665 to 1671; she was an ancestor of Mrs. Sally Pickman Dwight to whose estate the mug belongs. The fluted decoration is similar to that of other vessels of contemporary date already described; the handle is notched.

An early form of mug made in the Colonies was gourd-shaped, copied from the contemporary caudle cup. Such is the plain mug (Illus. 92) made the latter part of the seventeenth century by Jeremiah Dummer (1645–1718) of Boston. The very thin,

92. JEREMIAH DUMMER.  H. 3⅜ in.

solid flat handle terminates in a trifid end, similar to that on the end of the stem of the contemporary spoon. It is engraved with the initials F for I E

93. WILLIAM COWELL. H. 3⅛ in.

John and Elizabeth Forland, and was given to the First Baptist Church, Boston, in 1729 by John Forland, a tobacconist who was born in 1650; his wife became a member of that church in 1686.

Belonging to Mr. Philip Leffingwell Spalding is a mug (Illus. 93) similar to the straight-sided caudle cup with the same fluted base and corded band; it was wrought by the same maker William Cowell (1682–1736) of Boston.

Another early type of mug (Illus. 94), made by John Coney, is of the same shape as the contemporary class of the New England beaker with the flat bottom. It has a notched rat-tail on the handle and as it is very small it may have been used as a dram cup. Engraved on the bottom is: "S. Russell" for Samuel Russell who married Eliza-

94. JOHN CONEY. H. 2⅜ in.

beth daughter of Thomas Elbridge; he was the
donor in 1725 of a tankard to the First Congregational Church at Marblehead, Massachusetts,
which was made into a plain plate in 1852.   His
brother-in-law John Elbridge, collector of the
port of Bristol, England, presented the old brass
chandelier to St. Michael's Church in the same
town.   Also engraved upon the side is : " Eliza
Russell Treuett," for Samuel Russell's daugh-

ter who married
Benjamin Trevett:
their grandson was
Captain    Samuel
Russell Trevett who
so gallantly distin-
guished himself at
the battle of Bun-
ker Hill where he
commanded a com-
pany of artillery.
The mug belongs
to Mrs. Elizabeth

95. WILLIAM COWELL.  H. 4 in.

Hooper Betton, the seventh in descent from
Samuel Russell.

Another of this type (Illus. 95), with a
moulded base, was made by William Cowell
(1682–1736) of Boston.   It belongs to the Meth-
odist Episcopal Church of Hull, Massachusetts,
and was originally given in 1724 to the Church
of Christ at Hull which was dissolved in 1789.   It
is engraved with the initials $\frac{B}{E\ E}$ doubtless for

Edward and Experience Battles who were married in 1707. Considering that this type is simply the beaker of which so many specimens are in the New England churches, it seems somewhat strange that so few fitted with handles, as mugs, are to be found therein. As domestic cups, however, they seem to have enjoyed great popularity early in the eighteenth century, judging from the numbers that are extant. They vary considerably in height, doubtless being used for numerous purposes.

96. BENJAMIN BURT. H. 5¼ in.

An inverted bell-shaped mug (Illus. 96) typical of the beaker of this shape, belongs to the First Parish Church, Universalist, at Saugus, Massachusetts, and was a legacy to the Third Church of Christ at Lynn in 1774 from Samuel Jenks. It was made by Benjamin Burt (1729–1805) of Boston, a son of John Burt (1691–1745), who married Joan the daughter of John Hooton and Sarah Wye. The inventory of his estate amounted to $4788.52: his will mentions Joseph Veazie, Caleb Swan (1754–1816) of Boston, Samuel Waters, and his trusty friend Joseph Foster (1760–1839) of

Boston who was made executor. They were all very probably his apprentices.

An early type of mug has a plain slightly tapering cylindrical body, with or without a moulding encircling the body; this came into vogue in England toward the end of the seventeenth century and was in fact a copy of the contemporary English tankard, of a smaller size and without the cover. The bases and lips are usually moulded.

Of this description is the mug (Illus. 97) with a plain body and a flat notched disc upon the handle-end, made by John Allen (1671–1760) and John Edwards (1670–1746) of Boston

97. ALLEN AND EDWARDS. H. 4¼ in.

who were brothers-in-law. It seems not improbable, from the fact that it was given to the First Baptist Church, Boston, by Mrs. Sarah Jeffers, that the initials AC may be those of Anne Clarke who married in 1713 David Jeffries.

Belonging to Mrs. Charles H. Joy is a mug (Illus. 98) of the same shape, made by John Coney, with an unusually wide reeded band encircling the body and the base, which is char-

acteristic of the
cylindrical and
barrel-shaped mugs
that came into fash-
ion at the end of
the eighteenth cen-
tury. The thin flat
solid handle is
reeded and has
a notched rat-tail
running down the
back. The mug is
inscribed : "Ex
dono EL ad EG."

98. JOHN CONEY. H. 3⅞ in.

Mr. George S. Palmer owns the mug (Illus.
99) engraved with the name "M. Tucker," with
scalloped work above the moulded base. It was
made by a New York silversmith, Bartholomew
Schaats (1670–1758), "a descendant of that interesting character, Domine Gideon Schaats,

99. BARTHOLOMEW SCHAATS. H. 3½ in.

who, after being
ordained by the
Classis of Amster-
dam, came to New
Amsterdam in 1652
in the ship *Flower
of Guelder* under
contract with the
patron Johannis
van Rennselaer
'to be missionary
to the Indians,

teacher of the catechism, and schoolmaster for old and young,' and later, in 1657, became minister of the church at Beverwyck (Albany), which charge he held until his death in 1694." *

A mug (Illus. 100) made in 1739 by Peter Van Dyck (1684–1750) of New York and belonging to the First Presbyterian Church, Southamp-

ton, on Long Island, has no moulding at the lip — a characteristic not seen in the New England mug with the tapering body and one seldom adopted by the New York silversmiths. The width of the flat solid scrolled handle is also unusual. In the same church is a pair of

100. PETER VAN DYCK. H. 5⅞ in.

similar mugs, made in 1729 by John Hastier (admitted as freeman 1726), New York, having the lips moulded, which served as a model for that made by Peter Van Dyck.

William Cowell (1682–1736) of Boston made a mug (Illus. 101) with a moulding encircling the body, a gift in 1727 to the First Church of Christ, Hartford, Connecticut, whose first minister was Rev. Thomas Hooker. It is en-

* (R. T. H. H.)

graved with the in-
itials A W for Abi-
gail Woodbridge
wife of the Rev.
Timothy Wood-
bridge, the minis-
ter of the church
in 1687, at the time
Governor Andros
came to demand
the Charter of the
Colony and when
that document was

101. WILLIAM COWELL.  H. 5 in.

snatched from the deliberations in the meeting-
house and hidden in the famous Charter Oak;
he was one of the founders of Yale College.
This mug was sold in 1815 for fifteen dollars to
Dr. Jeremiah Bradford and was bought in 1883
from his grandson by Mr. William R. Cone who
presented it to the church.

A mug (Illus. 102) of this type has a double-scrolled handle with an acanthus leaf on the shoulder and is engraved with the initials $^S_{S\ I}$ doubt-less for Samuel Stevens, for his

102. WILLIAM SIMPKINS.  H. 4⅝ in.

N

daughter Mary married Joseph Warren — father
of General Joseph Warren the noted physician
and ardent patriot killed at the battle of Bunker
Hill, "the first Revolutionary martyr of rank"
to fall.   The initials EW engraved at a later
date are those of Judge Ebenezer Warren, a
brother of General Warren, from whom it has
descended to Mr. William W. Vaughan, a great-
grandson.  It was
made by William
Simpkins (1704–
80) of Boston who
married Elizabeth
Symmes : he was
appointed consta-
ble in 1743 but de-
clined to serve and
paid the fine ; 3d
sergeant of the
Artillery Company
1743, ensign 1757.
His son Thomas
Barton Simpkins

103. MUNSON JARVIS.  H. 4¼ in.

(1728–1804) of Boston was also a silversmith.

Belonging to the Congregational Church,
Greens Farms, Westport, Connecticut, is a mug
(Illus. 103) the legacy in 1765 of Mrs. Abigail
Couch, the daughter of Joshua Jennings of Fair-
field one of the signers of the first covenant of
that church in 1715.   It was made by Munson
Jarvis (1742–1825) a blacksmith of Stamford,
Connecticut, son of Samuel Jarvis also a black-

smith. He was a loyalist who fled in 1783 to St. John in New Brunswick, where he passed the remainder of his life: he became a vestryman of the Episcopal church and a member of the Provincial Assembly. (G. M. C.)

104. PAUL REVERE. H. 5½ in.

Mrs. Ellerton L. Dorr is the owner of the cylindrical mug (Illus. 104) hooped like a barrel, made by Paul Revere (1735–1818) of Boston. Similar mugs in the shape of a barrel were common in England at the end of the eighteenth and at the beginning of the nineteenth century.

A plain mug (Illus. 105) made by Lewis Cary (1798–1834) of Boston, with a feather scroll in relief on the shoulder of the handle, belongs to the Misses Cruft. It was given to their

105. LEWIS CARY. H. 4½ in.

grandparents, Edward and Elizabeth (Storer) Cruft, by President John Adams when he went from Quincy to attend the convention held in Boston in 1820 which brought about the separation of Maine and Massachusetts: he was the guest of Mr. and Mrs. Cruft at their house on Pearl Street.    It will be recalled that Abigail Smith was the granddaughter of the second wife

of John Edwards (1670–1746) and married President Adams.

A different type of mug made its appearance in England early in the eighteenth century and is seen in large numbers in the colleges of Oxford and Cambridge.    It has

106. WILLIAM POLLARD.  H. 4½ in.

a plain tapering body rounded at the bottom, with a low moulded base.    Of this variety is the mug (Illus. 106) in the First Church at Boston. William Pollard (1690–1746) of Boston wrought the mug : he was the grandson of Anne Pollard who came in the fleet with Winthrop to Charlestown.    Upon the invitation of Blackstone (the first settler of Boston who sold to the Town his forty-four acres of land — now Boston Common) Anne Pollard came in the first boat load and was the first white woman to set foot on Boston

soil. She lived to be 105 years old and her portrait at the age of 103 belongs to the Massachusetts Historical Society. As William Pollard's uncle Jonathan Pollard married Mary
Winslow, it may be assumed that he was apprenticed to her brother Edward Winslow.

Belonging to
the First Parish
Church at Beverly
in Massachusetts,
is a mug (Illus. 107)
of the same de-
scription but the
sides are more in-
curved, giving it a
slightly bulbous or
"bellied" appear-
ance. The mug is
inscribed: "The
legacy of the Rev$^{nd}$:
M$^{r.}$ Tho: Blowers

107. JOHN BLOWERS. H. 5⅜ in.

To the First Church in Beverly dec$^d$: June the
17th 1729." Rev. Thomas Blowers was the
second pastor of the parish. The mug has a
hollow handle, and while it bears no maker's
mark it was probably made by his son John
Blowers (1710–48) of Boston who married Sarah
Salter. They were the parents of Sampson
Salter Blowers who, with Adams and Quincy,
was junior counsel in 1770 in the defence of the
British soldiers concerned in the "Boston Massacre," and who, as a loyalist, went to England

in 1774 and returned to Boston in 1778; after imprisonment at Boston he went to Halifax, Nova Scotia, where he became chief-justice of the supreme court and died October 25, 1842 at the age of 100 years, 7 months, 4 days.

The type of mug with a "bellied" body was first introduced into England about 1725 and three, with the London date-letter for 1725–26, made by William Fleming, are in the collection of the Emperor of Russia. Mugs of this description continued to be made throughout the century and the tendency was toward a more bellied body and a higher moulded base, as in the mug (Illus. 108) with a double scrolled handle and an acanthus leaf on the shoulder; it is engraved with the Kitchen arms. Three of these mugs are in the Tabernacle Church and three belong to the South Church, at Salem, Massachusetts. That the name "can" was frequently applied to this variety, and possibly to other shapes also, is evidenced by Edward Kitchen's will of July 5, 1765: "I will and bequeath to the Church the Rev^d Mr. Huntington is ye Pastor of

108. DANIEL BOYER. H. 5 in.

six Silver Pint Cans with the three half Moons and the Sun engraven thereon wrote upon them the Gift of Edward Kitchen to said Church." They were all wrought by Daniel Boyer (1725–79) of Boston, son of James Boyer (1700–41) a Huguenot silver-

109. LONDON, 1779–80. H. 5¼ in.

smith who came with the Sigourneys and Johonnots from La Rochelle, France, and who married the daughter of Daniel Johonnot. Daniel Boyer was clerk of the market, 4th sergeant of the Artillery Company in 1762 and a member of the Old South Church: he married Elizabeth daughter of John Bulfinch, and two of his daughters married Joseph Coolidge junior (1747–1821) a silversmith, an ardent Son of Liberty and one of the "Boston Tea Party."

In the Congregational Church at Hamilton, Massachusetts, is a mug (Illus. 109) with the London date-letter for 1779–80, made by J. Denzilow. It was a gift from Hon. Symond Epes whose widow Mary Whipple became the third wife of Edward Holyoke president of Harvard College. As a matter of fact Symond Epes's bequest was a large tankard, which came into the possession of the church after his widow's death in 1790; and in 1821 "on account of its being a vessel exceedingly inconvenient for yᵉ use of yᵉ sisters of yᵉ church" the tankard was exchanged for "two silver cans." His son the "young and pale Major Samuel Epes" was the donor of three similar mugs, made by Benjamin Burt (1729–1805) of Boston, to the South Church at Ipswich, Massachusetts. The house built about 1680 by Captain John Whipple senior, and occupied by Symond Epes from 1715 to 1741, is still standing at Hamilton and now belongs to Mr. Nathan Matthews whose wife was a collateral descendant. The house has been restored and modernized, but most attractively so under the skilful hand of Mr. Norman Morrison Isham.

110. SAMUEL SOUMAINE.    H. 4½ in.

In the Presbyterian Church of Rehoboth and Pitts Creek in Maryland, founded in 1683, was a mug (Illus. 110) made by Samuel Soumaine of Philadelphia which is now in the rooms of the Presbyterian Historical Society at Philadelphia. It is engraved with the initials

K
R A  for Robert and Anne King.  She married
for her third husband George Holden clerk of
the county court of Accomack in Virginia: it
was presented to
the church in 1780
by Anne Holden.
The donor was the
daughter of Rev.
Francis Makemie
the founder of or-
ganized Presby-
terianism in the
Colonies.  He had
come from Scot-
land to Virginia
about 1682 and
engaged in the
West India trade;
in 1707 he was ar-

111. E. Davis.  H. 6½ in.

rested and imprisoned for preaching in New
York and he died in Boston in 1708.

One of the few mugs (Illus. 111) of this
variety, with a moulded band encircling the
body, was made by E. Davis of Newburyport,
Massachusetts, and belongs to Mr. George S.
Palmer.

Occasionally a mug (Illus. 112) with the
bellied body is found with a cover, but unless
the cover bears the maker's mark it seems ques-
tionable as to whether it may not have been
added at a later date.  The mug is engraved

with the Storer arms and the initials $\begin{smallmatrix}S\\E\,M\end{smallmatrix}$ for Ebenezer and Mary (Edwards) Storer who were married in 1723 : it belongs to Mr. Alfred Bowditch. It was once owned by Miss Mercy

Shiverick Hatch, a noted beauty, whose portrait by Stuart is in the possession of Mr. Charles P. Bowditch. The maker was John Potwine (1698–1792), the son of John Potwine a physician and Huguenot refugee from Portou in France who had married Sarah, a daughter of Edward Hill. John Potwine was born in Boston; he was

112. JOHN POTWINE.  H. 6⅞ in.

a member of the Old South Church and married Mary Jackson April 20, 1721; he moved to Hartford in Connecticut, in 1737; thence to South Coventry, where his wife died, and where he ran a general merchandise store, as he did after he moved to East Windsor; he died in Scantic where his son was pastor of the Congregational Church.

Another of this type of mug with a cover, belonging to Mrs. Charles W. Eliot, was made by Benjamin Pierpont (1730–97) of Boston. He was a nephew of Rev. James Pierpont the second pastor at New Haven; a member of the Brattle Street Church in 1758; married to Elizabeth Shepard March 29, 1759; he was clerk of the market in 1766.

# TWO–HANDLED CUPS

ILLUSTRATIONS of such early two-handled cups as were made in England prior to the Commonwealth period and still exist, may be seen in Mr. Jackson's "History of English Plate." The large silver-gilt cup and cover (Illus. 113), with the London date-letter for 1677–78 and

113. London, 1677–78. H. 10 in.

the maker's mark RC, was presented to the Cathedral of St. John the Divine at New York by Mrs. George Bromley Ironside. It belongs to a class of vessel which was highly popular for hot drinks in England in the late Stuart period. In form and decoration of the base it is like the straight-sided caudle cup of 1687–88 previously described. It is inscribed: "The guift of Edward Ironside Esquire In memory of his name and Kindred To the Reverend ffather in Christ Gilbert Ironside Lord Bishop of Bristoll 1661." The two shields of arms engraved upon it are those of the see of Bristol impaling those of Ironside, and the see of Hereford impaling those of Ironside. The cup was bought in 1677–78 with a bequest of twenty pounds contained in Edward Ironside's will proved in 1663.

At Trinity College — where Governor John Winthrop and the Puritan divine John Cotton were educated — is a covered bowl with two handles, with the London date-letter for 1697–98, which is decorated with spiral fluting.

Edward Winslow (1669–1753) of Boston made a two-handled cup with a cover (Illus. 114) similar in shape and decoration to the inverted bell-shaped beaker already described. The surbase is vertically fluted; the gadrooned borders of the base and cover are fluted in the same manner, as is also the band encircling the upper part of the body. Engraved upon one side of the cup are the Lowell arms, it having belonged to James Russell Lowell and doubtless to his

114. EDWARD WINSLOW. H. 11 in.

forebears; it is now owned by his grand-daughter Mrs. Lois B. Rantoul.

The two-handled English cup with cover (Illus. 115), the gift of Samuel Ledlie to Christ Church at Hartford, Connecticut, belongs to a class of cup which was introduced into England by the French Huguenot silversmiths who sought refuge there after the revocation of the Edict of Nantes in 1685. The type was fashion-able from about 1699 to 1740 and most of the makers were of French origin or descent. This specimen was made in 1726–27 by Isaac Riboulau one of those Anglo-French craftsmen. The vase-shaped body is divided into two sections by a plain moulding; the applied leaf and strap decoration on the lower part of

115. LONDON, 1726–27. H. 11 in.

the body and on the cover is much more re-
strained than that of most cups of its kind, which
are often embellished with ornate vertical straps
characteristic of the Louis XIV school of metal-
workers. An English cup with harp-shaped
handles made by Paul Crespin in the same year
1726–27, and almost identical with the Hartford
cup, is engraved with the crown and cipher of
the Empress Elizabeth the daughter of Peter
the Great. It is in the famous collection of the
Emperor of Russia in the Winter Palace, at
Petrograd.

At the beginning of the eighteenth century
the earlier embossed decoration was practically
abandoned and the fashion turned to one of
greater simplicity in the reign of Queen Anne
— much silver being perfectly plain, and when
ornamented the decoration consisted of fluting,
gadrooning and "cut-card" work. The fashion
inclined toward greater ornamentation at the
end of the reign of George I.

Belonging to the First Parish, Medford, Massachusetts, is a cup (Illus. 116) which may have
had a cover originally. It bears the London
date-letter for 1714–15 and the maker's mark
for Joseph Clare. On one side are engraved the
arms of the Royall family and on the opposite
side is the inscription : "The Gift of the hon^{ble}.
Isaac Royall Esq^{r} to the Church of Christ in Medford." Colonel Isaac Royall, the well-known
loyalist, was representative from Medford to the
general court and for twenty-two years was a

116. LONDON, 1714–15. H. 6 in.

member of the council; he was appointed briga-
dier-general in 1761, the first to bear that title in
America. His daughter Elizabeth married Sir
William Pepperell, second baronet. A portrait
group of the donor with his wife and child Elizabeth, his sister Penelope Royall, and his wife's
sister Mrs. Mary Palmer, painted by Robert
Feke in 1741, hangs in the reading-room of
Austin Hall at Harvard University. Although
exiled from his home, he never forgot the country which he left in 1775 "with great reluctance,"
and in his will he bequeathed 2000 acres of land
in Worcester county, Massachusetts, to found the
first law professorship at Harvard College. He
also left to the Church at Medford ten pounds
sterling to purchase a piece of plate, namely, the

o

baptismal basin made by Benjamin Burt (1729–1805).   A baptismal basin made by Thomas Edwards (1701–55) was Isaac Royall's gift in 1747 to St. Michael's Church, Bristol, Rhode Island, and is engraved in the centre with the Royall arms.   The interesting old Royall house built by his father, the old Antigua merchant who came to Medford in 1737, with its slave quarters

117. London, 1725?   H. 10¾ in.

has been restored by the Royall House Association which acquired it by purchase.

A cup with cover (Illus. 117) of this description, made by George Wickes (entered at Goldsmiths' Hall in 1721), is without a London date-letter. It is engraved in a circular panel with the arms of Hancock impaling those of Henchman, as on the standing cup in the First Church, Boston, — the gift of Lydia Hancock. In her will dated October 30, 1765 and proved November 21, 1777 Lydia Hancock bequeathed to her mother, Elizabeth Henchman, her plate "excepting a Silver Bowl, a Silver Spout Cup and a large two Handled Silver Cup which I give to my Nephew John Hancock Esq." It belongs to Mr. Frederick Goddard May, a descendant of John Hancock. There is a tradition that the cup was once owned by Thomas Hutchinson, the unpopular governor of Massachusetts, whose suspected actions in favor of the king, shortly before the Revolution, led to the sacking and burning of his mansion.

A Colonial example (Illus. 118), similar to the Hancock cup, was made by Peter Feurt who came from New York in 1727 and died in Boston in 1737. It is referred to in the will of Edward Mills junior dated May 24, 1732 : "to Henry Hope a silver cup with his coat of arms and mine engraved thereon." Upon one side are the arms of Mills of Harscombe, as on the plate made by Jeremiah Dummer which Edward Mills bequeathed, as "my salver," to John Merritt, by

118. PETER FEURT.  H. 9 in.

whom it was given to King's Chapel, Boston,
of which he was a vestryman.  Below the
arms is the motto NEMO SINE CRIMINE VIVIT
and engraved below this : "Ex Dono Henricus
Hope armiger."  Above the moulded band
which divides the body is engraved : "The gift
of Mrs. G. Apthorp to her Great Grand Daugh-

ter Sarah Apthorp Morton." Grizzel Apthorp
was the donor to Christ Church at Cambridge,
Massachusetts, of the English baptismal basin.
Sarah Apthorp Morton a poet, called "the
American Sappho," married Perez Morton a
Revolutionary patriot; he was speaker of

119. London, 1760–61. H. 14½ in.

the house, attorney-general of Massachusetts 1811–32; and a delegate to the state Constitutional Convention in 1820. The cup belongs to Miss Una Gray, a descendant.

The cup (Illus. 119) owned by the Metropolitan Museum of Art, New York, with the London date-letter for 1760–61 and made by Samuel Courtauld, illustrates the extravagant ornamentation in the French rococo style of Louis XV which was popular in England from 1725–60. Fortunately, in the Colonies, the silversmiths did not adopt extravagance in decoration, but it is quite possible that they were not capable of executing it. Occasionally some vessel is found, like the embossed sugar bowl made by Paul Revere, which is interesting and unique.

A cup (Illus. 120) bearing the London date-letter for 1770–71, with an inverted pear-shaped body, has a gadrooned edge on the base. It is inscribed: "Given to The First Church in Boston by Anne E. and Caroline M. Beale Easter Day Nineteen

120. London, 1770–71. H. 6⅜ in.

Hundred April Fifteenth." Engraved upon one
side are the Beale arms and the date 1770.

A plain oviform cup (Illus. 121) with reeded
edges, a high cover with a vase-shaped finial,

121. JOSEPH LORING. H. 11¾ in.

and two square-shaped handles, now belongs to
the Museum of Fine Arts at Boston. It is inscribed: "The gift of Mr. William Johnson
to Brattle Street Church Boston 1707." It was

made about 1790 from the original gift of silver. The maker was Joseph Loring (1743–1815) who was born in Hull, Massachusetts, but moved to Boston, where he married Mary Atkins; he lived in Court Street and had his shop in Union Street. He was 2d sergeant in the Artillery Company in 1791.   When 1st lieutenant he was a prisoner on Long Island for nine months but returned to Boston in 1777.   His son Henry Loring (1773–1818) of Boston was also a silversmith.

# CHALICES

STRICTLY speaking, the chalice is the only vessel in the Colonial churches never used for domestic purposes. It is almost the earliest ecclesiastical vessel known. It is quite impossible to attempt an adequate description of the English mediæval chalice because of their rarity, which arises from the great destruction of all vessels associated with the Mass, at the Reformation. The earliest piece of silver, whether ecclesiastical or secular, with an English hall-mark is the chalice with paten-cover at Nettlecombe, Somerset, bearing the London date-letter for 1479. To appreciate the various shapes of the bowls, stems, knops and bases up to the time of Queen Elizabeth, the numerous books in bibliography must be referred to and the illustrations studied.

In Holy Trinity Church, Wilmington, Delaware, is a chalice (Illus. 122) which, in an American church, is the nearest approach of any in shape, to the Pre-Reformation chalice. This, however, was not made until about 1718 at Gothenburg in Sweden. The bowl, gilt inside, is supported on a plain hexagonal stem divided by a round knop, separated into twelve horse-

shoe-shaped sections engraved with foliage.
The inscription, translated, reads : " Take and
drink, this is my blood.   The gift of the mining

122. GOTHENBURG, 1718.   H. 9⅜ in.

company of Falun to Holy Trinity Church at
Christina in Pennsylvania, A.D. 1718.  Assessor
and mine master, Andrew Swab.  Magister Eric
Björk, pastor of Falun, formerly at Christina in
Pennsylvania."  Rev. Eric Björk was the pastor
of that Swedish Lutheran church, built in 1698
and still standing, until he was recalled to
Sweden by Charles XII in 1713 when he became
pastor of the church at Falun in Sweden —
where are the oldest copper mines of Europe.

Each of the Post-Reformation chalices was
provided with a "cover of silver appointed also
for the ministration of the Communion bread."
This paten-cover has a circular foot, frequently
engraved with a date, which closely fits over the
rim of the body.  There are, of course, depar-
tures from this orthodox type of Post-Reformation chalice but these are generally confined to
definite areas in England.

A marked departure from the orthodox type
of Elizabethan chalice may be seen in the historical vessel of St. Andrew's Church at Norwich in which many distinguished Puritans
received the communion.  It was made in
1568–69 by Peter Petersen an accomplished
Dutch silversmith who had settled in that ancient city and was buried in that church.  It was
in this cup that such Puritans as John More,
Nicholas Bounde and Yates received the sacrament.  Tradition also associates John Robinson, the leader of the Puritans who crossed to
Leyden before their departure for America, as

minister of the church, though this is unsupported by substantial evidence.  Another Elizabethan chalice, made in Norwich in 1568, belongs to Heachem Church in Norfolk in England, where Captain John Rolfe, the Colonist who married Pocahontas, was baptized.  Most of the Elizabethan chalices were decorated with an interlacing band of strap-work filled with arabesques, which Hans Holbein the younger helped by his designs for silver-work to popularize in England ; such may be seen in every county in England and Wales. A chalice of this kind, dated 1591–92, is in the church of St.

123. London, 1611–12.  H. 8¼ in.

Mary Magdalene at Ecton in the county of Northampton — the ancestral home of the Franklins.

In the reign of James I the chalice retained its Elizabethan form, but displayed a tendency to become larger and the engraved decoration was frequently abandoned. Belonging to St. Peter's Church, Perth Amboy, New Jersey, is a chalice (Illus. 123) of that period, bearing the London date-letter for 1611–12, which is the earliest example in a Colonial church. It is engraved: "E H 1612" and is thought to have been presented nearly a century later by the widow of Rev. John Talbot, rector of the church. This and the next chalice follow the outline of the Elizabethan chalice. The body is encircled with a plain moulding; in the middle of the short stem is a compressed knop; the edge of the moulded base is stamped with an ovolo ornament. The paten-cover is engraved with the same band as the chalice and has a reel-shaped handle-foot. The Perth Amboy chalice is very like that of 1567–68 at Christ's College, Cambridge, in which Milton and other famous men received the sacrament.

In St. John's Church (Elizabeth City Parish) Elizabeth City County, Hampton, Virginia, is a plain chalice (Illus. 124) bearing the London date-letter for 1618–19 and two patens of the same date, with the maker's mark RG. These have been used in the communion service for nearly three hundred years — longer than any

124. LONDON, 1618–19. H. 8½ in.

vessels in any other American church. There are a very few vessels made at an earlier date but they did not come into the possession of the churches until much later. The deep bell-shaped body of the chalice is supported by a short double reel-shaped stem on a moulded base; traces of the original gilding are visible. This is inscribed "The Commvnion Cvpp for Sⁿᵗ Marys Chvrch in Smiths Hvndred in Virginia." The chalice and two patens were bought with a legacy of Mrs. Mary Robinson of "Mark lane in the parish of St Olave Hart Street, London" under her will of February 13, 1617 which reads: "I give and bequeath towards the helpe of the poore people in Virginia, towards the building of a Churche & the reduceinge of them to the knowledge of God's word,

the sum of two hundred pounds, to be bestowed
at the discreation of my cozen, Sir John Wolsten-
holme, knight, with the advice and consent of
four others of the chiefest of the Virginia Company, within two yeares next after my decease."
These vessels were originally in "Smith's hundred" so called from Thomas Smith treasurer of
the Virginia Company. It is not known how they
came into the possession of Hampton Church.

With the in-
crease in popula-
tion, the English
chalice became
larger in the time
of Charles II. The
same shape was re-
tained — a beaker
or deep bell-shaped
body, supported
on a stem divided
by a compressed
knop — and it was
fitted with a paten-
cover. When not
plain the decora-
tion followed that
of the contempo-
rary domestic plate.
Decorated chalices
of that period are
in Westminster
Abbey.

125. ENGLISH, 1660. H. 11¾ in.

An English chalice (Illus. 125) of this type, made about 1660, originally belonged to James- town Old Church in Virginia but is now in

126. LONDON, 1694–95.   H. 9⅞ in.

Christ Church in Bruton Parish at Williamsburg. It was the gift in 1661 of Colonel Francis Morrison deputy - governor of Virginia during the absence in England of the governor Sir Wil- liam Berkeley. It was in this chalice that many gener- ations of Virgin- ians, conspicuous in the history of their state, re- ceived the com- munion.   It   is appropriately in- scribed : " Mixe not holy thinges with profane."

A massive chal- ice with a paten- cover (Illus. 126) is spirally fluted at the base of the

body like contemporary domestic vessels; the
knop on the stem is fluted, as is also the edge of
the moulded base. The paten-cover is in two
stages, both spirally fluted, and has a plain reel-
shaped handle-foot. The chalice bears the London date-letter for 1694–95 and the maker's
mark R. It belongs to Westover Parish, Charles
City County, Virginia. Sarah Braine, the donor,
was a conspicuous figure in her day, as she was
in sympathy with the rebellion of Nathaniel
Bacon and the only woman excepted from the
free and general pardon granted by the General
Assembly in 1677. She was four times married,
first to Lieutenant-Colonel Thomas Stegge the
younger, who was an uncle of William Byrd the
founder of the Byrd family in Virginia. Her
fourth husband was Edward Braine a wealthy
merchant of London. William Byrd refers in a
letter to the return of Mr. and Mrs. Braine
from England in 1685 with "30 servants and
£1,000 worth of goods."

Small silver chalices and patens for private
communion were seldom made in England prior
to the early years of the nineteenth century.
Probably the earliest are in the London church
of St. James's, Piccadilly, where there are three
dated 1683–84, one being for the use of the
rector and the other two for the curates. The
church of St. John's, Westminster, contains a
chalice and paten of 1729–30. These facts
render doubly interesting the little English
chalice and paten of 1722–23 (Illus. 127) for

P

private communion, in St. Peter's Church at Perth Amboy, New Jersey. The chalice is also notable because of the engraved representation of the Crucifixion — an extremely rare symbol on English ecclesiastical vessels of Post-Reformation times. It has a bell-shaped body, gilt inside, on a high stem with a moulded base and is inscribed in a laurel wreath on the bowl: "Hic est Calix Sanguinis mei Novi, et Eterni Testamenti, Mysterium Fidei, Qui pro Vobis, et pro Multis Effundetur, In Remissionen Peccatorum." The base is inscribed: "Sanguis Meus est Vere Potus." The donor was Mrs. Talbot, the widow of Rev. John Talbot, who presented them in 1728.

127. LONDON, 1722–23.
H. 4¾ in.

The practice of engraving sacramental plate and decorating church ornaments and vestments with the sacred trigram was common in the mediæval church in England. It was abandoned at the Reformation but revived on plate at the end of the seventeenth century: throughout the next century it became exceedingly common. A chalice (Illus. 128) with this decoration belongs to Mapsico Church, Charles City County,

Virginia. It has the London date-letter for
1731–32 and the maker was probably Thomas
Tearle. This was a legacy in 1727 from Colonel

Francis Lightfoot
of Sandy Point,
in Charles City
County, Virginia.

The Colonial sil-
versmiths very sel-
dom copied the
conventional
Post-Reformation
English chalice
and paten-cover.

A chalice (Illus.
129) made by John
Edwards (1670–
1746) of Boston,
was the gift in
1724 of Captain
Thomas Tudor to
Christ Church at
Boston. Tradi-
tion says it was in
the belfry of that
church, erected in
1723 and still
standing in the
North End, that
the lanterns were
hung on the night
of the 18th of

128. London, 1731–32.  H. 10⅞ in.

129.    JOHN EDWARDS.    H. 9 in.

April in 1775 as a signal of the British march to Lexington and Concord : "One if by land and two if by sea." William Dawes and Paul Revere roused the countryside on that memorable night.    While the silver wrought by Paul Revere is always sought for, largely for the name it bears, it should not be forgotten that the father of William Dawes was also a silversmith. In this connection it may not be amiss to insert the following poem :

## WHAT'S IN A NAME

### HELEN F. MORE

(Before the Battle of Lexington, William Dawes and Paul Revere were both despatched to rouse the country, Dawes starting first.)

I am a wandering bitter shade,
Never of me was a hero made,
Poets have never sung my praise,
Nobody crowned my brow with bays,
And if you ask me the fatal cause
I answer only, "My name is Dawes."

'Tis all very well for the children to hear
Of the midnight ride of Paul Revere;
But why should the name be quite forgot
Who rode as boldly, and well, God wot?
Why should I ask? The reason is clear:
My name was Dawes and his Revere.

When the lights from the Old North Church flashed out,
Paul Revere was waiting about,
But I was already on my way;
The shadows of night fell cold and gray
As I rode, with never a break or pause,
But what was the use, when my name was Dawes?

History rings with his silvery name;
Closed to me are the portals of fame.
Had he been Dawes and I Revere,
No one had heard of him, I fear,
No one has heard of me, because
He was Revere, and I was Dawes.

The inverted bell-shaped chalice (Illus. 130)
with a high domed cover, a twisted finial and a
stem encircled with a moulding, was made by
John David (1736–98) of Philadelphia. It belongs to St. Peter's Church, Lewes, Delaware,
and is inscribed as the gift of Hon. John Penn in
1773; it was, however, bought with money
realized from the estate of Henrietta Sims, at
the same time as the flagon already described.

John Penn, called the "American Penn," was a tory at the time of the Revolution and his estate was the largest that was forfeited, the claim amounting to £944,-817. The Quakers, as a body, while generally passive were thought to give secret "aid and comfort to the enemy," and very few of them became refugees at the close of the war. Congress was, however, suspicious of them and in 1776 eleven of the leading Quakers of Philadelphia were banished to Fredericksburg in Virginia, as were John Penn, the governor, and Benjamin Chew.

130. JOHN DAVID. H. 12 in.

In St. Mary's Church, Burlington in New Jersey, is a French chalice (Illus. 131) of the second half of the seventeenth century, with a plain bell-shaped

131. French, 1650–1700. H. 9⅜ in.

body enclosed in an ornate frame decorated
with acanthus leaves, three cherubs' faces in
relief and embossed symbols of the Passion,

on a matted ground.  The top of the baluster stem is reel-shaped, with a cut ring in the middle; the decoration of the base is similar to that on the frame;  the border is enriched with open acanthus leaves, with a wire edge.  The remains of an old inscription are visible under the edge. Inscribed in one line is:  "The Gift of Mrs. Cartherine Bovey of fflaxley in Gloucestersheire to St Marys Church att Burlington in new Iersey in America."  Mrs. Catharina Boevey, the remarkable and talented woman who gave this chalice, was the daughter of John Riches a wealthy merchant of London.  She was born in 1669 and at the age of fifteen married William Boevey of Flaxley Abbey, in Gloucestershire, and was left a widow, without children, at the age of twenty-two.  Catharina Boevey was the reputed original of Sir Roger de Coverley's "Perverse Widow" in the *Spectator*, written by Steele. She was "a very learned, most exemplary, and excellent woman" and after a life of good works, died at Flaxley January 18, 1726.  A monument by James Gibbs, showing her medallion portrait, was erected in Westminster Abbey by her friend and executrix, Mrs. Mary Pope who had lived with her for forty years.  This chalice, together with a plain English paten of about 1705, also the gift of Mrs. Boevey, was brought from England in 1709 by the rector Rev. John Talbot who had previously held the living of Fretherne in Gloucestershire where he had come in touch with the donor.

The French chalice (Illus. 132) of the time of
Louis XIV was made at Paris in the last quarter
of the seventeenth century.  The plain bell-

132. PARIS, 1675–1700.  H. 10¼ in.

shaped body is enclosed in a frame of acanthus
leaves and supported by a tall baluster stem enriched with oval bosses and acanthus leaves in
relief; the plain base is decorated with a border
of the same leaves.   The acanthus leaves on the
bowl and base are characteristic of French ecclesiastical plate of the second half, and especially of the last quarter, of the seventeenth
century.   It was a gift in 1758 to the Old South
Church, Boston, from Anthony Bracket the
well-known landlord of the famous Boston
tavern, the "Cromwell's Head" in School Street.
It was there that George Washington stayed for
two weeks in 1756; Paul Jones and Lafayette
were also guests at that tavern.   It seems not
improbable that this chalice may have been a
piece of the communion silver of the little church
of the French Huguenots in School Street and that
it may have come into Anthony Bracket's possession at the dissolution of the society in 1748.

A plain copy of this French chalice, made by
Paul Revere (1735–1818) of Boston, is inscribed
in a circular panel: "The Gift of the Rev$^d$ M$^r$
Tho$^s$ Prince to the South Church in Boston who
was Ordained Pastor of said Church Oct: 1$^{th}$
1718 & died Oct: 22. 1758 Æ 72."   With allu-
sion to the backsliding of some of his flock
during Whitefield's visit and to the coming expedition to Louisburg, the Rev. Thomas Prince
thus expressed himself: "The heavenly shower
was over; from fighting the devil they must
turn to fighting the French."

The donor was the son of Samuel Prince and his second wife, Mercy, daughter of Governor Thomas Hinckley; he married Deborah Denny from Coombs in England. As a youth he began collecting public and private papers relating to the civil and religious history of New England and at his death had amassed a most valuable collection which he bequeathed to the Old South Church. It was stored in the church and upon the occupation of the church by the British, in 1775–76, many of these papers were unfortunately destroyed. Rev. Thomas Prince's only daughter, Sarah, married Lieutenant-Governor Moses Gill the donor in 1796 of a pair of plain standing cups to the First Congregational Church at Princeton, Massachusetts — a place where the worthy pastor was the largest owner of land; when incorporated in 1759 it was named Prince-town and later Princeton. Moses Gill was active in public affairs; representative of the general court at Salem in 1774; executive councillor; lieutenant-governor of Massachusetts and acting governor from 1799 until his death May 20, 1800. Portraits by Copley of Moses Gill and his two wives are in the possession of the Rhode Island School of Design, at Providence.

# BAPTISMAL BASINS

ONE sacred piece of furniture in the English church which the Pilgrims and Puritans did not bring with them across the Atlantic was the font, though they were believers in the rite of baptism. In adopting baptismal basins or bowls they were anticipating the action of Cromwell's parliament which ordered the use of basins and the removal of fonts from the parish churches, in the hope that all suspected superstitions connected with the rite of baptism would be suppressed. In lieu of fonts the churches in America were provided with basins, bowls or dishes. In the early days of Christianity in New England, any domestic vessel of wood, pewter, porcelain or glass was requisitioned for use in the rite of baptism. Basins or bowls of silver were introduced early in the eighteenth century and, like the flagon, they are significant of the growing prosperity of the Colonists. The basins are shallow and vary little in height which is seldom more than three inches. The earliest were doubtless made for domestic use, to take the place of the large pewter chargers. The bowls made for baptismal purposes were somewhat deeper. Very many

of the churches never possessed baptismal basins
of silver.

None of the silver baptismal basins of the
Dutch churches in the State of New York followed a custom occasionally met with in the
Dutch Reformed churches in Holland.  This
custom consisted of engraving or embossing a
representation of the Baptism of Christ upon
them.  A basin so decorated, made by a Delft
silversmith in 1668, is in the Oude Kerk at
Delft.  The Lutheran church at Haarlem contains a baptismal basin with the same sacred
subject done in relief; it was made in 1656 at
Haarlem by a silversmith believed to be an
Englishman, Thomas Rosewell.

In the South Reformed Church at New York
City, which was until 1812 the senior member of
the Collegiate Dutch church of New York, is
the earliest dated baptismal basin (Illus. 133) in
a Colonial church.  It has a deep inverted cone-
shaped depression and a wide flat rim with
a moulded edge.  The poetical verse, in Low
Dutch, in explanation of the inner meaning of
baptism, was composed by Dominie Selyns one
of the most eminent of the divines who came
from Holland to the early church.  The basin
was bought by the congregation in 1694, at a
cost of sixty-three Holland guilders, and was
made by Jacobus Van der Spiegel, the earliest
native silversmith of New York.  Mr. Halsey
says : "The plate made by Jacobus Van der
Spiegel carries with it memories of its maker's

military services along the Albany frontier, as well as of the days when fear of the capture of New York by the French was ever terrifying to

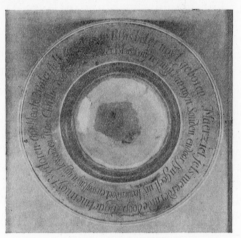

133. Jacobus Van der Spiegel.  D. 10⅜ in.

its citizens.  We find his name on the list of 'yᵉ people sent to Albany' on the 13th of March, 1689, upon orders from Leisler to protect the northern frontier against the impending French invasion, also his commission as ensign in Captain Walter's company in the same year."

The earliest baptismal basin (Illus. 134) in a New England church is undoubtedly in the First Parish (Unitarian) Cambridge, Massachusetts, and was made by Jeremiah Dummer (1645–1718) of Boston.  It has a deep depression with a domed centre, and a wide flat rim upon which

is inscribed : "Ex dono Pupillorum 1695." It
was presented to Rev. William Brattle (who was
ordained pastor of that church November 25,
1696) undoubt-
edly for domes-
tic use, as is in-
dicated in his
will of June 21,
1716 which con-
tains the fol-
lowing clause :
" I    bequeath
and present to
the Church of
Christ in Cam-
bridge    for    a
baptismal basin,
my great silver
basin,    an    in-
scription upon
which I leave

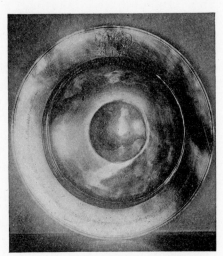

134. JEREMIAH DUMMER.   D. 14¾ in.

to the prudence of the Rev^d. President [John
Leverett] and the R^d Mr. Simon Bradstreet."
The inscription is : "A Baptismall Basin consecrated, bequeath^d & presented to the Church
of Christ in Cambridge, his Dearly beloved
Flock, by the Rev^d M^r W^m Brattle Past^r of the
S^d Church : Who was translated from his Charge
to his Crown, Feb^r 15 : 1716/17." Thomas Brattle
principal founder of the Brattle Street Church at
Boston was a brother of William Brattle and
treasurer of Harvard College for twenty-five years.

A similar basin for domestic purposes, in the
Old South Church, Boston, made by John Coney
(1655–1722) of Boston, is engraved on the rim
with large foliated mantling and the arms of
Clarke. It had belonged to William Clarke
whose wife Mary Withington later became the
wife of Gurdon Saltonstall the well-known governor of Connecticut. Gurdon Saltonstall occu-
pies the unique position of a man for whom the
law of the Colony of Connecticut was repealed
in order that he might step from the pastorate
of a church to the governorship of the Colony,
succeeding Governor Winthrop upon his death,
November 27, 1707. In Madam Mary Saltonstall's will of March 24, 1728 is this clause: "I
Give to the Brick South Church when built (at
its Dedication if I live not to see it and do it
myself) my Silver Basin on which it shall be
written that it is my Gift vizt or the Gift of
Mary Saltonstall to us." Two silver beakers,
made in 1794 from a tankard given by Governor
Gurdon Saltonstall, are in the First Congregational Church, New London, Connecticut. The
maker was John Proctor Trott (1769–1852) of
New London a man of prominence in the community, and the son of Jonathan Trott (1730–
1815) of Boston who moved in 1772 to Norwich,
where he kept the Peck Tavern for a short time,
before settling in New London where he died.
    An unusually large baptismal basin 17 inches
in diameter, made by John Coney, belonging to
the Second Congregational Society of Marble-

head, Massachusetts, is like the Saltonstall
basin. The donor, John Legg, one of the 114
householders of Marblehead in 1674, died October 8, 1718, aged 74. Rev. Edward Holyoke,
first pastor of the church, resigned in 1737 to become president of Harvard College, and held the
office for thirty-two years. In this basin was
baptized Agnes Surriage, a poor girl employed
at the "Fountain Inn" of Marblehead, whose
youth and beauty attracted Sir Charles Frank-
land collector of His Majesty's customs who
made her his mistress; but during the great
earthquake in Lisbon she saved his life and he
then made her his wife. The story has been
related by Oliver Wendell Holmes in the poem,
"Agnes." The Marblehead Historical Society
owns the famous house of Colonel Jeremiah Lee
which was built in 1768 at a cost of ten thousand pounds. The house has one of the finest
panelled rooms in the country and the large
hall and fine stairway are still hung with the
original wall paper, in panels, representing Roman ruins.

The large deep baptismal basin (Illus. 135)
with a narrow flat rim, made by Philip Syng
(1676–1739) of Philadelphia, was the gift in
1712 of Robert Quary to Christ Church, Philadelphia, with the flagon by the same maker and
two circular English plates of the last quarter
of the seventeenth century; he also gave to
St. Mary's Church, Burlington, New Jersey, the
fine covered beaker, already described.

Q

A baptismal basin (Illus. 136) with a deep body nearly hemispherical, on a plain flat base,

135. PHILIP SYNG.  D. 14¾ in.

belongs to the First Reformed Church of Tarry-town, New York, at the entrance to "Sleepy Hollow" made famous by Washington Irving in his story of Ichabod Crane in the "Legend of Sleepy Hollow." The donor of this basin, Fredryck Flypse, lord of the manor of Philipsburgh, was born in 1626 and died in 1702. His second wife

136. JACOB BOELEN.  D. 10½ in.

was Catharina Van Cortlandt and the church bears a tablet which commemorates its erection in

1699 by "Frederick Philipse and Catharine Van Cortlandt." She was the donor to that church of a beaker with the mark of Haarlem and the date-letter for 1655: her brother Jacobus Van Cortlandt married Eva the adopted daughter of Frederick Philipse her husband. In 1699 Frederick Philipse bought from his father-in-law the fifty acres of land now included in Van Cortlandt Park, the same land which was conveyed to the city of New York by the direct descendant of Jacobus and Eva Van Cortlandt. The present Van Cortlandt house, built by their son Frederick Van Cortlandt, has been restored and appropriately furnished by the New York Society of the Colonial Dames. The basin was wrought by Jacob Boelen of New York who made in 1707 a pair of tall beakers, engraved with the figures of Faith, Hope and Charity, belonging to the New Utrecht Reformed Church, Brooklyn. His son Hendrik Boelen made a similar beaker belonging to the Reformed Church, Flatlands, Long Island, and a pair in the Reformed Church at Bergen, New Jersey.

A plain baptismal basin (Illus. 137) made by John Potwine (1698–1792) of Boston, has a deep depression with a rounded bottom and it seems probable that the basin was supported by a wooden frame when in use. The wide rim, with a moulded edge, is inscribed in a foliated panel: "The Gift of Capt Eleazar Dorby to y$^e$ New South-Chh of Christ in Boston 1730." The New South Church, founded in 1719, no

137. JOHN POTWINE. D. 13½ in.

longer exists and the communion service has been generously and wisely given to the Museum of Fine Arts, at Boston.

Of the same type, but with a domed centre, is the basin in the First Congregational Church at Kittery, Maine, made in 1759 by Samuel Minott (1732–1803) of Boston. The rim is engraved with the Pepperell arms and inscribed: "The Gift of the Hon^ble Sir William Pepperrell Baronet, Lieu^t General of his Majesty's Forces, & of the Province of the Masachusetts, &c. &c. to the first Church in Kittery." Sir William Pepperell was the celebrated victor in 1745 of Louisburg, the "Dunkirk of America." The standards which he captured from the French at Louisburg were "borne in triumph from Kensington Palace to the city and were suspended in St. Paul's Cathedral, amidst the roar of guns and kettle-drums, and the shouts of an immense multitude." Sir William Pepperell was selected as commander of that expedition by Governor

William Shirley whose name is inscribed on the silver service given by George II to Trinity Church at Boston. It is said that he received the appointment when George Whitefield, the famous preacher, was a guest at his house. Whitefield chose the motto, *Nil desperandum Christo duce*, for the New Hampshire flag. Sir William Pepperell was created a baronet by King George II, in 1746. A portrait of him by John Smibert is in the possession of Mrs. Underhill A. Budd of New York and the sword which he wore at Louisburg is in the rooms of the Massachusetts Historical Society of Boston. Sir William Pepperell died July 6, 1759 and his only son died in his father's lifetime. His daughter Elizabeth married Nathaniel Sparhawk and their son William was created a baronet in compliment to his distinguished grandfather whose name he assumed. A portrait by Copley of William and Elizabeth Pepperell, two of the children of the second baronet, hangs in the Longfellow house at Cambridge.

The large plain baptismal basin (Illus. 138) was made by Daniel Russell of Newport, Rhode Island. Its shape is most unusual and the two large rings at the ends are attached to loops. It was the legacy of Nathaniel Kay in 1734 to Trinity Church, Newport, Rhode Island. Nathaniel Kay came from England as collector of the royal customs and held that office for many years after the accession of Queen Anne. He appears to have been an innkeeper as well as

138. Daniel Russell. L. 14¾ in.

collector of customs at Newport.  He was one
of the signers of the petition to Queen Anne in
1713 by the "minister, churchwardens, and
vestry of the Church of England in Newport,"
praying that a bishop be appointed over the
Church of England in the Colonies.  His tombstone (restored by the vestry in 1865) in the
graveyard of Trinity Church, is inscribed:
"This covers the dust of Nathaniel Kay, Esq.
collector of the King's customs in Newport,
whose spirit returned to God on the 14th day of
April A. D. 1734, after it had tabernacled here 59
years.  He, after an exemplary life of Faith &
Charity, did by his last will, at his death, found
and largely endow two Charity Schools in Newport & Bristol within his collection."  Nathaniel
Kay was the donor to St. Michael's Church
Bristol, Rhode Island, of a paten made by
Edward Winslow (1669–1753); also of a plain
chalice of Colonial make.  He bequeathed to
St. John's Church (formerly King's Church) in

Providence, Rhode Island, a tall cylindrical flagon made by Jonathan Clarke of Newport which is inscribed: "An Oblation from Nathaniel Kay a publican for the use of the blessed Sacrament in the Church of England in Providence Lux perpetua Credentibus Sola 1734." A flagon by the same maker was also bequeathed by him to St. Paul's Church in Narragansett, now Wickford, Rhode Island.

In St. James's Parish (St. James's Church, Herring Creek), Anne Arundel County, Maryland, is a baptismal basin (Illus. 139) made by David Hennell with the London date-letter for 1751–52. It is chased with scrolls and flowers in the rococo style so common on English plate between 1725 and 1760; and is inscribed: "Ex dono Gulielmi Lock Armigeri, A : D : 1732." and in Greek is the last part of the fifth verse of St. John, chapter iii. William Lock was justice of the Provincial court of Maryland in 1727 and died May 9, 1732. His will con-

139. LONDON, 1751–52. D. 9⅛ in.

tains the following legacy: "I give ten pounds sterling to St James Parish to be laid out in Plate as the Minister shall think most proper to be paid in a twelve months time after my decease." His

140. LONDON, 1761–62.  D. 13 in.

legacy was not fulfilled until about twenty years after his death. William Lock's daughter Sarah married Samuel Chew : her portrait by Gustavus Hesselius is in the possession of the family of her descendant, Miss Elizabeth Chew Williams.

The plain baptismal basin (Illus. 140) with a gadrooned edge, in Christ Church, Cambridge, Massachusetts, with the London date-letter for 1761–62, was made by Daniel Smith and Robert Sharp. It was a gift in 1761 from Grizzel Apthorp, the widow of Charles Apthorp of Boston, "the greatest and most noted merchant in this continent," who was paymaster and commissary of the British land and naval forces in America. He was warden of King's Chapel, Boston, and his monument, done by Henry Cheere of London, may still be seen there. A portrait of Charles Apthorp by Robert Feke is in "The Brook," a club of New York City, and Mrs. Apthorp's portrait by the same artist be-

longs to Mr. Isaac R. Thomas. Rev. East
Apthorp, rector of Christ Church from 1761 to
1765, was the son of Charles and Grizzel Apthorp. The house which he built at Cambridge
is still standing and was familiarly known as the
"Bishop's Palace," as he was thought to aspire
to the episcopate.

A baptismal basin (Illus. 141) made by Freeman Woods of New York, has a beaded edge, a
form of decoration found on English plate from
1775 to 1815. It is inscribed on the rim in
one line: "The Gift of the Rev^d Ezra Styles,
D.D. L.L.D. President Yal. Coll. to the Congregational Church in North Haven, 1794." Rev.
Dr. Ezra Stiles, son of Rev. Isaac Stiles pastor
of the church, was graduated at Yale in 1746 and
was a tutor of the college from 1749 until 1755.
He was ap-
pointed presi-
dent of Yale
College in 1777
and remained
in that office
until his death
May 12, 1795.
A silver tank-
ard which was
given to Ezra
Stiles by his
pupils on Janu-
ary 1, 1755 be-
longed to the

141. FREEMAN WOODS. D. 10⅝ in.

late Mrs. Kate Gannett Wells. It was made
by Samuel Casey (1724–73) of Newport, Rhode
Island, who moved to South Kingston about
1750 where he was presumably in business
with his brother Gideon Casey, a silversmith.
Samuel Casey was apparently a sober, indus-
trious and respectable member of the community and worked steadily at his trade in
which he was a skilled craftsman. After the
Spanish silver dollars came into use as currency,
imitations soon appeared and became so common that a penalty of death was pronounced
upon any person who should counterfeit them
or knowingly put any such counterfeit in circu-
lation. Great was the surprise of his fellow
townsmen when Samuel Casey with several
others was arrested October 6, 1770 for counter-
feiting. There was grave doubt in the minds of
the jury as to his guilt; but by instructions of
the court he was sentenced to be hanged as
the principal culprit, and the others received
minor sentences. But his friends did not believe
him guilty and on the night of November 3,
1770, so disguised that they could not be recog-
nized, they broke into the jail and liberated
him, and he escaped on horseback. Although
£100 reward was offered for his apprehension it
was never claimed nor was the culprit ever re-
taken. (G. M. C.)

The plain basin (Illus. 142) made by Paul
Revere (1735–1818) of Boston, is mounted on a
low foot; the rim is engraved with arms within

a scrolled and foliated panel as on the flagon by
the same maker. Both were presented to the

142. PAUL REVERE. D. 14⅛ in.

Hollis Street Church, Boston, the basin in 1761
and the flagon in 1773, by Zachariah Johonnot
a distiller and merchant. He was one of the
Sons of Liberty and died in 1784, aged 83.
His second wife was Margaret daughter of Rev.
Andrew LeMercier minister of the French
Protestant Church — the little church of the
French Huguenots — where until its dissolution,
the Johonnots, Boutineaus, Faneuils, Baudoins
and Sigourneys worshipped.

Early in the nineteenth century a small baptismal basin on a base was made both of silver
and Sheffield plate in New England. One of
this type, of silver, (Illus. 143) made by Lows,
Ball & Co. of Boston, has a classical border surrounding the base. It was a gift in 1804 to the
Second Parish, Worcester, Massachusetts, from
Mrs. Mary Thomas, the wife of the patriot
printer Isaiah Thomas who was born in Boston

January 19, 1749.   After serving an apprenticeship to Zechariah Fowle he went to Halifax
and later was engaged by Robert Wells, principal bookseller in the Carolinas, at Charleston,

143. Lows, Ball & Co.  D. 9 in.

where he married
Mary   Dill.   He
removed to Boston
in 1770 and issued
the first number of
the  *Massachusetts
Spy* July 17, 1771.
An active member
of the Sons of Lib-
erty, he took part
in  the  battle  of
Lexington  and  a
few days after that
event with the assistance of General Joseph
Warren, moved his printing outfit to Worcester,
where he became postmaster.  Most of the
Bibles and school books used throughout the
country emanated from his press : he was the
founder of the American Antiquarian Society in
1812 and died April 4, 1831.

## PATENS AND SALVERS

THE English chalices, as noted, had paten covers which fit closely over the lip to serve as dishes for sacramental bread. A separate paten was first made in England about the year 1615. It had a narrow flat rim and a shallow depression; the foot was generally reel-shaped in the earlier examples. The bases of the later Stuart patens were frequently trumpet-shaped and are sometimes called truncated. In the reign of Charles II the form of the later patens was adopted in a larger size with a wide rim richly decorated in the style of the period, and was used as a salver for domestic purposes; it is usually called a tazza.

An early Colonial tazza (Illus. 144) made by Timothy Dwight (1654–91) of Boston, belongs to the estate of Sally Pickman Dwight and is engraved in a pricked ornament with the initials $\frac{B}{TM}$ for Thomas and Mary Barton who were married in 1710. It rests on a trumpet-shaped foot with a flat base; the broad rim with a moulded edge is richly engraved with a running border of leaves, tulips and carnations inter-spersed with four animals, the elephant, lion,

unicorn and camel.   The combination of various
flowers and animals in decoration may be seen
in the embossed ornamentation of the time of
Charles II.   Belonging to the same estate is
a plate, or salver without a foot, made by John
Coney (1655–1722) of Boston.   The broad rim

144. TIMOTHY DWIGHT.   D. 11⅛ in.

with a moulded edge is engraved with three
cherubs' heads which spring from branches of
tulips and other flowers, while the initials $\begin{smallmatrix}R\\C\ E\end{smallmatrix}$
are enclosed in similar branches.

To the Northern Diocese of Virginia was presented in 1856 by Hugh Munroe of Mobile,
through the Rev. B. B. Leacock, a paten (Illus.

145), bearing the London date-letter for 1691–
92, with a plain centre and an embossed gadrooned edge.  The original inscription, which
surrounds the arms of Sir Edmund Andros, is:
"EX DONO D<sup>NI</sup> EDMUNDI ANDROS, EQUITIS, VIR-
GINIÆ GUBERNATORIS ANNO DOM. MDCXCIV.  IN

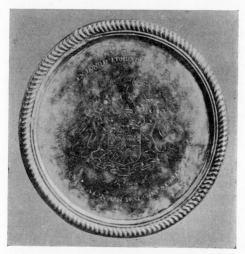

145. LONDON, 1691–92.  D. 11 in.

USUM ECCLESIÆ IACOBI POLIS."  Sir Edmund
Andros, the donor of the paten to Old Jamestown Church in Virginia, was the able but unpopular Colonial governor, first, of the Province
of New York (1674–81), secondly, of the Provinces of New England (1685–89), and lastly, of
Virginia (1692–98).  He was the son of Amias
Andros, marshall of the ceremonies to Charles

I, born in 1637 and made gentleman-in-ordinary in 1660 to the ill-fated Elizabeth, queen of Bohemia. Major Edmund Andros succeeded his father in 1674 as bailiff of Guernsey and in 1681 was knighted by Charles II: he died February 27, 1713–14 and was buried at St. Anne's, Soho.   This paten is used in the celebration of the Holy Communion at every diocesan convention in Virginia, where it is taken by the bishop.

A large plain paten (Illus. 146) with a truncated base and gadrooned borders, belongs to St. John's Church (Elizabeth City Parish) Elizabeth City County, Hampton, Virginia.   It bears the London date-letter for 1698–99 and the maker's mark for Richard Syngin.   A similar paten made by John Allen (1671–1760) and John Edwards (1670–1746) of Boston belongs to Mrs. Richard H. Morgan and is engraved in

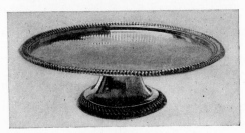

146. LONDON, 1698–99.   D. 9¾ in.

the centre in feathered mantling with the Coffin arms.

A plain English paten of 1725–26 which has

associations with America, is at Corpus Christi
College, Cambridge. This was the gift of an
American alumnus, James de Lancey of New

147. BILLIOUS WARD.  D. 7¼ in.

York, who held such public offices as acting
governor of the Province of New York, lieutenant-governor and chief justice. The plain
paten (Illus. 147) with a moulded edge and supported on a trumpet-shaped foot is inscribed:
"Trinity Church In Memory of Rev. Philo
Shelton Easter 1826." It belongs to Trinity
Church, Southport, in the town of Fairfield,
Connecticut, and as *Trinity Church* in the inscription was engraved at an earlier date it
may be inferred that it was part of the original
communion service of that church presented in
1762 by that generous churchman St. George
Talbot. The silver was presumed to have been
carried off by the British when they destroyed
the church in 1779. St. George Talbot was a
resident of New York City and had business
relations in Stamford; he presented to St.

R

John's Church of that town a paten with a
gadrooned edge and a high base, made by John
Coddington (1690–1743) of Newport, Rhode
Island, a grandson of Governor William Cod-
dington, and a great-grandson of William and
Anne Hutchinson who were forced to leave
Boston at the time of the Antinomian Con-
troversy.

Rev. Philo Shelton was graduated at Yale
College in 1775 and at the first ordination, held
by Bishop Seabury August 3, 1785 at Middletown, Connecticut, he with three others received
deacon's orders. As the Bishop's hands were
laid upon him first, he enjoyed the distinction of
being the first clergyman episcopally ordained
in the United States of America. He died
February 27, 1825. The maker of the Southport
paten was Billious Ward (1729–77), the first
master of the Masonic Lodge of Guilford,
Connecticut, the son of William Ward (1705–61)
a silversmith who died of smallpox while visiting
his intimate friend, Rev. Samuel Andrews, rector
of the Episcopal Church at Wallingford. William Ward (1678–1767), the grandfather of
Billious Ward, was also a silversmith.

The conventional paten of the English Church,
used in most of the Episcopal churches of the
Colonies, was not generally adopted by the New
England churches. The vessels used for bread
in the sacrament are usually shallow plates or
circular dishes, such as were used as alms basins
in many churches: in size they do not differ

and they may have been used for either purpose.

In St. Peter's Church at Albany, New York, is a circular alms basin, 12 inches in diameter, made by Francis Garthorne in 1711–12 which is engraved with the cipher and royal arms of Queen Anne. It is part of a service of five pieces, given by her, and is inscribed: "The Gift of Her Majesty, Ann, by the Grace of God, of Great Britain, France, and Ireland and of Her Plantations, in North America, Queen, to Her Indian Chappel, of the Onondawgus." Besides the service of five pieces presented by Queen Anne to Trinity Church, New York, she was the donor of eleven chalices to Episcopal churches in the states of New York, New Jersey, Pennsylvania and Rhode Island.

In the Second Church at Boston are two similar basins, 15 inches in diameter, with curved rims and moulded edges, dated 1711, the gifts of Thomas Hutchinson and of his half-brother Edward Hutchinson, upon which are engraved the Hutchinson arms. Thomas Hutchinson a prosperous merchant was a conspicuous man in the official and commercial life of Boston and prominent in the Artillery Company: he was the father of Governor Thomas Hutchinson. The maker of the dishes was Edward Winslow (1669–1753) of Boston whose father had allied himself with the Hutchinson family by marriage.

A circular shallow dish (Illus. 148), belonging to the Museum of Fine Arts at Boston, is inscribed: "The Gift of the Hon^{ble} Thomas

Hancock Esq$^r$ to the Church in Brattle Street
Boston 1764." The donor married Lydia the
daughter of Daniel Henchman in whose book-
shop he was employed and to whose business he

148. SAMUEL MINOTT. D. 13⅜ in.

eventually succeeded; he left a large fortune to
his nephew John Hancock. The Hancock arms
are engraved upon the dish; and also upon a pair
of beakers made by Nathaniel Hurd (1729–77)
of Boston, which Thomas Hancock bequeathed
in 1764 to the Lexington Church of which his
father, Rev. John Hancock, was pastor from
1698 to 1752. Samuel Minott (1732–1803) of
Boston, the maker of the dish, was a strong
tory, and an addresser of Hutchinson in 1774;

he was arrested by order of the Massachusetts council in 1776. He was a member of the Brattle Street Church and married Elizabeth Davis.

The heart-shaped dish (Illus. 149) is probably Spanish, about 1690–1700. It has a gadrooned rim of hollow flutings; and inside of this is a border, in slight relief on a matted ground, decorated with sprays of foliage. The initials on the bottom $\frac{F}{I\ R}$, are probably those of Captain John Flavel and his wife Rebecca. He was a mariner and apparently cruised as a privateer, about the year 1700, in the West Indies and on the Spanish main; the inference is obvious. This dish belongs to St. Philip's Church, Charleston, South Carolina.

149. SPANISH, 1690–1700.   L. 12½ in.

In the reign of George I the tazza or salver with a foot was supplanted by the more orthodox salver on three small feet. Of this type is the circular salver (Illus. 150) with the London date-letter for 1740–41 made by Robert Abercrombie and belonging to Mr. C. Hartman

150. LONDON, 1740–41.    D. 6 in.

Kuhn. Salvers are seldom found in the churches but in the First Parish at Weston, Massachusetts, is a small salver with the London date-letter for 1766–67 made by Ebenezer Coker or Edward Capper; and another, 12¾ inches in diameter, of 1755–56, made by Richard Rugg or Robert Rew. Both of these were given by Mrs. Catherine Maria Barrell, the daughter of Artemas Ward. He was the donor of the circular dish to the Arlington Street Church at Boston.

Such salvers were made of various size and shape. A Colonial example (Illus. 151) octagonal in section, is owned by Mr. Hollis French. It was made by Jacob Hurd (1702–58) of Boston, the son of Jacob Hurd and Elizabeth daugh-

151. JACOB HURD.    D. 6¼ in.

ter of Captain Peter Tufts of Medford. He was
1st sergeant of the Artillery Company in 1745 and
prominent in the militia, becoming captain of a
Boston company. His son Nathaniel Hurd (1729–
77) was a silversmith and eminent engraver; his

152. DUBLIN, 1720–21. D. 8⅜ in.

son Benjamin Hurd (1739–81) wrought the baptismal basin given in 1774 by Mr. John Morey
to the First Parish in West Roxbury, Massachusetts — over which society the famous Unitarian divine and abolitionist, Theodore Parker,
was settled in 1837. Captain John Parker, his
grandfather, commanded the company of minute-
men at Lexington who were fired upon by the
British on that memorable day—April 19, 1775.

In the First Church at Boston, Massachusetts, is a plain circular dish (Illus. 152) with a
scalloped edge divided into twenty parts.  Engraved in the centre are the arms of Weld impaling those of Harstonge, the original owners.
It is inscribed on the bottom : "Given to the
First Church in Boston by William F. Matchett
and Sarah A. Matchett 1905."  The plate has
the Dublin date-letter for 1720–21 and was made
by Robert Harrison.  It is the only piece of
Irish silver in a New England church.   Such
dishes were made in large numbers by the Dublin
silversmiths in the early years of the eighteenth
century but examples by English silversmiths
are comparatively rare;  three made by the
latter are in the Spanish and Portuguese synagogue at London.

# DRAM CUPS OR TASTERS

THESE small vessels were formerly used in England for tasting and sampling ale, wine and spirituous liquors. They varied in size from less than a quarter of a pint to a half pint which was merely a "taste." While mention may be found of tasters in wills at the latter end of the fourteenth century, no examples are known of earlier date than one of the seventeenth century, dated 1638–39, which is shown in Mr. Jackson's "History of English Plate." In New England wills they are occasionally called wine tasters but usually "dram cups." Richard Webb of Boston, by his will dated July 1, 1659 bequeaths to his son Nehemiah "one silver wine taster"; Robert Sanderson (1608–93) mentions in his will a "dram cup" and John Clarke of Boston in his will of 1690 mentions "3 dram cups." This name may have been derived from "dram" meaning as much spirituous liquor as is usually drunk at once; or from the word "drachm" which is one-sixteenth of a pint. Both appear to be applicable.

Belonging to Dr. Samuel A. Green is a dram cup (Illus. 153) made by Robert Sanderson

153. SANDERSON AND HULL.
H. ⅞ in.

(1608–93) and John Hull (1624–83) of Boston, engraved with the initials $_{I}^{G}{}_{A}$ for Joseph and Ann Gerrish who were married prior to 1673. The Rev. Joseph Gerrish succeeded Rev. Antipas Newman as pastor of the Wenham church: he married the daughter of Richard Waldron a major in the Indian war 1675–76 and one of the councillors for New Hampshire in 1680.

Mr. Dwight Blaney is the owner of a dram cup (Illus. 154) with the initials $_{S}^{P}{}_{M}$ made

154. BENJAMIN SANDERSON. H. 1 in.

by Benjamin Sanderson (1649–78) of Boston a son of Robert Sanderson. The identity of the maker's mark would seem to be established beyond doubt by that on the standing cup belonging to the First Church, Boston, the gift of John Sunderland, a parchment maker; his son John Sunderland married Mary Viall whose sister Mercy was the wife

155. EDWARD WINSLOW. H. 1 in.

of Benjamin Sanderson.   The latter would have been likely to be commissioned to make the cup.

Edward Winslow (1669–1753) of Boston was the maker of a dram cup (Illus. 155) with plain scrolled handles which also belongs to Mr. Blaney.

# SALTS AND SALTCELLARS

"SALT was formerly obtained by the evaporation of sea-water, and was, therefore, a costly although indispensable commodity. It has very generally been regarded with veneration and together with bread, has figured in the sacred rites of many nations. Salt was formerly considered a safeguard against witchcraft, and in ancient folklore was said to be always absent from the unholy feasts and orgies of witches and demons; from this probably came the notion that it was unlucky to spill salt, a superstition illustrated in the painting of the Last Supper by Leonardo da Vinci, who has depicted the ill-fated Judas in the act of upsetting the salt." (C. J. J.)

The salt or saltcellar (the derivation of the latter indicates that it should be spelled seller, a salt holder; hence the word salt is redundant) was, in England during the Middle Ages, the most important article of plate that was used on the tables of the rich and noble. Examples of great elaborateness and in a variety of designs most unusual, from the middle of the fifteenth to the seventeenth century, are to be found in all the books describing English plate.

Mr. Jackson dwells at some length on the erro-
neous tradition of the salt having been used to
divide the lord and his noble guests from the
inferior guests and menials. The salt was
placed in the middle of the high table where the
host was seated with his guests on his right
and left according to precedence; consequently
when these seats were filled others were obliged
to sit at the tables below.

The English salt (Illus. 156) belonging to
Harvard University, is spool-shaped and bears

156. LONDON, 1629? H. 3¼ in.

some resemblance in outline to the hour-glass
salt of the fifteenth and of the early sixteenth century. The diameter of the base is $6\frac{1}{2}$ inches, and
of the top 6 inches. The only ornamentation
is in the volutes of the three brackets which are
fixed on the broad rim for the purpose of sup-
porting a napkin. The illustrations heretofore
shown of this particular salt have been upside
down, the brackets being shown as feet. The
initials $\begin{smallmatrix} G \\ I\ E \end{smallmatrix}$ on the base are those of Jose and
Elizabeth Glover who were married about
1629. This salt had belonged to Mrs. Glover's
father Rev. Nathaniel Harris, canon of Hereford. Rev. Jose Glover with his family sailed
from London in 1638 with the intention of setting
up the first printing press at Cambridge. He
had made a contract with Stephen Daye who
came on the same ship; but Glover died on
the passage over, consequently Stephen Daye
achieved the honor of being the first printer in
America. Richard Harris was a brother of Mrs.
Glover and was graduated in 1640 at New
College, Oxford, for which he had been fitted at
Winchester College under the care of his uncle,
John Harris the warden. He came to America,
probably in the same ship with Henry Dunster,
who became president of Harvard College in
1640 and married Mrs. Glover in 1641. Richard
Harris was one of the first tutors of Harvard
College, and upon the death of his sister in 1643
the salt came to him and he bequeathed the

"Great Salt" to the college, at his death in 1644.
This was the most common form of salt of the
time of Charles II and of particular interest is a
duplicate of the Harvard College salt, with the
London date-letter for 1664–65, which belongs
to Winchester College, where Richard Harris's
uncle was warden.

The earliest type of salt that appears to
have been made by the New England silversmiths is called "trencher" as it was placed be-
side the trencher. An Elizabethan plain circular salt dated 1580 is not unlike the trencher
salt except that it is nearly twice the height of
the latter. Very few made prior to the time of
Charles II are extant: they were of various
shapes; triangular, oval, round, octagonal and
quatrefoil. A circular trencher salt, with spiral
flutings similar to the borders on other contemporary vessels, was made in England between
1690 and 1715. A Colonial example (Illus. 157)
made by John Coney (1655–1722) of Boston,
is engraved with
the initials S M for
Sarah Middlecott,
the daughter of
Richard and Sarah
(Winslow) Middle-
cott, who married
Louis Boucher of
Boston March 26,
1702. He was a
merchant of dis-

157. JOHN CONEY.  H. 2⅛ in.

158. LONDON, 1706–07.    H. 1¼ in.

tinction and resided part of the time in Paris where he owned considerable property: he was lost at sea in 1715. The saltcellar has been presented to the Museum of Fine Arts in memory of her mother Abigail Brigham Hill, by Miss Harriet A. Hill, a descendant of Sarah Middlecott. A portrait of Sarah Middlecott Boucher painted by Blackburn, is in the possession of Mrs. Alexander S. Porter. An oval trencher salt (Illus. 158) with the London date-letter for 1706–07 and the maker's mark illegible, belongs to Mr. Hervey E. Wetzel. A similar pair made by John Burt (1691–1745) belonging to Miss Emily Sever, was shown in the 1911 exhibition at the Museum of Fine Arts, at Boston.

A type of saltcellar made in England from 1740 to 1780, designated as "tripod," has a circular bowl with a rounded bottom resting on three feet. The terminations and shoulders of the feet vary in design; but the rim of the saltcellar is usually gadrooned and is

159. LONDON, 1764–65.    H. 1¾ in.

everted. The salt-
cellar (Illus. 159)
with the London
date-letter for
1764-65 made by
R. and D. Hennell,
is one of a pair
given to the Mu-
seum of Fine Arts
by the Misses
Catharine Lang-

160. DANIEL PARKER. H. 1½ in.

don Rogers and Clara Bates Rogers. The terminations of the feet are shells and the shoulders
are foliated. Belonging to Mrs. L. B. Taft is a
similar saltcellar (Illus. 160), with moulded feet
and shoulders, made by Daniel Parker (1726-85)
of Boston. He was one of the fifteen Sons of
Liberty whose names encircle the punch bowl
made by Paul Revere.

Pierced saltcellars fitted with colored glass
linings were made
in England be-
tween the years
1760 and 1790.
They were pierced
in a variety of
pleasing designs
and they were often
overlaid with ro-
settes and festoons,
after the style used
in the decoration

161. LONDON, 1766-67. H. 2 in.

s

of furniture by the brothers Adam.   The shapes
were usually oval or circular and the feet were of
various designs.   An oval saltcellar (Illus. 161)
made by Richard Mills is one of a set of four,
with the London date-letter for 1766–67, belonging to Mr. Philip Leffingwell Spalding.   The
rim is beaded and the four feet are claws grasp-
ing balls — a type of foot very commonly used

162. Caleb Swan ?   H. 2¼ in.

on furniture made in the second half of the
eighteenth century.   This variety of English
saltcellar seems never to have been made in
the Colonies — very probably for the reason
that similar less expensive salts of Sheffield plate
found a ready sale here, if we may judge from
the number of examples extant.   Pierced work
is more particularly mentioned under Other
Objects.

The boat-shaped saltcellar (Illus. 162) was a
form commonly made in England between the

years 1775 and 1820; many had rings suspended from volutes instead of the slender loop-shaped handles; the bodies are shaped like a canoe and the bases are oval. This pair belongs to the Worcester Art Museum and was probably made by Caleb Swan (1754–1816) of Boston.

# SPOONS LADLES FORKS

THE spoon is a utensil of very great antiquity. The ancient Egyptians used spoons made of pottery, wood, slate, ivory and bone; and spoons of bronze and the precious metals were made by the Greeks and Romans. The Lord commanded Moses to make golden spoons for the Tabernacle. Spoons of some sort were used commonly in Christian and mediæval times : the bowl and stem were wrought in one piece.

A very early Christian spoon, illustrated in Mr. Jackson's "History of English Plate," belongs to the British Museum; the bowl is elliptical, while others of approximately this period have a nearly circular bowl; the stem is quite flat and bears much resemblance to the modern fiddle-pattern spoon except that the angular shoulders which appear on the latter, just above the bowl, are not seen in the early Christian spoon.

A spoon of very great interest made at the end of the twelfth century is the English mediæval "Coronation Spoon" which forms part of the regalia preserved in the Tower of London and has been used at recent coronations for

the oil for anointing the sovereign.  It is of
silver-gilt,  10¼ inches in length, and has been
used, in all probability, at the coronation of
the English sovereigns for seven hundred years.
Mr. E. Alfred Jones fully describes and illustrates the spoon in his "Old Royal Plate in the
Tower of London"; the bowl is more like that
of the spoon of Charles II, while the elaborate
stem terminates in a seal-shaped knop.

The bowls of the early spoons up to the
middle of the seventeenth century were, as a
rule, more or less fig-shaped with the narrowest
part next the stem; the short stems were round,
square, hexagonal and sometimes quite flat;
and most of the terminations were knops with
various designs, such as acorns, diamond-points,
owls, and other objects.  A bust of the Blessed
Virgin, sometimes used to surmount the stem,
gave rise to the name "maiden head" spoons;
these were made up to the accession of Queen
Elizabeth in 1558.

The "Apostle" spoon was made to a considerable extent in England in the sixteenth and
seventeenth centuries.  The stems were surmounted with figures of the twelve apostles
and sometimes a thirteenth was added which
was called the "Master" spoon.  A complete
set of these, with the "Master" spoon, made in
1536-37 by one maker, is illustrated in Mr. E.
Alfred Jones's catalogue of the collection of the
late Mr. J. Pierpont Morgan.

The "seal top" spoon enjoyed great popu-

larity in England for a longer period than any
other type and appears to have been made
principally during the last half of the sixteenth
century and throughout the seventeenth century. The stems terminate in an ornamental
knop with a circular disc on the top, resembling
the article used for sealing letters with wax.

During the period when the seal top spoon
was made the bowl appears to have been
undergoing an almost imperceptible change.
This change, however, becomes more noticeable during the time of Charles I and of the
Commonwealth, when the bowl is broader next
the stem and narrower at the end, being quite
the reverse of the fig-shaped bowl but somewhat more oval.

A spoon which is of more interest to Americans
was the "Puritan" spoon, sometimes called a
"slip-stem." This made its appearance in England during the Commonwealth period and on
account of its extreme simplicity undoubtedly
appealed to the Puritans. The bowl is ovoid
— a form that became firmly established at
the time of the Restoration in 1660 and has so
continued with only slight changes, such as
making the bowl somewhat more pointed at
the end; the stem is quite flat with the end
stumped. A Puritan spoon (Illus. 163) made
by John Hull (1624–83) of Boston, is the
earliest known Colonial spoon and belongs to
the Essex Institute of Salem, Massachusetts.
On the back, where the stem and bowl meet, is

a horizontal ridge
and a short V-shaped
tongue on the bowl.
There is no record
of the original owner-
ship but the initials
B
W H may be those
of William and Han-
nah Brown of Salem
who were married in
1664.

At the beginning
of the reign of
Charles II, a spoon
made its appearance
with a stem quite
flat and thin, and
much wider; the
end, still wider and
thinner, was orna-
mentally outlined by
being cleft into three
parts; it is termed a
"trifid" or notched-
end spoon. The
clefts vary; the end
is sometimes divided

163.  John Hull.  L. 7 in.

into three nearly
equal parts; sometimes the centre part is much
wider and turned forward. A long V-shaped
tongue extends down the back of the bowl: the

164. COLONIAL.
L. 6¾ in.

tongues vary somewhat in design but usually consist of a centre and two side ribbings; this may be considered the precursor of the rat-tail spoon which is less elaborate. A Colonial example (Illus. 164) belonging to the First Baptist Church, Boston, is without a maker's mark. The V-shaped tongue is treated as the centre stem of the acanthus leaf ornament. "The patterns appear to have been raised on the surface by means of steel dies, with which the spoons were stamped when heated, after having been shaped with the hammer." This spoon was later inscribed: "WS to the Baptist Church 1727." The initials are those of William Snell a weaver of Boston who died November 10, 1726 at the age of 91. By his will he left a legacy to that church, of which he was a member, amounting to "forty one pounds, together with twelve ounces of Plate and twelve pennyweight." On May 8, 1727 the Church voted: "that the twelve ounces of plate should be made into a handsome Cup with his name upon it and

as left by him to ye Church in his last will and
Testament.  But one Spoon be Reserved with
his name upon it for ye use of ye Lord's Table."
The "cup" is a plain mug, with a tapering body
encircled with a moulded band, made by Benjamin Hiller (1687–1739) of Boston, a deacon of
the church in 1719.  He was clerk
of the Artillery Company in 1716
and 4th sergeant in 1717: he
married Elizabeth Russell, the
grand-daughter of Rev. John Russell the second pastor.  In the
church are two similar mugs made
by Benjamin Hiller, the gifts of
Joseph and Mary Russell, the
parents of his wife.

In the First Parish (Unitarian)
Tyngsboro, Massachusetts, is a
spoon (Illus. 165) made by John
Coney (1655–1722) of Boston,
with a different trifid end and a
bowl, with a ribbed V-shaped
tongue, decorated with scrolls
similar to the spoons made by
John Edwards.  It is inscribed
on the stem: "1st Ch. T. by S.
Winslow, 1790."  The initials
W
I E  are those of Joshua Winslow

and his wife Elizabeth Savage
who were married February 8,
1720–21; portraits of them are in

165.  JOHN CONEY.
L. 7⅝ in.

166. JOHN EDWARDS. L. 7½ in.

the possession of their descendant, Mr. Arthur Winslow. Sarah Winslow was the daughter of Colonel Eleazer and Sarah Tyng, for whose family the town was named, and married John Winslow, the son of Edward Winslow the silversmith, and the brother of Joshua Winslow.

A spoon made its appearance in England at the end of the seventeenth century which was similar to the trifid-end spoon, but the clefts were omitted and the end was waved. A pair of "wavy-end" spoons (Illus. 166) made by John Edwards (1670–1746) of Boston, belonging to the First Church, Boston, is engraved $\begin{smallmatrix} T \\ O \ C \end{smallmatrix}$ for The Old Church. A long V-shaped ribbed tongue extends down the centre of the back of the bowl which is ornamented with scroll-work in low relief. A wavy-end spoon (Illus. 167) made by John Coney, has a

plain rat-tail which succeeded the more elaborate V-shaped tongue of the earlier spoon.   This
form of rat-tail commonly obtained during the
first quarter of the eighteenth century in England but in our country is often found at a
much later date.   The initials
MW are those of Mary Wil-
loughby of Salem who married
Thomas Barton in 1710: the
spoon belongs to the estate of
Sally Pickman Dwight.

A change in the upper half of
the stem of the spoon, which
lasted for nearly three quarters
of a century, occurred in England in the eighteenth century,
about 1705.   The end of the
stem became much thicker than
any other part and rounded, but
still turned forward; a sharp
ridge runs down the centre of
the front for some distance making the sides concave; the lower
part of the stem is narrower than
in the earlier type of spoon.   A
pair of spoons (Illus. 168) of this
description with a plain rat-tail
and the initials $\frac{B}{T\,M}$ for Thomas
and Mary (Willoughby) Barton
who were married in 1710, belongs to the estate of Sally Pick-

167. JOHN CONEY.
L. 7⅞ in.

man Dwight.    They were made by Jeffrey
Lang (1707–58) of Salem, Massachusetts, whose
sons, Richard Lang (1733–1820) and Edward
Lang (1742–1830) were also silversmiths.

In the second quarter of the eighteenth century the stem-end underwent a further change
— the ridge was shortened
and the concavities dis-
appeared — as in the spoon
(Illus. 169) made about
1760 by S. Barrett of Nantucket.    A double-drop is
on the back of the bowl;
it is engraved : "Solomon
Gardner" and belongs to
Mr. Dwight Blaney.

Early in the reign of
George II the rat-tail disappeared and an ornament
was substituted resem-
bling that on the front
end of the stem but on
a smaller scale; this is
termed the "double-drop"
and was common up to the
middle of the eighteenth
century.    A spoon (Illus.
170) with this ornament
on the bowl and with the
front ribbed like the Lang
spoons, was made by

168. JEFFREY LANG.   L. 8 in.    Jacob Hurd (1702–58) of

169. S. BARRETT.
L. 8¼ in.

Boston. It is engraved with the Green crest and: "Joshua Green"; he was born in 1731 and was an ancestor of the owner Dr. Samuel A. Green.

Jacob Hurd stamped his mark on a plain eighteenth century French silver spoon and fork, which once belonged to Esther Wheelwright, the great-granddaughter of the Rev. John Wheelwright, who was captured when seven years old by the Abenakis tribe of Indians at Wells in Maine; Esther was placed by the French governor, the Marquess de Vaudreuil, in the celebrated Ursuline Convent at Quebec where these are still preserved. In "True Stories of New England Captives" by Miss C. Alice Baker is a graphic description of Esther Wheelwright's captivity and a reference, probably to these very

170. JACOB HURD.
L. 8¼ in.

171. L. 8¼ in.
THOMAS SKINNER.

articles.   It seems that in January 1754 Esther Wheelwright's nephew from Boston went to see her and gave her a miniature portrait of her mother.   According to the records of the convent he presented the community with some "fine linen, a beautiful silver flagon, and a knife, fork and spoon, of the same material."

The front of the spoon (Illus. 171) marked $\frac{B}{I\ L}$, is like the Lang spoons but shows a change in the double-drop on the back of the bowl; the ribbing of the lower drop is omitted.   It was made by Thomas Skinner (1712–61) of Marblehead, Massachusetts, and belongs to Mr. Dwight Blaney.

Various forms of rococo ornament were used on the backs of the bowls of spoons made in England about the middle of the eighteenth century, which were probably introduced from France; these consisted of shells and scrolls.   A spoon (Illus. 172) belonging to the Museum of Fine Arts, Boston, is inscribed: "Church in Brattle Street"; the front is ribbed like the Lang spoons and the bowl shows the scallop-shell ornament.   "In the Dark Ages, a scallop shell

fastened to the hat was the accepted sign
that the wearer had made a pilgrimage to
the Holy Land." The spoon was wrought by
Joseph Edwards junior (1737–83) of Boston,
the son of Joseph Edwards a stationer; and
the grandson of John Edwards,
(1670–1746).

An unusual spoon, probably
never made in the Colonies, was
introduced into England before
the middle of the eighteenth
century and was fashionable for
about thirty years; it is called
" scroll-headed " and is also
known as the "Onslow pattern"
— probably so called after Mr.
Arthur Onslow speaker of the
House of Commons in the reign
of George II. The end of the
stem is not turned forward as in
the spoons previously shown but
is curled back in the manner of
an Ionic volute, while the upper
side is moulded with a series of
quite deeply-cut curved members
which converge to a point part
way down the stem. A ladle
(Illus. 173) with the scroll-headed
stem, owned by Mrs. B. M. Jones,
bears some indistinguishable
marks.

172. L. 8 in.
JOSEPH EDWARDS JR.

This turning back of the stem-

173. ENGLISH. L. 11 in.

end, which for nearly three quarters of a century had turned forward, became a general fashion in the reign of George III and has continued to the present day; the end was rounded, as in the earlier examples. Spoons of this form have become known as the "Old English" pattern. A pair of spoons (Illus. 174) of this description with a chased border of short oblique lines, called "feather-edged," has a rococo shell ornament on the bowl; it was made by William Homes junior (1742–1825) of Boston the son of William Homes (1717–83) and belongs to Mr. Dwight Blaney. Other decorations used on this type of spoon were the bright-cut engraving and the beaded edge.

A pair of spoons (Illus. 175) made by Joseph Loring (1743–1815) of Boston, shows a variation in the stem-end; this is pointed, a form common in Scotland and Ireland. The decoration of "bright-cut" engraving consists of indented or zig-zag lines —

common on English plate
from Anglo-Saxon times.
On the back of the bowl
is a rococo scroll acanthus
leaf. The initials T E P
are those of Theophilus

175. JOSEPH LORING. L. 9 in.

and Elizabeth (Greenleaf)
Parsons who were married
January 13, 1780, and to
whose granddaughters, the
Misses Parsons, the spoons

174. WILLIAM HOMES JR.
L. 8¼ in.

T

belong.  Theophilus Parsons was chief justice of Massachusetts and by his contemporaries was considered the most learned lawyer in the country.   A pint mug of the bellied shape, made by John Coburn (1725–1803) of Boston, in the

176.  DANIEL ROGERS.
L. 8¼ in.

First Parish Falmouth, now Portland, Maine, was presented in 1775 to the pastor the Rev. Samuel Deane by twenty-one young men of the parish whose initials are inscribed upon it ; Theophilus Parsons was one of the donors. Rev. Samuel Deane was a poet awarded by Harvard College in 1760 a prize for having written the best English ode on the death of George II and the accession of George III.

Spoons engraved with a death's head and the legends, "Live to Die" and "Die to Live," came into fashion in England shortly after the Restoration ; they were called "funeral" spoons as they were presented upon such occasions, not perhaps to be used but in memory of the dead.

In New England wills bequests
of spoons are so common as to
lead one to think that the custom
was perpetuated in this manner
in the Colonies and that contemporary spoons, intended for use,
were given. Made by Daniel
Rogers (1753–92) of Newport,
Rhode Island, is a pair of spoons
(Illus. 176) which appears to be
of a type purely Colonial in design; the stem-end is "clipped"
on the top and sides and resembles a coffin. This design may
have been introduced to exem-
plify more clearly a funeral
spoon. One is inscribed: "Sam¹
Gidds ob. 1777 Æ 59 BG" and
the other: "Joanna Good ʰᵉ ob.
1775 Æ 52 BG"; they belong to
Mr. Dwight Blaney.

The "fiddle" pattern spoon
(Illus. 177) made its appearance
early in the nineteenth century:
the stem-ends were frequently
plain and the shoulders, just
above the bowl, were often right-
angled; the bowl is decidedly pointed. The
makers were Davis, Palmer & Co. of Boston.

177. DAVIS, PALMER
& Co.
L. 8¾ in.

A form of decoration, not unusual in America,
consisted of an embossed sheaf of wheat or a
basket of flowers, as on the spoon (Illus. 178)

which has a scallop shell on the back of the bowl; it was made by Edward Watson of Boston. Both spoons belong to the Museum of Fine Arts, Boston.

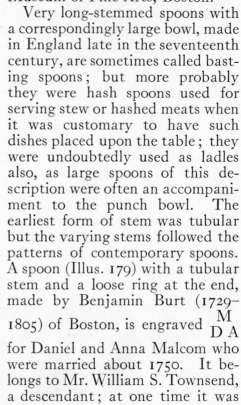

178. L. 8¾ in.
EDWARD WATSON.

Very long-stemmed spoons with a correspondingly large bowl, made in England late in the seventeenth century, are sometimes called basting spoons; but more probably they were hash spoons used for serving stew or hashed meats when it was customary to have such dishes placed upon the table; they were undoubtedly used as ladles also, as large spoons of this description were often an accompaniment to the punch bowl. The earliest form of stem was tubular but the varying stems followed the patterns of contemporary spoons. A spoon (Illus. 179) with a tubular stem and a loose ring at the end, made by Benjamin Burt (1729–1805) of Boston, is engraved $\begin{smallmatrix} & M \\ D & A \end{smallmatrix}$ for Daniel and Anna Malcom who were married about 1750. It belongs to Mr. William S. Townsend, a descendant; at one time it was owned by William Mackay one of the Sons of Liberty whose name is inscribed on the punch bowl made by Paul Revere.

In England tea spoons were not made until the end of the seventeenth century. Spoons of that size, somewhat heavier, were made in small numbers early in the reign of Charles II but were probably used by children or for sweetmeats or eggs : the intermediate size (now called a dessert spoon) originated at the same time ; both followed the designs of the large spoons.

An interesting spoon made during the eighteenth century was that with a pointed end which is barbed ; the stem is round and the bowls are pierced in various designs. They were made in England in the three sizes but only the small size appears to have been made to any extent in New England. Mr. Jackson thinks that they were not made as strainers for tea nor the long pointed stem used to free the spouts of teapots of leaves ; but that they were used to remove the cloves and lemon seeds from punch, the stem being used to spear the slices of lemon which floated on the top. For whatever purpose they were originally made, it seems quite probable that they must have been found

179. L. 16 in.
Benjamin Burt.

very convenient for removing any leaves that chanced to get into the tea cup; and the stem will penetrate, to a considerable extent, the spouts of many teapots. Of this description is the pierced spoon (Illus. 180) made probably by Jeffrey Lang (1707–58) of Salem, Massachusetts, which belongs to the estate of Sally Pickman Dwight.

The only pierced spoons in an American church are the pair (Illus. 181) made by Paul Revere (1735–1818) of Boston (or by his father) belonging to the Second Church, Boston, and acquired after 1730; they were doubtless used to remove sediment, or cork from the wine.

180. L. 5¾ in.
JEFFREY LANG?

They have rat-tails on the backs of the bowls, and the stem-ends are turned forward and ribbed.

Caddy spoons, the bowls made in the shape of shells, leaves, scoops and various other designs, were used to transfer the tea from the caddy to the teapot.

181. PAUL REVERE.
L. 4⅞ in.

A marrow scoop (Illus. 182) made by Thomas Tolman, with the London date-letter for 1764–65, belonging to the estate of Sally Pickman Dwight, was the common form made in England; but occasionally a stem of this kind had a spoon termination.

Ladles for soup or punch with plain hemispherical bowls, or often in the shape of shells, had stems similar to contemporary spoons; and ladles correspondingly smaller were made for sugar and sauces. A distinctive type of punch ladle, made throughout the Georgian period, had stems of turned hard wood, such as ebony or chestnut; and later, delicate slender stems of whalebone twisted and tipped with silver. The bowls were of various forms and sometimes a coin was inserted in the bottom. Jacob Marshe made the ladle (Illus. 183) with the London date-letter for 1793–94 which has an oval bowl with an everted lip at one side. It

182. L. 8⅞ in.
LONDON, 1764–65.

belongs to Mr. Dwight Blaney as does also the Colonial ladle (Illus. 184) perhaps made by George Hanners junior (1721–60) of Boston; it has a turned wooden stem rivetted into a silver socket with two twisted supports for the bowl.

183. LONDON, 1793-94.
L. 14½ in.

Ewers and basins for rose-water were an indispensable adjunct of the dining-table before the middle of the seventeenth century, when the common use of forks was unknown and when meat and fish, fowl and fruit, were conveyed to the mouth by the fingers, a proceeding which necessitated frequent washing of the hands. Shakespeare was familiar with the use of these vessels, for in "The Taming of the Shrew" Gremio in speaking of his house describes it as richly furnished with plate and gold, and with "basins and ewers to lave her dainty hands." As the custom of providing guests with silver forks became general after the restoration of Charles II the original use of silver rose-water dishes and ewers declined, and what was deemed a necessity in Tudor and Jacobean times became a luxury after 1660. It was Swift who said : "Fingers were made before

forks, and hands before knives." Forks were
made with two, three or four prongs, the number of prongs being no cri-
terion as to date; though
at the end of the eighteenth
and the beginning of the
nineteenth century, most
of the silver forks had four
prongs.  The stems fol-
lowed the designs of con-
temporary spoons; occa-
sionally a fork is found
with a spoon at the other
end.

A spoon and a fork (Illus.
185) with wavy-ends, were
perhaps made by John
Coney (1655–1722) of Bos-
ton, as they bear his initials
in a small rectangle.  The
initials MW are those of
Mary Willoughby, born in
1676, an ancestor of Sally
Pickman Dwight to whose
estate they belong.  The
front and back of the stems
are engraved in foliated
scroll-work suggestive of
the French decoration of
the Louis XIV period.

A pair of plain large forks
(Illus. 186) with wavy-ends

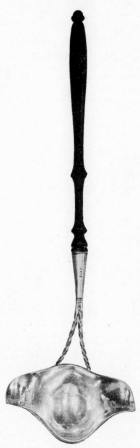

184. George Hanners Jr. ?
L. 14 in.

185. John Coney?
L. 4¼ in.

bears the initials HA for Hannah Arnold who married Rev. Samuel Welles, September 15, 1719. They constituted a portion of her wedding silver and were presented to the Museum of Fine Arts, Boston, by the late Mr. Winthrop Sargent, a descendant. The maker of the forks, John Noyes (1674–1749) of Boston, was 4th sergeant of the Artillery Company in 1699, ensign 1704; he was elected constable April 19, 1704 but declined to serve and David Jesse (1670–1705) served instead.

186. John Noyes.
L. 7¼ in.

Forks do not seem to have been made to any extent by the Colonial silversmiths and none of the succeeding patterns which are represented by the spoon stems have come under the writer's observation. Steel forks and knives with bone, ivory or silver handles, were doubtless in common use in the Colonies in the eighteenth century.

# CANDLESTICKS SNUFFERS SCONCES

THE earliest candlesticks were surmounted with a pricket and the candle was pressed down over this projection which held it upright. Cathedral candlesticks made of wood and various kinds of metal are almost invariably of that description. Only a few of the candlesticks, made in England during the first half of the seventeenth century have escaped the melting pot; but those illustrated in books on English plate show them to have had cylindrical tubes for holding the candles, and circular bases; near the middle of the stem was a projecting pan for catching the drippings. A pair of embossed candlesticks of this description, with the London date-letter for 1663–64, that formed part of the gift of Charles II to the Czar Alexis in 1663 is illustrated in "Old English Plate of the Emperor of Russia" by Mr. E. Alfred Jones.

For a few years after the Restoration there was a spasmodic revival of the quasi-Gothic taste and candlesticks were made in the form of clustered pillars — a style adapted from mediæval architecture. A pair of pricket candlesticks, in Salisbury Cathedral, with the London date-letter for 1663–64, is similar in the lower

half to the candlestick (Illus. 187) made by Jeremiah Dummer (1645–1718) of Boston, with
eight engaged columns or shafts grouped to-

187. JEREMIAH DUMMER.   H. 10¾ in.

gether in the form of a square. A square projecting nozzle surmounts the top and a similar larger projecting flange masks the junction of the column with the circular foot which rests on a square moulded base. Upon the four corners of the base are engraved the arms of Jeffries, Lidgett, Clarke and Usher: and on the bottom are the initials $\begin{smallmatrix} I \\ D\ E \end{smallmatrix}$ for David Jeffries, a merchant of Boston and his wife Elizabeth Usher whom he married September 15, 1686. Elizabeth Usher was the grand-daughter of Peter Lidgett (also a rich merchant of Boston and partner in many voyages with John Hull) and the daughter of John Usher lieutenant-governor of New Hampshire. Tradition says that the pair of these candlesticks was presented by David and Elizabeth Jeffries to their son John Jeffries upon his marriage in 1713 to Anne Clarke, when her family arms were added. This candlestick belongs to Mr. William A. Jeffries, the seventh in direct descent. The great-grandson of David Jeffries was Dr. John Jeffries surgeon-general of His Majesty's forces in America at the time of the Revolution: in 1785 he made a notable balloon trip from England to France in company with Blanchard. This was the first crossing of the English Channel by air.

A candlestick (Illus. 188) with the maker's mark IC in a small rectangle, shows great similarity to the work of John Coney (1655–

1722) of Boston.   Were it not for the insertion
of the baluster stem it would resemble to a
greater degree the early English candlestick of
tubular form.   The maker would appear to have
had in mind the dripping pan on such candlesticks when he added the projecting fluting

188. John Coney?   H. 6⅛ in.

above the foot.
The fixed
nozzle is fluted
and at the
junction of the
tubular top
with the bal-
uster stem is
a cut ring.
This candle-
stick belongs
to the estate of
Sally Pickman
Dwight; en-
graved upon
the base are
the initials
RA.

Towards the
end of the sev-
enteenth cen-
tury cast can-
dlesticks with
a stem of the
baluster form
came into fa-

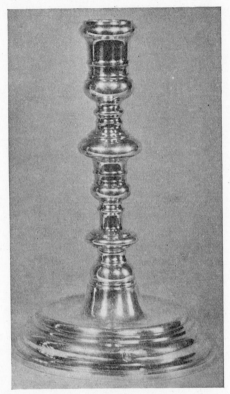

189. JOHN CONEY.   H. 6¼ in.

vor in England, as they were more easily made
than those that had to be hammered.

One of a pair of candlesticks (Illus. 189) belonging to the estate of Sally Pickman Dwight,
was made by John Coney. The tubular tops
were usually fitted with removable nozzles to

catch the drippings, but in most instances they
have been lost.   A candlestick (Illus. 190) is

190. JOHN BURT.   H. 7 in.

one of a pair made by John Burt (1691–1745)
of Boston.  The baluster stem and domed base
are octagonal in section.  The candlesticks

are inscribed : "Donum Pupillorum 1724" and
with much other silverware were given to
Nicholas Sever of
Kingston, Massa-
chusetts, a tutor
at Harvard Col-
lege from 1716 to
1728. The Rev.
William Warren
Sever, a descend-
ant, presented the
candlesticks    to
the college.

191. LONDON, 1741–42.  H. 8⅜ in.
THOMAS DANE.

One of a pair
of    candlesticks
(Illus. 191) with
the London date-
letter for 1741–42
and the maker's
mark for John
Gould,    has    a
baluster-shaped
shaft with the
middle section in
the form of a
vase ; the fixed
nozzle is wavy in
outline. Of very
great interest is
the fact that these
candlesticks also bear the stamp of Thomas
Dane (1724–96) of Boston.  He did not make

U

them but he undoubtedly imported or perhaps bought the pair from some loyalist who fled the country at the time of the Revolution. With

no intention to deceive, Dane merely put his stamp upon them to show that they had passed through his hands, and to serve as an advertisement. The candlesticks are engraved with the initials RGA for Rufus Greene Amory and are owned by Mrs. George W. Harrington, his descendant. When Queen Victoria's father, the Duke of Kent, visited Boston he was present at the wedding of Nancy Whitelock Geyer to Rufus Greene Amory, February 13, 1794.

192. SHEFFIELD, 1783–84. H. 11½ in.

In the latter

half of the eighteenth century, much taller
candlesticks were made in England. They
were often in the form of a Corinthian column
with the capital and base of that order. Many
others, designed in a variety of forms, were
decorated with festoons and medallions in the
Adam style. A candlestick (Illus. 192) with
a rectangular shaft tapering toward the square

193. LONDON, 1777-78.  H. 3½ in.

base is surmounted by a vase to hold the candle;
it is representative of a classical type common
in England. It bears the Sheffield date-letter
for 1783–84 with the makers' mark for John
Parsons & Co. and belongs to Mrs. F. C. Martin.

Small bedroom candlesticks were made in
England from the end of the reign of Charles II
up to the early part of the nineteenth century.
The conical extinguisher has, at the side, a hook

which fits into a small eye attached to the inner edge of the handle; the snuffers, in the form of scissors, fit into a slot in the middle of the stem. The plain candlestick (Illus. 193) with beaded edges has the London date-letter for 1777–78 and the makers' marks for John Crouch and Thomas Hannam.   It belongs to Miss M. H. Jewell.

In early times the thick wicks of candles were made of a soft material; consequently a pair of snuffers was indispensable.   In the nineteenth century a hard wick was invented which was entirely consumed by the flame. The earliest snuffers were quite flat throughout, like scissors, and the two pans formed a heart; probably there were other shapes.

Belonging to Mr. Dwight M. Prouty is a pair of snuffers (Illus. 194) with the London date-letter for 1725–26, made by John Bignell.   The two limbs are of unequal length; the longer, having a pointed end for removing "thieves" from the candle, contains the pan; while the shorter has the cutting edge, the shutter fitting into the pan.   The stand or tray bears the London date-letter for 1724–25 and the maker's mark for Anthony Nelme who made a plain paten in St. Mary's Church at Burlington, New Jersey, the gift of Mrs. Catharina Boevey; and also a paten, the gift of Maximilian Boush to Donation Church, Lynnhaven Parish, Princess Anne County, Virginia.   The snuffers and tray are said to have been the property of Edward Holland mayor of Albany, New York.

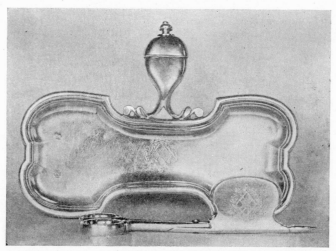

194. LONDON, 1725–26.  L. 7½ in.

John Burt (1691–1745) of Boston made a pair
of snuffers and a tray (Illus. 195) as an accom-

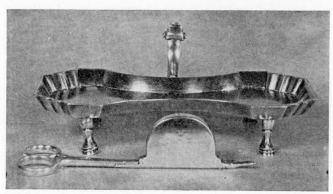

195. JOHN BURT.  L. 7¼ in.

196. LONDON, 1705–06. H. 11½ in.

paniment to a pair of candlesticks of baluster form which are octagonal in section. All the objects are engraved with the initials W D S for Daniel and Sarah (Hill) Warner who were married December 15, 1720; they belong to Miss Evelyn Sherburne, a descendant. Daniel Warner was justice of the peace 1740; and councillor 1754–79.

In the reign of George III, snuffers were made with three small feet which raised them above the tray and made it much easier to take them up with the thumb and forefinger.

While silver candle brackets and sconces are known to have been made at an early date, it was not until the reign of Charles II that their use became general in the great houses of England.    After

the accession of Queen Anne, the fashion of
lighting the walls of rooms by means of sconces
waned.  On account of the destruction of so
much plate in England few sconces now exist.
One (Illus. 196) belonging to Mrs. William W.
Vaughan, with the London date-letter for 1705–
06, was made by Francis Garthorne.  A hook,
affixed on the back, permits hanging it on
the wall; scratched on the back is : "Iames
Iarvis" and below the name is : "Wins."  The
embossed ornamentation is on a matted ground.
It is an interesting illustration of Louis XIV
decoration on English silver.  The form, copied
in tin, was made to a considerable extent in New
England in the early days;  and reproductions
are abundant in the antique shops.

One of a pair of candle brackets (Illus. 197)
belonging to the writer, is unusual.  The cylindrical tube for the candle is similar to that on
the candlestick with a baluster stem; below it
the dripping-pan is affixed to the removable
stem which fits into a socket on the circular
plate.  The brackets are attached to wooden
frames enclosing scrolls of paper quill-work and
flowers which sparkle in the candle-light.  One
of these sconces is shown in the new edition of
"Furniture of the Olden Time" by Miss Frances
Clary Morse;  they were probably made by
Ruth Read as the initials RR with the date
1720 are engraved on the dripping-pans.  She
was the daughter of John Read a distinguished
lawyer born in 1679 in Fairfield, Connecticut,

who came to Boston in 1722; of him President
John Adams said : "he had as great a genius and
became as eminent as any man." The maker
of the silver bracket was Knight Leverett
(1703–53) of Boston, the great-grandson of

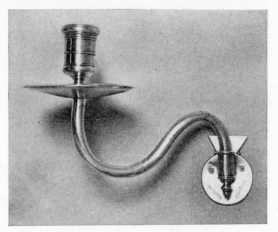

197. Knight Leverett.  H. 5⅜ in.

Governor John Leverett upon whom Charles II
conferred the order of knighthood, which fact
undoubtedly accounts for the Christian name of
the silversmith. John Leverett, president of
Harvard College, was the uncle of Knight
Leverett who was constable in 1728, scavenger
1742 and 3d sergeant of the Artillery Company
in 1736.

# PORRINGERS

THE name applied in our country to the shallow circular bowls with a single flat handle suggests that their use was for porridge. Some writers have held that the porringer was used for heating brandy and other liquors : that it was designed for any such purpose is inconceivable for, putting it so near an open fire would have been likely to damage the porringer, to say nothing of the impossibility of holding the handle after the contents had become hot. Furthermore the porringer is difficult to pour from as the sides of the interior of the body are concave ; besides a red-hot iron or poker was the method invariably used in the early days of the porringer for the purpose of heating liquors. It is of course not improbable that porringers may have been used over spirit lamps if an emergency arose for heating something in a hurry. In all probability they were used in the early days, much as they are today, for children's food of a soft nature ; and doubtless they were a convenience in time of illness for serving broth and other food. It is more than likely that by the beginning of the eighteenth century they were used in the Colonies as sugar bowls ; as were small bowls and caudle cups in England before the covered sugar bowl became the fashion.

It has been noted under the subject of caudle cups that in England the name porringer was frequently applied to caudle cups, but it never appears to have been used to designate what is here called a porringer : there the name applied to such vessels is surgeons' "bleeding-bowls," as they were used for catching the blood when the custom prevailed in the seventeenth and eighteenth centuries for surgeons to bleed their patients. Mr. Jackson illustrates in his "History of English Plate" one bearing the Norwich hall-mark for 1689 on the handle of which are pricked the initials IAW for John A. Worrell who was master of the Barber Surgeons of Norwich in 1693. Whether bleeding-bowls were ever in use in England for domestic purposes has perhaps not been proved to the contrary but at all events they do not seem to have been a common article. Two of these porringers, dated 1696–97 and 1710–11, given to English churches early in the nineteenth century, are used as alms basins. It seems highly probable that some surgeon, having one in the family, found it useful for catching the blood ; it could be easily carried in the pocket ; hence its adoption by the profession. Would not this custom eventually lead to the abandonment of their use for domestic purposes ? No one familiar with the unpleasant associations would care to see them on the breakfast table !

The very interesting small porringer (Illus.
198), 4⅞ inches in diameter, bears the London
date-letter for 1637–38, the lion passant, the
leopard's head, and as the maker's mark a heart

198. LONDON, 1637–38.   L. 1¾, W. 1¾ in.

enclosing three indistinct devices. The small
handle is trefoil in form; the foils, pierced with
semi-circles, surround the centre trefoil pierc-
ing with a tiny circle below. The initials $\begin{smallmatrix} D \\ H\ E \end{smallmatrix}$

on the slightly domed bottom are those of
Henry Dunster the first president of Harvard
College and of his first wife Elizabeth Harris,
the widow of Jose Glover, whom he married in
1641. Henry Dunster died at Scituate February 27, 1658–59 but no reference is made to the
porringer in his will and the inventory of his
estate only shows the item: "plate of divers
sorts £38.18.o." Mr. Charles H. Baker, the
grandson of Samuel Dunster of Attleboro a descendant of Henry Dunster, has fittingly presented it to Harvard University. In his will
Henry Dunster directs that his body be taken
to Cambridge and placed by the side of his wife
in the old burying ground, which lies between
the First Parish and Christ churches and recalls
the lines of Oliver Wendell Holmes:

> "Like Sentinel and Nun, they keep
>     Their vigil on the green:
> One seems to guard, and one to weep,
>     The dead that lie between;"

As the handle affords the best means for the
discrimination of porringers, their shapes being
alike though differing in size, the illustrations
are of the handle only: the English types are
shown first, as comparisons with the Colonial
handles can thus best be made. Belonging to
Messrs. Crichton Brothers is a porringer (Illus.
199), probably made by John Ruslin, which
bears the London date-letter for 1682–83; it is
pricked with the initials $_I^S{}_C$ and the date 1693.

Judge A. T. Clearwater is the owner of the porringer (Illus. 200) which is 3¾ inches in diameter, made by Timothy Ley, with the London date-letter for 1691–92. Another porringer (Illus. 201) belonging to Messrs. Crichton

199. LONDON, 1682–83. L. 2½, W. 2⅝ in.

Brothers, made by William Andrews, bears the London date-letter for 1701–02; it is pricked with the initials $\begin{smallmatrix} & S & \\ T & & M \end{smallmatrix}$.

One of a pair of porringers (Illus. 202) with the London date-letter for 1743–44, was made by Thomas Farren who wrought numerous vessels described in "The Old Silver of American Churches." They are engraved with the initials MS for Martha Salisbury whose mother died in London in 1743 and whose husband was Nicholas Salisbury. These were bequeathed to the Worcester Art Museum by Stephen Salisbury, a Boston merchant who moved

200. LONDON, 1691–92.
L. 1½, W. 1¾ in.

201. LONDON, 1701–02.  L. 3, W. 2¾ in.

to Worcester about 1850 and generously endowed that museum.

The porringer (Illus. 203) belonging to Mrs. Charles H. Joy, is one of a pair made by William Vincent and bears the London date-letter for 1780–81. The handle is much like those of scrolled pattern which were so abundant in New England at that time. On the bottom is : "B. Joy" for Benjamin Joy a prominent physician of Boston and a subscriber to the fund raised among the merchants and other citizens to build the frigate *Boston*. Benjamin Joy married the daughter of Joseph Barrell, an eminent Boston merchant who built in Somerville the superb old mansion designed by Bul-

202. LONDON, 1743–44.  L. 2¾, W. 2⅜ in.

finch and supplied with glass from the first works
erected in Boston. Mrs. Joy has two tapestries
loaned by Mr. Barrell when Washington was
given a reception in Concert Hall at Boston
in November 1789; one was hung on the wall
as a background, the other served as a carpet
for Washington to
stand upon in re-
ceiving the guests.

In New England
"three pewter por-
ringers" are men-
tioned in the will
of Olyvar Mellows
in 1638. Again we
have no means of
knowing whether
they were porrin-
gers or caudle cups!
But in the will
of William Paddy

203. LONDON, 1780–81.
L. 2¼, W. 2⅜ in.

dated September 9, 1658 he leaves to his wife "a
new Silver Cawdell Cup and porringer" which
implies that a distinction was made between the
two articles in New England. It is greatly to be
regretted that no porringer made by the earliest
Colonial silversmiths exists : it may be assumed,
however, that the handles made by Jeremiah
Dummer would be likely to follow the designs of
those made by Robert Sanderson and John Hull
with whom he served his apprenticeship. As the
earlier caudle cups and tankards were somewhat

smaller than those made later it seems only natural that such would be the case with por-ringers, the handle being of a corresponding size. It should not, however, be inferred that no small porringers were wrought after the larger size made its appearance. The centres of the bottoms of nearly all porringers are domed to add strength by making the surrounding portion somewhat heavier and consequently less sus-ceptible to dents which would be likely to occur in an entirely flat bottom, for an article that was in such constant use.

To place a date on any particular Colonial handle is futile, for it is merely guesswork; and to state when one variety of handle came into fashion or disappeared is absurd. One can only be guided by the working period of the makers, aided by the initials of husband and wife. The very charming handles pierced in a great variety of designs are a most interesting study. If a thousand porringers could be brought together for examination, doubtless valuable data could be derived which would be of great importance. Very probably each maker used a design differing slightly from his neighbor's; but apprentices might feel justified in copying the designs of their masters.

Belonging to the Worcester Art Museum is a Colonial porringer (Illus. 204) 4$\frac{1}{8}$ inches in diam-eter, made by Jeremiah Dummer (1645–1718) of Boston, a bequest to the museum from Stephen Salisbury. Unfortunately the initials

P
E A have not been identi-
fied. The small size and
the light weight, together
with the signs of age,
would seem to show that
it was of earlier date than
the larger porringer with
the distinctly geometric
handle; the dimensions
of the bowl and handle

204. JEREMIAH DUMMER.
L. 1¾, W. 2 in.

are much the same as those of the English
porringer of 1637–38. The design would indicate that it was the prototype from which
was derived the scrolled handle commonly made
during the eighteenth century.

A similar porringer (Illus. 205), 4¼ inches in
diameter, was made by René Grignon who died
in 1715 at Norwich, Connecticut. He was a
Huguenot silversmith who settled in East
Greenwich the later part
of the seventeenth cen-
tury and in 1696 went
to Boston where he be-
came elder of the French
Church. Benjamin Gri-
gnon a silversmith, prob-
ably his father or brother,
was in 1685 "not ad-
mitted nor approved of
by ye selectmen of Bos-
ton to be an inhabitant

205. RENÉ GRIGNON.
L. 1¾, W. 2 in.
x

of ye Towne" and settled at Oxford, Massachusetts. That there was some business connection between René Grignon and David Jesse
(1670–1705) is shown by the payment of £5 to
the former by the administrator of the latter's
estate. The in-
itials $\begin{smallmatrix} R \\ I\ E \end{smallmatrix}$ are prob-

ably those of James
and Elizabeth
Rayner who were
married on October
25, 1692. The
porringer belongs
to Mrs. John Ber-
tram Read, a de-
scendant.

Owned by the
estate of Mrs. Sally
Pickman Dwight
is the porringer
(Illus. 206) $4\frac{1}{8}$

206. PETER OLIVER. L. $2\frac{1}{4}$, W. 2 in.

inches in diameter, with the initials $\begin{smallmatrix} B \\ T\ M \end{smallmatrix}$ for
Thomas and Mary Barton who were married in
1710. It was made by Peter Oliver (1682–1712)
of Boston and bears some resemblance, in outline and in the piercings, to the English handles
of the late seventeenth century.

Made by an early Colonial silversmith with
initials BF, is a porringer (Illus. 207) $4\frac{3}{8}$ inches
in diameter, belonging to Miss Edith D. Beck;

207. BF. L. 2⅛, W. 2½ in.

the initials DH are those of Dorothy Harben, probably the mother of Dorothy Harben Forster who married Thomas Alleyne in 1755. The handle is quite similar in piercing and outline to that on the English porringer of 1691–92; the heart appears in three of English design.

Mr. R. T. Haines Halsey is the owner of a porringer (Illus. 208) 5½ inches in diameter, made by Jeremiah Dummer, with the initials $\begin{smallmatrix}B\\C\ M\end{smallmatrix}$. The "geometric" handle bears no resemblance in piercings or outline to those of the English porringers and seems to be of distinctly Colonial design.

By the same maker is a handle (Illus. 209) almost identical in design, excepting that the

208. JEREMIAH DUMMER.
L. 2⅞, W. 3¼ in.

209. JEREMIAH DUMMER.
L. 2½, W. 3 in.

three upper circles on each side have been cut open thus giving it a lighter appearance. The initials $_T^S{}_R$ are those of Thomas and Rebecca (Eldrige) Smith who were married prior to 1697: Rebecca Eldrige married (ii) Josiah Sanders and at her death the porringer was left to her granddaughter Rebecca Salisbury who married Daniel Waldo. It belongs to Mrs. George E. Francis, a descendant.

Almost an exact duplicate of this handle (Illus. 210) was made by Edward Winslow (1669–1753) of Boston. The only difference is that the two middle circles are not cut into scrolls. The initials $_L{}^B{}_S$ are those of Louis Boucher and his wife Sarah Middlecott whom he married March 26, 1702; the por-

210. EDWARD WINSLOW.
L. 2⅞, W. 3⅛ in.

ringer may have
been a wedding gift
from Edward Wins-
low to Sarah Mid-
dlecott, his cousin.
It belongs to Miss
Harriet L. Clapp,
a descendant.

Samuel Vernon
(1683–1737) of
Newport in Rhode
Island, a second
cousin of Edward

211. SAMUEL VERNON. L. 2¾, W. 3⅛ in.

Winslow, made a porringer (Illus. 211) of the
same design, which belongs to Mrs. Trumbull

Hartshorn. The initials $\begin{smallmatrix} & P & \\ N & & S \end{smallmatrix}$ are those of Na-

thaniel and Sarah (Clark) Paine who were

212. JOHN CONEY. L. 2⅞, W. 3 in.

married June 25,
1713. Nathaniel
Paine's sister mar-
ried Samuel Ver-
non in 1725.

Owned by the
estate of Mrs. Sally
Pickman Dwight is
a porringer (Illus.
212) made by John
Coney (1655–1722)
of Boston, with the

initials $\begin{smallmatrix} & B & \\ T & & M \end{smallmatrix}$ for

Thomas and Mary Barton who were married
in 1710. While the general design is the same
as Mrs. Francis's porringer made by Jeremiah
Dummer, variations will be noted: the ovals
next the body are slightly scrolled; the pair of
quatrefoils are straight lines on three sides;
and the circle near the top is changed to a trefoil.
All the handles made by John Coney, so far
noted, are exactly like this; also one made by
David Jesse (1670–1705) and one dated 1740
made by Thomas Millner (1690–1745) of Boston.
Perhaps Jesse and Millner were Coney's apprentices.

An unusually large porringer with a cover
(Illus. 213) is 6¾ inches in diameter and while
it is without a maker's mark, it was probably
made by John Coney; the handle is like
that made by Coney except that the two usual
piercings at the outer edge of the broadest part

213. JOHN CONEY?    L. 2¾, W. 3⅛ in.

of the handle are omitted. The initials $\begin{smallmatrix}B\\T\ M\end{smallmatrix}$ are those of Thomas and Mary Burroughs of Boston and the date 1680 is probably that of their marriage: their daughter Mary born in Jamaica, Long Island, married in 1718 Brinley Sylvester, the grandson of Nathaniel Sylvester who in 1659 settled at Shelter Island which he and his brother Constant had purchased in 1651 of Stephen Goodyear. Nathaniel Sylvester was the son of the celebrated poet Joshua Sylvester "translator of the divine rapsodies of Du Bartas of whose fame, in the age of Elizabeth and James, the Puritans were anxious guardians": he married Grizzle the daughter of Thomas Brinley of Datchet, in the county of Bucks, the parish well known to the readers of Shakespeare's "Merry Wives of Windsor." To the Shattuck and Southwick fugitives, Nathaniel Sylvester gave protection and shelter from the bloody persecutions in Massachusetts under the successive rule of Governors Endicott and Bellingham, whose zeal for the honor of God overcame all tenderness for their fellow creatures. Mr. Sylvester Dering, a direct descendant, has presented the porringer to the Metropolitan Museum of Art, New York.

Andrew Tyler (1692–1741) of Boston made a porringer (Illus. 214) with a handle identical with Coney's, excepting that he has substituted a circle for the trefoil. It belongs to Mr. Dwight Blaney. By the same maker is a handle

214. ANDREW TYLER. L. 2¾, W. 3 in.

(Illus. 215) of the "scrolled" variety which in its proportions is more like the geometric handles of Dummer, Winslow and Vernon than the more elongated handles of Coney and of Tyler. The initials

$$\begin{array}{c} H \\ B\ M \end{array}$$

are those of Benjamin and Mary Hammatt who were married May 9, 1734; on the bottom is: "Benjamin Pemberton" who was born March 13, 1696, the son of Benjamin and Elizabeth (Dixie) Pemberton: the latter became the wife of Edward Winslow the silversmith in 1712. The porringer is owned by Miss Helen Temple Cooke.

A decided similarity is noticeable in the handles of three of the English porringers and cf the handle (Illus. 216) made by John Edwards (1670–

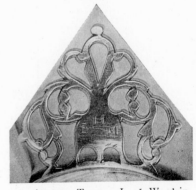

215. ANDREW TYLER. L. 2⅝, W. 3⅛ in.

1746) of Boston who undoubtedly served his apprenticeship in London from 1684 to 1691. It is engraved: "M : Storer 1724." Mary Storer was John Edwards's daughter and the wife of Ebenezer Storer; her first child was born in

216. JOHN EDWARDS. L. 2⅜, W. 2⅝ in.

1724. As it bears the earliest mark used by John Edwards it seems probable that the porringer had previously been used by his children. It belongs to Mrs. T. D. Townsend, a descendant.

217. JOHN EDWARDS. L. 2⅜, W. 2¾ in.

A handle (Illus. 217) by the same maker, resembles in its broadest part those of the English porringers. The initials $\begin{smallmatrix} B \\ T\ M \end{smallmatrix}$ are those of Thomas and Mary Barton who were married in 1710; it is owned by the estate of Sally Pickman Dwight.

Handles almost identical in design, with trifling variations, were made by William Cowell (1682–1736) and Andrew Tyler (1692–1741).

Edward Winslow (1669–1753) of Boston made the scrolled handle (Illus. 218) with the initials SG for Stephen Gorham (1683–1743) who married Elizabeth Gardner in 1703: it belongs to Mrs. J. D. Brannan, a descendant. A comparison with the scrolled handle made by Andrew Tyler shows the elimination of the scroll at either side of the broadest part; otherwise it is the same. John Edwards, Samuel Vernon and a few other silversmiths made similar handles. Porringers with scrolled handles were made in abundance throughout the eighteenth century apparently by every silversmith and the variations are not worth noting. In later porringers the two centre piercings next the bowl were usually omitted.

218. EDWARD WINSLOW.
L. 2¾, W. 2½ in.

It requires a very vivid imagination to understand the application of "keyhole" to this design; the top piercing is like some escutcheons.

# CASTERS

THE caster appears to have received its name from the act of "casting" salt (or pepper) from the receptacle; hence the tops are pierced for that purpose. In the Elizabethan and Jacobean periods the large salts were often provided with covers sometimes made for pepper. As separate articles of plate, casters do not appear to have been made in England before the latter part of the seventeenth century. The small caster, as well as the pepper box with a handle, is often called a muffineer in England as it was used to sprinkle salt on hot buttered muffins; the larger are called casters or dredgers. The latter term is applied to similar receptacles used in our kitchens for sprinkling flour over meats and for other purposes. The earliest form is cylindrical.

A caster (Illus. 219) of this shape is one of a pair made by William Gamble bearing the London date-letter for 1701–02 and belongs to Miss Harriet L. Clapp: the mate has been presented by Miss Harriet A. Hill to the Museum of Fine Arts at Boston. It has a gadrooned border surrounding the very flat base; the pierced bell-shaped top has a fluted and turned finial

from which radiate leaves of "cut-card" work.
Below the gadrooned edge the cover is attached
to the body with a bayonet joint; fastened

to the cover, on opposite
sides, are two small
brackets so shaped as
to exactly fit the mould-
ing surrounding the lip;
a single opening in the
moulding permits the
insertion of a bracket
before turning to se-
curely fasten the cover.
Both casters bear the
initials $\mathrm{I}\ \overset{F}{\phantom{I}}\ \mathrm{S}$ for John and
Sarah (Boucher) Foye
who were married Oc-
tober 23, 1729. John
Foye was the grandson
of John Foye captain
of the *Dolphin* on the
voyage to London No-
vember 26, 1687. As his
father John Foye mar-

219. LONDON, 1701–02.  H. 6 in.    ried Sarah Lynde November 16, 1699 it is
probable that the pair of casters originally belonged to John Foye's parents.   Sarah Boucher
was the daughter of Louis Boucher and Sarah
Middlecott whose initials are on the porringer
made by Edward Winslow.  The Foyes lived

at Charlestown where the Navy Yard now is and in fitting up their bridal chamber they sent to Paris for damask of orange color because of their admiration for William of Orange. At the burning of Charlestown by the British in 1775 the Foye house was destroyed but the silver was saved by throwing it into the well.

A fine Colonial example (Illus. 220) of this type, owned by Mr. George S. Palmer, has a broad flat base of bold gadrooning, with a band of acanthus leaves surrounding the body; the top is similarly fluted. The maker was Garrett Onclebagh of New York, who wrought in 1697, for the Reformed Dutch Church at Flatbush, Long Island, a pair

220. GARRETT ONCLEBAGH.
H. 5⅛ in.

of tall cylindrical beakers engraved with interlacing bands of flowers, and oval panels containing figures of Faith, Hope and Charity. "He was of an old and socially prominent New York family and an active member of the

Dutch Church. His standing in the community was high, for he was elected to the office of assistant alderman for the successive years 1700–03. Onclebagh became involved in certain factional disputes and lost the favor of the people, which he regained but fell from grace, as upon his

221. JOHN EDWARDS. H. 3⅛ in.

election to his former office in 1713 his colleagues on the board passed the following resolution : 'Whereas Garrett Onclebagh who was lately Elected to serve in the Office of Assistant of the North Ward of this City for the year Ensueing is A Person of Evil fame and Reputation and hath been Convicted of Coyning the Current Money of this Province and since hath also been Convicted of Champerty, it is therefore the Opinion of this Court that the said Garrett Onclebagh is not qualified to serve in the said Office and it is ORDER'D (Nemine Contra Dicente) that the Mayor and Recorder do refuse to swear him into Office.'" (R. T. H. H.)

John Edwards (1670–1746) made a plain caster or pepper box (Illus. 221) with a scrolled

handle which is notched.  The initials $\begin{smallmatrix} & L \\ C & S \end{smallmatrix}$ are
those of Charles and Sarah (Warren) Little who
were married at Plymouth October 9, 1712; it
belongs to Miss Frances M. Lincoln a descendant in the fifth generation.  Sarah Little married
November 21, 1728 at Kingston, as her second
husband, Nicholas Sever to whom the candlesticks made by John
Burt were presented.

A similar caster
(Illus. 222) with a
pierced domed cover
and a plain scrolled
handle is owned by
Mr. Dwight Morti-
mer Prouty and was
made by William
Cowell (1682–1736)
of Boston.   The in-
itials $\begin{smallmatrix} & N \\ I & M \end{smallmatrix}$ are those
of Rev. John Norton

222. William Cowell.  H. 2¾ in.

and his wife Mary Mason who were married
November 27, 1678; they were the parents of
Elizabeth Norton who married the Hon. John
Quincy.  A tankard made by John Edwards
engraved with the Norton arms, the gift of
Elizabeth Quincy to her daughter Lucy Tufts,
wife of Dr. Cotton Tufts, belongs to the First
Congregational Society at Quincy, Massachu-
setts, to which it was a gift in 1872 from Quincy

223. LONDON, 1702–03.
H. 4 in.

Tufts the grandson of Lucy Tufts.

Owned by Mrs. James A. Garland is an octagonal caster (Illus. 223) with the London date-letter for 1702–03.

An octagonal caster with a scrolled handle (Illus. 224) made by John Burt (1691–1745) of Boston, is engraved with the date 1732 and with the initials EH, undoubtedly for Elizabeth Henchman whose daughter Lydia was the wife of Thomas Hancock. It belongs to Mrs. L. B. Taft.

Vase-shaped casters were made in England by the beginning of the eighteenth century. The

224. JOHN BURT. H. 3¾ in.

lower part is hemispherical and the upper part curves inward; the tops are dome-shaped. A caster (Illus. 225) owned by Judge A. T. Clearwater bears the London date-letter for 1726–27 : it was made by Starling Wilford. The body is fluted and chased in the style of the rococo period.

A Colonial caster (Illus. 226) of this type, belonging to Mr. George S. Palmer, is octagonal in section, like many made in the eighteenth century : it was wrought by Arnold Collins of Newport in Rhode Island. The initials $\begin{smallmatrix} U \\ D\ A \end{smallmatrix}$ are those of Daniel and Anstis Updike who were married in 1720. A chocolate pot of pear-shaped outline with the spout made as an extension of

Y

225. LONDON, 1726–27. H. 7¾ in.

226. ARNOLD COLLINS.   H. 6½ in.

the lip, and the London date-letter for 1725–26, was presented to Daniel Updike of Newport, for twenty-four years attorney-general of the Colony, by his friend George Berkeley bishop of Cloyne, "the professor of an ideal philosophy and the projector of a Utopian scheme for evangelizing and educating the Indians." Dean Berkeley (as he then was) came to New England in 1728 and with him came John Simbert the painter, who planned the original Faneuil Hall at Boston and infused the love of his art into such men as Copley and Trumbull. These familiar lines were written by Berkeley :

"Westward the course of empire takes its way;
   The four first acts already past,
A fifth shall close the drama with the day;
   Time's noblest offspring is the last."

The caster (Illus. 227) owned by Mr. and Mrs. Henry W. Cunningham was made by Rufus

Greene (1707–77) of Boston, the maker in 1729 of a pair of tall cylindrical flagons belonging to Christ Church at Boston. The initials $_S^I{_R}$ are those of Samuel and Ruth (Chapin) Jackson who were married in 1722; the later initials $_S^T{_R}$ are those of Simon and Ruth (Jackson) Tufts who were married June 11, 1747. A portrait in water color of their daughter Ruth Tufts was painted by Copley and belongs to her descendant, Mrs. William Brewster. Captain Simon Tufts, born in Medford, married as his second wife Rebecca Lloyd of Charleston.

At the time of the Revolution he was living there as a merchant and was in command of a schooner when the British fleet was off the coast. At the battle in the harbor in July 1776, when General William Moultrie commanded the land forces on Sullivan's Island, Captain Tufts and his schooner did such effective work in helping to save the day that the Provincial Congress of South Carolina passed him a vote of thanks.

Cruet frames were made in the eighteenth century

227. RUFUS GREENE.
H. 4¼ in.

to hold a pair of glass cruets for oil and vinegar, two silver casters for Jamaica and Cayenne pepper and a third for either sugar or salt.

228. LONDON, 1747–48.   H. 9½ in.

The cruet frame (Illus. 228) owned by Mr. J. Templeman Coolidge bears the London date-letter for 1747–48 and was made by Samuel

Woods. While the casters are plain, the stand on three shell feet and the panel containing the arms are in the rococo style.

Mrs. Isabella (James) Gozzaldi owns a cruet frame with the London date-letter for 1761–62 made by Edward Aldridge and Company. The casters are of glass as well as the three cruets which bear silver labels marked "lemon," "soy" and "vinegar"; the silver tops are foliated.

# CHAFING DISHES

STANDS with spirit lamps were used in England as early as the reign of Queen Anne. In New England wills and inventories the word applied to them is chafing dish. They are now frequently called braziers.

229. JOHN CONEY. H. 3 in.

Belonging to the estate of Sally Pickman Dwight is a pair of chafing dishes (Illus. 229) made by John Coney (1655–1722) of Boston, with the initials $\frac{P}{W\ E}$ perhaps for William and Elizabeth (Eastwick) Pickman who were married in 1673. The cylindrical body with an everted

lip is pierced in
a scrolled design;
the three silver
claws originally
grasped wooden
balls. It has a
solid bottom with
a moulded rim
upon which rests
a circular pierced
disc (Illus. 230)
held in place by
a removable bolt
passing through

230. JOHN CONEY. D. 4 in.

the centre piercing, and secured by a nut
screwed on the under side; the flame came
through the piercings. By the same maker is
a chafing dish (Illus. 231) belonging to Mr.
Norman W. Cabot. Silver balls have undoubtedly replaced those originally of wood.

231. JOHN CONEY. H. 3½ in.

At a later date many were fitted with turned
wooden handles rivetted into silver sockets; the
bodies continued to be wrought in the same
general shape as Mr. Cabot's chafing dish but
the lip became more everted. The principal
variations are in the piercings, in the scrolled
arms and in the feet. A chafing dish (Illus.
232) made by John Potwine (1698–1792) of

232. JOHN POTWINE. H. 3¼ in.

Boston, owned by Mrs. George F. Richardson,
has scrolled feet resting on wooden balls.

A chafing dish (Illus. 233) with shell feet, and
scrolled arms extending much further from the
body, is one of a pair owned by the estate of
Mrs. Theodore Lyman. It bears the London
date-letter for 1743–44 and was made by Richard
Gurney & Co. who wrought in 1759–60 a
bellied tankard belonging to the Independent or Congregational Church at Charleston,
South Carolina. The tankard is engraved with

233. LONDON, 1743–44. H. 3⅜ in.

the initials $\begin{smallmatrix} S \\ I\ M \end{smallmatrix}$ for Josiah and Mary Smith. Josiah Smith, deacon of the church for forty years, was a successful merchant and in 1775 made large loans to the government; he was appointed cashier of the United States Bank at Charleston in 1790.

The dish cross (Illus. 234) with the London date-letter for 1773–74, made by William Penstone, belongs to Judge A. T. Clearwater. Such were made in England during the latter half of

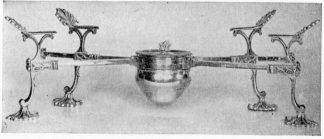

234. LONDON, 1773–74. L. 12¼ in.

the eighteenth century: the four horizontal
bars are joined to two circular revolving rings
which encircle the spirit lamp; the shell feet
and bracket arms are furnished with pierced
sliding sockets fitting the bars, which enables
dishes of various sizes to rest on the arms.
Like the chafing dishes they served the purpose
of keeping the food hot and prevented injury to
the polished table.

The pierced Irish dish ring erroneously called
a potato ring, a common article in Ireland after
1750, "was used throughout the dinner to support in turn the earthenware soup bowl, the
wooden potato bowl, the glass fruit dish and
the silver punch bowl."

# TEAPOTS KETTLES URNS

SYDNEY SMITH said: "Thank God for tea! What would the world do without tea?—how did it exist? I am glad I was not born before tea."

"The earliest mention of tea by any Englishman is believed to be contained in a letter from Mr. Wickham, an agent of the East India Company, written from Firando in Japan on the 27th June 1615, to Mr. Eaton, another agent of the Company, resident at Macao, asking for a pot of the best sort of Chaw: the term Chaw, from the Chinese ch'a, being the expression used at that time by Europeans in speaking of tea. In Mr. Eaton's accounts of expenditure, at a subsequent date, occurs the entry: 'three silver porringers to drink chaw in.' It was not, however, until the second quarter of the seventeenth century that the use of tea began in England. Upon its introduction it was drunk exclusively on account of its medicinal properties and the price ranged from £6 to £10 per pound. In his diary of 1660 Pepys says that he sent for a cup of tea, 'a China drink of which I had never drunk before.'" (c. j. j.).

Teapots of Oriental ware were naturally the

first to come into use in England and un-
questionably the tea brewed in porcelain or
earthenware is best.   They were more liable to
destruction and the wonder is that so many of
the charming little teapots made in England
and sent to America still exist; only because
they were treasured with so much care can
explain it.   The Oriental teapots were copied by
the English craftsmen in silver.

At first apparently no difference in size was
made in the English teapot, coffee pot and
chocolate pot; but after several years the teapot
was made lower and in later years broader.   In
the late eighteenth and early nineteenth century
teapots were made in many different shapes.

The earliest English silver teapots were of
tapering cylindrical shape and had the handles
at right angles to the tapering cylindrical spouts.
The single-scrolled wooden handles fitted into
silver sockets, to the upper one of which the conical cover was sometimes hinged.   They were
tall and did not differ from the same objects intended for coffee and chocolate.   It seems highly
probable that no distinction was made as to their
use and that one of these pots answered all requirements; how one chose to designate it was
decided by the use to which it was being put at
the moment.   O that Alice's soliloquy "what *does*
it call itself, I wonder?" could be answered!

In the Victoria and Albert Museum is a
teapot of this description which is 13¼ inches
in height; it is the earliest example known and

bears the London date-letter for 1670–71. Fortunately an inscription enlightens us as to its name: " This siluer tea : Pott was presented to $y^e$ Com$^{tte}$ of $y^e$ East India Cumpany by $y^e$ Right Hono$^e$ George Lord Berkeley of Berkeley Castle A member of the Honourable & worthy Society and A true Hearty Louer of them 1670."

The Colonial silversmiths do not appear to have copied the tall early English teapots sometimes called lantern-shaped; the nearest approach to them is the cylindrical coffee pot of the middle of the eighteenth century.

The cylindrical teapot (Illus. 235) belonging to Mrs. Nathaniel Thayer and made by Paul Revere (1735–1818) of Boston, perhaps best

235. PAUL REVERE. H. 6 in.

illustrates the type that was likely to have been
evolved from the tall cylindrical teapot first
made in England. The straight spout and the
handle sockets are fluted; the flat bottom, the
shoulder and the edge of the low domed cover
have gadrooned borders; the hinge is affixed
to the cover and to the shoulder, forming a
right angle.

More in accordance with the modern idea of a
teapot were the smaller pots made in England

236. JOHN CONEY. H. 8 in.

at the end of the seventeenth and early in the
eighteenth century; these had the handles at
right angles to the spouts which were in the
form of a duck's neck curving quite closely to
the body. The teapot (Illus. 236) engraved
with the arms of Perkins, made by John Coney
(1655–1722) of Boston, is pear-shaped in outline
—like the English pot of the early eighteenth
century. The domed cover with a turned finial
is hinged to the upper handle socket close to
the lip of the teapot; the scrolled handle is
of wood and the spout is in the form of a duck's
neck. It is in the Clearwater collection at the
Metropolitan Museum of Art, New York.

A very near approach to this Coney teapot
was made by the silversmiths of New York and
vicinity: it is quite typical of the English pots
made during the first quarter of the eighteenth
century. The lower part of the plain body is
more compressed and larger round; the neck
has been lengthened and a moulded band divides
them. The teapot (Illus. 237) made by I.
Ten Eyck of Albany belongs to Mr. George S.
Palmer. The domed cover with a moulded
band is hinged to the outer part of the socket;
the wooden knob is held in place by a silver
ornamental bolt; the scrolled wooden handle
terminates in a tongue; the duck-neck spout
extending further from the body is capped in
such a way as to give it the appearance of a
bird's beak. The caps on English teapots were
frequently hinged.

237. I. TEN EYCK.   H. 7 in.

A teapot of this variety (Illus. 238), made
perhaps by Josiah Austin (1719–80) of Charlestown, seems to fit in some particulars, between
the teapots just described. The outlines of
the body are unbroken as in the Coney teapot
but the neck is lengthened as in that by Ten
Eyck. The principal difference is in the domed
and moulded cover of undulating outline. The
wooden knob is missing and the ornamental
silver bolt has slipped down. It is engraved
with the Cushing arms and belongs to Mrs.
Robert N. Toppan.

A globular teapot on a moulded foot came into

238. Josiah Austin? H. 5⅜ in.

fashion in England early in the eighteenth
century, a variety made up to about 1770. A
gold Scotch teapot of that form, of about the
date 1735, belongs to Mr. Leopold de Rothschild;
the spout is straight as in the earliest types.
Some teapots are literally globular but most of
those so designated are flattened at the cover
and base.

A Colonial specimen of the globular teapot
(Illus. 239) with a straight spout, has a detach-
able cover with a wooden knob. The only
ornamentation is the gadrooned edge of the
base, and of the shoulder and cover. The pho-

z

tograph was kindly furnished by the Towle
Manufacturing Co. of Newburyport, Massachusetts.

A teapot (Illus. 240) of this variety made by
Jacob Hurd (1702–58) of Boston, with a hinged
cover, is engraved on the shoulder with a narrow
border enclosing bellflowers; on the side are

239. COLONIAL.

the arms of Andrews ( ?). On the bottom is : "E.
Storer 1756" for Ebenezer Storer junior whose
mother was Mary Edwards the daughter of
John Edwards the silversmith.   It belonged to
the late Miss Georgiana G. Eaton, a descendant,
but has been given to the Museum of Fine
Arts, Boston, by her brothers, Messrs. Francis
S. and William S. Eaton.

The teapot (Illus. 241) owned by Mrs. George

240. JACOB HURD. H. 5½ in.

241. PAUL REVERE SENIOR. H. 5⅛ in.

W. Harrington is engraved with the initials
$\frac{T}{W\ B}$. Surrounding the hinged cover with a
wooden knob, is an engraved border of scrolls
with an angel's head in front; while the spout
is of the same general shape as that on the Hurd
teapot, the lower part of the opening is everted.
The maker was Apollos Rivoire (1702–54) a
Huguenot silversmith, born in Riancaud, France,
who came to Boston when thirteen years of age
and was apprenticed to John Coney; he angli-
cized his name to Paul Revere and was the father
of Paul Revere (1735–1818). A portrait of
the latter, painted by Copley, shows him holding
in his hands a teapot of this description which
he has apparently just finished.

Belonging to Mrs. L. B. Taft is a teapot (Illus.
242) with a hinged domed cover, surrounded by
engraved scrolls with a human mask in front;
on the bottom is the date "1766"; the silver
handle has ivory insulators which act as non-
conductors of the heat. It was made by Nathaniel Hurd (1729–77) of Boston, the son of Captain Jacob Hurd the silversmith; he is better
known as an engraver of prints and book-plates.
The following advertisement appeared in the
*Boston Evening Post*, December 27, 1762 : "Engraved and Sold by Nath. Hurd, a striking
likeness of his Majesty King George the Third,
Mr. Pitt and General Wolfe, fit for a Picture,
or for Gentlemen and Ladies to put in their
watches." The Harvard College book-plate,

with the seal of the college, was engraved by
Nathaniel Hurd. A portrait of him, painted by
Copley, has recently been acquired by the Cleve-
land Museum of Art, at Cleveland, Ohio.

242. NATHANIEL HURD. H. 5¾ in.

Owned by the estate of Sally Pickman Dwight
is a teapot (Illus. 243) made by John Coburn
(1725–1803) of Boston. The wooden handle
has a scroll termination; the spout has a large
shell support, and is much lengthened; the
shoulder is engraved with a border of scrolls
and flowers. The Pickman arms are engraved
upon the side and on the bottom are the initials: "LP to MP" for Love Pickman to her
daughter-in-law Mrs. Mary (Toppan) Pickman.

Love Rawlins became the wife of Benjamin
Pickman in 1731. He was a successful merchant of Salem and held many public offices;
representative and councillor, judge of the
superior court, colonel of the Essex regiment
and a member of the Committee of War in 1745.

243. JOHN COBURN.  H. 6¼ in.

His portrait painted by Greenwood is in the
Essex Institute at Salem.  A tankard made by
Daniel Parker (1726–85) of Boston was given by
Benjamin Pickman to the First Church of
Salem in 1759 but was transferred to the North
Church in 1772 when he presented to the latter
a baptismal basin made by Joseph Edwards
junior (1737–83) of Boston.  Mary Toppan
married Benjamin Pickman junior in 1762 : she

was the donor in 1802 to the North Church at
Salem of a pair of mugs made by Paul Revere
(1735–1818).  Portraits of Benjamin and Mary
Pickman painted by Copley in 1763 are in the
possession of their great-great-grandson Mr.
George Peabody Wetmore.

244. LONDON, 1759–60.  H. 6¼ in.

In England the form of teapot which came
after the globular type was an inverted pear-
shape.  Of this description is the teapot (Illus.
244) with the London date-letter for 1759–60,
made by William Grundy the maker of many
vessels described in "The Old Silver of American Churches."  The hinged domed cover is spirally fluted, as is the lower half of the body;
gadrooned edges surround the mouth and

245. BENJAMIN BURT. H. 7½ in.

base. Inscribed on the base are the names of
the various owners: "Rebecca, daughter of
Thomas Amory and Rebecca Holmes born 1725
died 1796 married Edward Payne; Rebecca
Lowell 1771–1842; Anna Cabot Lowell 1808–
1894; Sarah Putnam Lowell Blake 1843–99."
The name of the present owner, John Amory
Lowell Blake, is inscribed inside the cover.

A plain Colonial teapot (Illus. 245) with a
somewhat taller body and a higher domed
cover, made by Benjamin Burt (1729–1805) of
Boston, is engraved with the date 1765 and the
initials $\underset{P\ E}{S}$ for Peter and Elizabeth (Wendell)

Smith and belongs to Mrs. Charles W. Lord, a
descendant.    Elizabeth   Wendell    was    the
daughter of Jacob Wendell.   Peter Smith was
the son of Rev. Thomas Smith who went to
Falmouth in 1725 as chaplain of the troops.
He also preached to the inhabitants and became first pastor of the church, now the First
Parish, Portland, Maine, where he died in
1795.  His interesting journal has been published.

A great many teapots made in the last quarter
of the eighteenth century were oval or octagonal
in plan, with flat bases, vertical sides and straight
tapering spouts.   They were made of sheet
silver, soldered where the handle is affixed, and
were ornamented with bright-cut and engraved work consisting of bands of foliage,
medallions and festoons.   Small stands with
four feet were frequently made to support

246. London, 1780–81.  H. 4 in.

teapots of this kind to protect the polished tables from the heat. A teapot (Illus. 246) of this variety, belonging to Mrs. F. C. Martin, was made by William Vincent in 1780–81. It is oval in plan with narrow vertical panels at each side of the central serpentine panel; the fluted tapering spout is cylindrical; the hinged and flat cover is surmounted by a silver pineapple with leaves — the emblem of hospitality; the silver handle has ivory insulators.

A Colonial teapot (Illus. 247) of much the same outline, made by Paul Revere (1735–1818),

247. PAUL REVERE AND SON.  H. 5½ in.

belongs to Mrs. Nathaniel Thayer. The original bill from Paul Revere and Son is dated April 8, 1789. The initials in the medallion MB are for Captain Moses Brown who died

at Newburyport, January 1, 1804 at the age of
62. He commanded several of the largest
privateers during the Revolution and distinguished himself on various occasions. At the

248. ZACHARIAH BRIGDEN. H. 6¼ in.

time the United States navy was established
the merchants of Newburyport built for the
government, by subscription, the ship *Merri-
mack* and placed in command Moses Brown
who received his commission as captain September 15, 1798.

An oval teapot (Illus. 248) ordered to commemorate the opening of the Charles River
bridge between Boston and Charlestown —
both river and town named for Charles I
— was fittingly made by Zachariah Brigden

who was born at Charlestown in 1734 and died at Boston March 19, 1787, less than a year after the making of the teapot. Engraved in an oval panel is a representation of the bridge and in a similar panel on the other side is inscribed: "Presented to Capt. David Wood, by the Proprietors of CHARLES RIVER BRIDGE, in Testimony of their entire Approbation of his faithful Services, as a special Director of that Work, begun A.D. 1785, and perfected A.D. 1786." The Charles River bridge is particularly worthy of mention as it was the longest bridge in the world when it was built, and constructed entirely of wood with the exception of the abutments. The architect was Captain John Stone of Concord but the credit of the undertaking must be given to that ingenious shipwright Lemuel Cox, the pioneer bridge builder of the United States, who considered the construction practicable. He not only built the bridge to Malden in 1787 and the Essex bridge at Salem but was invited to go to Ireland where he constructed the bridge over the Foyle, at Londonderry. The teapot belongs to a descendant of Captain David Wood, Mr. Henry H. Edes. The bright-cut and engraved borders and the festoons of flowers surrounding the panels are considerably more elaborate than is usual. The four ball feet were common on teapots, sugar bowls and cream pitchers at the beginning of the nineteenth century.

An oval teapot (Illus. 249) with curving body

and domed cover, bearing the Newcastle date-
letter for 1799–1800, made by Thomas Watson,
has a tray with the London date-letter for 1800–
1801 made by John Emes. These pieces were
part of a tea service originally belonging to a
magistrate of Sheffield, England, to whom they

249. NEWCASTLE, 1799–1800.   H. 6¼ in.

were presented by a mob which had attacked
and stoned his house through mistake during
some political strife, and desired to make amends.
They were presented to Mary Isabella (James)
Gozzaldi by the Hannah Winthrop Chapter of
the Daughters of the American Revolution
May 17, 1906.

Tea kettles at the time of Queen Anne were
made in the form of contemporary teapots,

and had pear-shaped bodies with spouts of the duck-neck type. The stand upon which the kettle rests is fitted with a spirit lamp for the purpose of boiling the water for use in the teapot. They follow the changing fashions of the teapot; the only difference is in the position of the handle and spout; and in the relative size of the two. Many of the time of George I and the early part of the reign of George II were of globular form.

A Colonial kettle (Illus. 250) of this variety was made by Jacob Hurd (1702–58) the maker of many teapots of the same form. The duck-neck spout with a moulded collar terminates in a bird's beak; the flat cover is surmounted by an ivory knob resting on a silver base and held in place by an ornamental bolt; the hinged handle is flat and solid; the stand rests on four scrolled claw feet from which spring four narrow arched mouldings to support the spirit lamp; two long silver pins, affixed to the base by chains, may be inserted into the rim of the body to fasten the kettle and stand together. It is engraved with the Lowell arms and owned by Mrs. Stanley Cunningham, the granddaughter of James Russell Lowell to whom it was a familiar object and doubtless in use when he received his literary friends at "Elmwood." It was at "Elmwood" that Thomas Bailey Aldrich lived during Mr. Lowell's visit to Spain and where he wrote the delightful stories of "Margery Daw" and "Prudence Palfrey."

Tea and coffee services, although made in England before the middle of the eighteenth century, are rarely found before the accession of George III.

250. JACOB HURD.   H. 9⅛ in.

251. PAUL REVERE. H. 7½ in.

251. H. 7 in.                    251. H. 9½ in.

Belonging to the Museum of Fine Arts, Boston, is a tea service (Illus. 251) which was made by Paul Revere (1735–1818) of Boston, consisting of an oval pot and tray, a cream pitcher on a square plinth base, and a vase-shaped sugar bowl. It was the gift of Mr. James Longley in 1896. The inscription is: "To Edmund Hartt Constructor of the Frigate Boston. Presented by a number of his fellow citizens as a Memorial of their sense of his Ability Zeal & Fidelity in the completion of that Ornament of the American Navy. 1799." Edmund Hartt, an original trustee of the Mechanic Charitable Association, lived on Ship Street in Boston opposite his shipyard which is now known as Constitution wharf — as there was built the famous *Constitution* the keel of which was laid in November 1794. The frigate *Boston*, so named because the funds were subscribed by the citizens of Boston, was built at Hartt's Naval Yard and launched June 12, 1799.

Tea urns took the place of kettles in the third quarter of the eighteenth century. Some were provided with spirit lamps while others were fitted with a socket in the centre of the urn into which was put a hot iron cylinder to preserve the heat. The heated water was used to replenish the teapot; occasionally the urn was filled with tea already made. An urn (Illus. 252) with the London date-letter for 1795–96 engraved with the initials AC, for

2 A

252. LONDON, 1795–96. H. 12¾ in.

Madam Anna Craigie, was bought at the
sale of her effects by Mrs. Abbott Lawrence to
whose granddaughter, Mrs. H. A. Lamb, it

now belongs. The ring handles hang from the
mouths of lions' heads ; the border is bright-cut.

A plain vase-shaped urn (Illus. 253) with

253. PAUL REVERE. H. 19 in.

looped handles, made by Paul Revere, is owned
by Mr. Gamaliel Bradford to whose great-grandfather it had belonged. It is inscribed: "To
Perpetuate The Gallant defence Made by Cap^t
Gamaliel Bradford in the Ship Industry on the
8^th. July 1800 when Attacked by four French Privateers in the Streights of Gibralter This Urn is
Presented to him by Samuel Parkman." Captain
Bradford was a descendant of William Bradford
the second governor of Plymouth Colony.

A Dutch urn (Illus. 254) with square-shaped
handles formed of two flat sections joined together with rosettes of quatrefoil shape, is
inscribed in a circular panel: "To Charles
Bulfinch Esq. Presented by the Catholics of
Boston Jan^y 1. 1806." Charles Bulfinch, the
noted architect of the Capitol at Washington,
of the State House at Boston and of many
other fine buildings, furnished gratuitously the
plans for the Church of the Holy Cross built
in 1803 on Federal Street. It was the earliest
Roman Catholic church erected in the United
States, with the exception of that at Newcastle
in Maine founded by John Cheverus. The
church at Boston was built through the efforts
of Father Matignon and John Cheverus who
became bishop of the diocese — and later a
cardinal — a man as much beloved by the
Protestants who contributed largely to the
fund, as by the Catholics. The two doves on
the top of the urn are thought to typify the
peaceful relations existing between the sects.

Miss Ellen S. Bulfinch, a granddaughter of Charles Bulfinch, has given the urn to the Museum of Fine Arts, Boston.

254. DUTCH, 1806. H. 13¼ in.

# TEA CADDIES

255. London, 1713–14.  H. 3⅝ in.

"CADDY (a corruption of catty from kati, the Malay word for a pound) the term applied to the small box, containing about 1⅓lb., in which tea was originally imported into England, is the name in general use for the box or canister in which tea is kept for use." *

It was not until early in the eighteenth century that tea caddies were generally used in England. The commonest form in the first quarter of the century was plain and of bottle shape; sometimes they were made with a sliding bottom so that they could be more easily filled. Apparently, the Colonial silversmiths did not make them.

A plain caddy (Illus. 255) rectangular in out-

* (C. J. J.)

358

line, made by William Ash, with the London date-letter for 1713–14, belongs to Mr. Dwight M. Prouty. The caddy is divided by a vertical partition to hold two kinds of tea; the sliding top, in two sections, enables the removal of either; the lock and key show that great value was placed on the contents.

Owned by Mr. Norman W. Cabot is a rectangular caddy (Illus. 256) of the bottle shape with moulded corners, bearing the London date-letter for 1724–25; the sliding lid has a removable cap; a shield of arms is engraved upon it. The caddy came into Mr. Cabot's possession through an ancestor's marriage with the Sewall family.

256. LONDON, 1724–25. H. 5 in.

A caddy (Illus. 257) in the rococo style, with the London date-letter for 1758–59 and made by Pierre Gillois, was originally one of a set of three — the centre caddy being of a larger size. Such were frequently made in England

for the purpose of holding three different kinds
of tea which were blended to suit the individual
taste.   The arms engraved upon it are thought

257. LONDON, 1758–59.   H. 5⅞ in.

to be the arms of Bulfinch impaling those of
Apthorp.   The caddy at one time belonged to
Thomas Bulfinch, the author of "The Age of
Fable" and "The Legends of Charlemagne":
it is now the property of Miss Ellen S. Bulfinch,
a descendant.

A larger caddy (Illus. 258) with the London
date-letter for 1792–93, owned by Mr. Dwight
M. Prouty, is oval like the contemporary teapots
and sugar bowls; it is decorated with garlands
and borders of bright-cut engraving.   In a panel

is the inscription: "JBC to JLC." It was made by Peter and Ann Bateman, the makers of a mug, dated 1799–1800, which was the gift

258. LONDON, 1792–93. H. 6½ in.

of Mrs. Anne Waring of Tranquil Hall near Summerville to the Congregational or Presbyterian Church (the "White Meeting") at Dorchester, South Carolina.

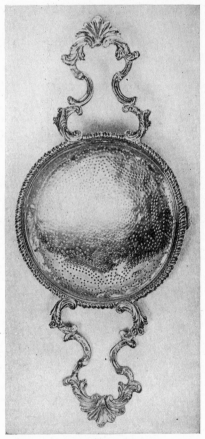

STRAINERS were made to a considerable extent in the Colonies by the last half of the eighteenth century; the bowls, about 4 inches in diameter, were pierced in various designs and the long handles reached across the lips of bowls or pitchers for straining punch; doubtless they also served as strainers for tea.

Belonging to Mrs. George W. Harrington is an English strainer (Illus. 259) upon which the marks are indistinct on

259. LONDON. L. 10 in.

account of the pierc-
ings ; the handles are
rococo. Attached to
one side of the bowl
is a projecting leaf to
fit over the lip of a
vessel.

A strainer (Illus.
260) with zigzag
handles, made by
Daniel Parker (1726–
85) of Boston is en-
graved with the in-
itials $\underset{B\ H}{H}$ for Benjamin Hall and his wife
Hepzibah Jones whom
he married May 3,
1752. It belongs to
Mr. Vernon H. Hall,
a descendant.

Another type of
handle, arched and
scrolled, is that on
the strainer (Illus.
261) made by Samuel
Edwards (1705–62) of
Boston, and engraved

260. DANIEL PARKER. L. 11¾ in.

with the initials $\underset{I\ E}{S}$·
It was probably a gift from the maker to his step-
brother Isaac Smith upon the latter's marriage

261. SAMUEL EDWARDS.   L. 11 in.

in 1746 to Samuel Edwards's niece Elizabeth Storer and it is owned by Mrs. T. D. Townsend, a descendant.    Samuel Edwards, the son of John Edwards (1670–1746), married August 23, 1733 Sarah Smith of Charlestown, the daughter of William and Abigail (Fowle) Smith; her mother became the wife of John Edwards in 1740. Sarah Smith's sister Mary married Ebenezer Austin and they were the parents of Ebenezer Austin (1733–1818) a silversmith at Hartford in Connecticut, after 1764. The value of Samuel Edwards's estate amounted to £3816.12.11½.

Belonging to Mr. George S. Palmer is an unmarked strainer (Illus. 262) with a single handle similar to that of a porringer.   Surrounding the

centre ornament is pierced: "Silvanus Jencks
August 26, 1772." Captain Silvanus Jencks
married July 11, 1772 in Providence, Freelove
daughter of Captain James Fenner.

262. COLONIAL.   D. 4¼ in.

# COFFEE AND CHOCOLATE POTS

"NEITHER coffee nor chocolate appears to have been known in England before the middle of the seventeenth century. The use of coffee seems to have originated in Abyssinia, whence it passed to Arabia and Turkey; it is said to have been known in Germany in the latter part of the sixteenth century. An entry dated 10th May, 1637 in Evelyn's Diary, refers to one Nathaniel Conopios, out of Greece, from Cyrill, the patriarch of Constantinople, as the first he ever saw drink coffee which custom came not into England till thirty years after (thirty is said to have been written in error for twenty)." (C. J. J.)

In "The Rape of the Lock" Pope wrote:

"Coffee, which makes the politician wise,
   And see through all things with his half-shut eyes."

"Chocolate, a preparation of cocoa mixed with sugar and some aromatic substance, such as vanilla, was brought into England shortly after the introduction of coffee. Columbus is said to have been the first to bring a knowledge of cocoa to Europe from the American continent, but it was not until the second quarter of the

366

seventeenth century that chocolate was used as a beverage in England. The earliest published reference to the sale of it in London occurs in the following announcement in the *Public Advertiser* of the 16th June, 1657: 'In Bishopgate Street, in Queen's Head Alley, at a Frenchman's house, is an excellent West India drink, called chocolate, to be sold, where you may have it ready at any time, and also unmade, at reasonable rates.'   In the course of half a century from its introduction, chocolate became a very fashionable beverage, but after the first quarter of the eighteenth century it appears to have fallen greatly out of favour."   (c. j. j.)

Like the teapot, the earliest form of chocolate pot and coffee pot was cylindrical, with the handle fixed at a right angle to the spout which was straight and tapering like the tall body, and sometimes called lantern-shaped.   In the Victoria and Albert Museum is one of the earliest known English coffee pots of this type; it bears the London date-letter for 1681–82 and was a gift to the East India Company.   It does not differ materially from the teapot made in 1670–71 except that the handle is opposite the spout; and it was in all probability used for tea.   The only distinguishing feature of the chocolate pot seems to be the hollow cylinder, on the cover, with a removable cap, to permit the insertion of a stick or brush to stir the contents that otherwise would thicken.

In the Clearwater collection at the Metropoli-

tan Museum of Art, New York City, is a chocolate pot (Illus. 263) conical in outline, made by
Edward Winslow (1669–1753) of Boston.   It is

263. EDWARD WINSLOW.   H. 9½ in.

engraved with the arms of Hutchinson, a family to which Winslow was closely related. The fluted base is similar to that of contemporary objects; the wooden handle is at a right angle to the duck-neck spout, the plain bulbous base of which has a V-shaped tongue terminating in a "cut-card" leaf; the domed cover, hinged and fluted, has an open "cut-card" ornament surrounding the cylindrical top; a removable cap with an acorn finial is attached to a chain fastened at the other end to the handle.

Chocolate and coffee pots of the pyriform or pear-shaped variety were made in England early in the eighteenth century; they were like the contemporary teapot but the neck was elongated. John Coney (1655–1722) of Boston made the chocolate pot (Illus. 264) belonging to Mrs. Robert Soutter, a descendant of William Downes and Elizabeth (Edwards) Cheever; their initials W $\frac{C}{D-E}$ in a panel of scrolls and acanthus leaves were doubtless engraved at the time of their marriage May 5, 1749; but the pot was without doubt a part of the silverware inherited from Elizabeth Edwards's mother, the wife of Thomas Edwards the silversmith. The duck-neck spout with a moulded collar terminates in the form of a bird's beak; a large "cut-card" leaf ornament is on the body. The finial is affixed to a small circular plate, made to revolve on a pin, covering the opening for the insertion of a stick. Constant wear evidently

2 B

264. JOHN CONEY.  H. 9½ in.

loosened the plate, for it is now soldered to the cover.

In England, somewhat later, the spout of the

chocolate pot was made as an extension of the body at the lip.   Such were also used for hot water or milk.   The covered jug (Illus. 265) of this description, with the London date-letter for

265.  London, 1794–95.  H. 11¾ in.

1794–95, made by John Robbins, is wrought after the fashion of a Roman vase and is decorated with bright-cut engraving. It belongs to Dr. C. W. Townsend. Many of this form were embossed with festoons of flowers and laurel leaves, tied with ribbons in the Adam style; and others were decorated with vertical acanthus leaves on the lower part of the body.

Tall cylindrical silver pots continued to be made in England during the second quarter of the eighteenth century. Belonging to Mr. William S. Townsend is a chocolate pot (Illus. 266) of this variety with a tapering body and domed cover, engraved with the Storer arms, and made by Zachariah Brigden (1734–87) of Boston who married Sarah the daughter of Thomas Edwards the silversmith. The latter's sister Mary Edwards married Ebenezer Storer to whom the pot originally belonged. The turned finial is affixed to a small plate to which is soldered a cylindrical tube that closely fits into the opening in the top of the cover, where the stick is inserted.

Of this description is the coffee pot (Illus. 267) owned by Mr. Munroe Chickering and made by Jacob Hurd (1702–58) of Boston. The Alleyne arms in a scrolled and foliated panel were probably engraved by Nathaniel Hurd who made a book-plate for Thomas Alleyne (who married in 1755 Dorothy Harben Forster) to whom the pot belonged.

In England in the middle of the eighteenth century the cylindrical coffee pot was superseded

266. Zachariah Brigden. H. 9¾ in.

by a form of pot which approximated, in form,
the pear-shaped teapot of the reign of Queen
Anne; the spouts were cast and extended much

267. Jacob Hurd.  H. 9 in.

further from the body; it was popular throughout the Georgian period.

A coffee pot (Illus. 268) with its domed and
moulded cover, is cone-shaped in outline.  It
bears the London date-letter for 1751–52 and
the makers' mark for William Shaw and William
Priest who made the tall cylindrical flagon and

pair of chalices with paten-covers belonging to
Stephney Parish, Somerset County, Maryland,
the gift in 1752 of Rev. Alexander Adams senior,
rector of that parish from 1704 until his death
in 1769.   The plain body is engraved in scrolled
and foliated panels with the arms and crest of
Peter Faneuil, the wealthiest Bostonian of his

268. LONDON, 1751–52.   H. 10½ in.

269. PAUL REVERE.    H. 11¾ in.

day, who gave to the town Faneuil Hall — the
"cradle of liberty."    His sister Mary Faneuil
married George Bethune and gave to Christ
Church at Cambridge in 1791 a plain paten engraved with the same arms.    The coffee pot has
been given in the name of Mrs. Jane Bethune

(Craig) Hawkins to the Museum of Fine Arts, Boston. A portrait of Peter Faneuil by Smibert is in the rooms of the Massachusetts Historical Society.

The coffee pot (Illus. 269) made by Paul Revere (1735–1818) of Boston, is more pear-shaped in outline; the edges of the base and cover are gadrooned. It belongs to Mrs. Thomas Bailey Aldrich whose husband depicted his youthful life in "The Story of a Bad Boy." His boyhood days were passed in the Nutter house, acquired by the people of Portsmouth as a memorial to the gifted author; and his wife and son have generously restored to it the furnishings familiar to "Tom Bailey" — including the table upon which he wrote the story.

The coffee pot (Illus. 270) by the same maker, owned by Mrs. T. D. Townsend, has a pronounced pear-shaped body with a rounded bottom supported on three spreading shell feet; small cream pitchers with three feet were popular in England between the years 1735–60.

A coffee pot (Illus. 271) belonging to Mrs. Robert Hale Bancroft, with the London date-letter for 1773–74, made by Francis Crump, is similar in form to the inverted pear-shaped teapots and sugar bowls made during the second half of the eighteenth century. The body, base and cover are embossed with festoons of flowers; the edges are beaded; the finial is an acorn in the cup. Engraved on the long plain neck is a shield of arms with the motto AIME LA VERTU.

270. PAUL REVERE.  H. 12 in.

Made by Paul Revere (1735–1818) is a coffee
pot (Illus. 272) of this variety with a gadrooned
border and edge on the circular foot; the domed

cover has a gadrooned edge and a pine cone finial. On one side are engraved the Warren arms in a medallion suspended from a festoon of

271. LONDON, 1773-74.  H. 14½ in.

272. PAUL REVERE. H. 13½ in.

leaves and flowing ribbon with crossed branches
below; on the other side in a similar ornament
are the entwined initials JAW for Dr. John

Warren and his wife Abigail, the daughter of
Governor John Collins of Newport. Dr. Buck-
minster Brown, a grandson of John and Abigail

273. AMERICAN. H. 13½ in.

Warren, bequeathed the coffee pot to the Museum of Fine Arts; the tradition that it was once owned by General Joseph Warren, killed at Bunker Hill in 1775, is probably correct since John and Abigail Warren were not married until 1777 — two years later.

In the last quarter of the eighteenth century some coffee pots were wrought after the fashion of the Roman vase. A plain coffee pot (Illus. 273) with this form of body and a long concave neck, is supported by a high circular foot and base resting on a square plinth; the spout, base and intersections are beaded — a popular decoration in England between the years 1775 and 1815. It belongs to Mrs. F. P. Garvan, and is probably American but without a maker's mark.

# SPOUT CUPS

THESE interesting cups sometimes called feeding cups are intended for use in time of illness; doubtless they were put to many other uses. The books on English plate do not comment on them and they may therefore be of Colonial origin.

A spout cup (Illus. 274) made by John Edwards (1670–1746) of Boston, bears much re-

274. JOHN EDWARDS. H. 5⅝ in.

semblance in the outline of the body to an
Oriental vase. The duck-neck spout at a right
angle to the wooden handle and the "cut-card"
leaves surrounding the finial of the low domed
cover, indicate that it was wrought early in
the eighteenth century. A small circular hole,
with a tiny cover turning on a pin, permits the
insertion of a stick to stir the contents.
Inscribed on the bottom is: "Ex dono D$^{ni}$
Johannis George 1706" and the initials $\begin{smallmatrix} & C \\ B & I \end{smallmatrix}$,
doubtless those of Benjamin Colman, the first
pastor of the Brattle Street Church, and of his
wife Jane Clarke. John George, a merchant of
Boston, proposed in January 1713 the "Erecting
of a Light Hous and Lanthorn on some Head
Land at the Entrance of the Harbour of Boston
for the Direction of Ships and Vessells in the
Night Time Bound into the said Harbour."
The General Court authorized the erection of a
lighthouse and it was completed September 14,
1716; for two hundred years Boston Light has
guided the mariner. John George married
Lydia Lee; after his death in 1714, she married
Rev. Cotton Mather; by his will he leaves £5
to Rev. Benjamin Colman, in whose church he
owned a pew. By Benjamin Colman's will of
1747 he ordered to be sold what little plate he
had. The spout cup was undoubtedly purchased
by Martha Salisbury whose initials also are on it.
It was bequeathed to the Worcester Art Museum
by Stephen Salisbury. Except in decoration it

does not differ from a chocolate pot shown by Mr.
Jackson; perhaps it was used for a like purpose.

John Allen (1671–1760) and John Edwards
(1670–1746) of Boston made a spout cup (Illus.
275) similar to the little English mug of 1688–
89; the shape and reeded neck are derived from

275. ALLEN AND EDWARDS. H. 5 in.

the stoneware jugs of the sixteenth century.
Engraved upon the side is a crest; the initials
$\begin{smallmatrix} D \\ C\ M \end{smallmatrix}$ are those of Caleb and Mary Davis who
were married in 1783; it belongs to Mrs. Alex-
ander Whiteside, a descendant.

2 C

A spout cup (Illus. 276) of the same shape, without a cover, which may have been lost, is engraved with the initials AS for Ann Simpson

276. SAMUEL HAUGH.   H. 3½ in.

who married Nathaniel Glover in 1750: it belongs to Miss Margaret C. Wyman, a descendant. The earlier initials T D cannot be identified. It was made by Samuel Haugh (1675–1717) of Boston, an apprentice of Thomas Savage (1664–1749); his aunt Sarah Haugh married Ephraim Savage, the uncle of Thomas Savage, who had previously married Mary the sister of Daniel Quincy (1651–90); his marriage to Margaret Cowell September 30, 1697 brought him into close connection with William Cowell (1682–1736). Samuel Sewall was his guardian.

Andrew Tyler (1692–1741) of Boston made a spout cup (Illus. 277) of similar form ; the initials $\frac{S}{I\ E}$ are those of Isaac and Elizabeth (Storer) Smith who were married in 1746; it belongs to Mrs. T. D. Townsend, a descendant.

277. ANDREW TYLER.  H. 4½ in.

Mrs. F. C. Martin owns the spout cup (Illus. 278) engraved with the Coffin crest. Its high domed cover and pear-shaped outline resemble

the Coney teapot.   The maker, Nathaniel Morse
(1685–1748) of Boston, was probably apprenticed
to Coney and in 1731 engraved the rare portrait
of Matthew Henry a Nonconformist divine.

278. NATHANIEL MORSE.   H. 5⅛ in.

The beaker-shaped spout cup (Illus. 279) belonging to the writer, probably never had a
cover.   The initials $_{I\ M}^{F}$ are probably those of

John and Mercy (Prence) Freeman who were
married in 1650. Mercy Freeman died at Har-
wich in 1721 and the maker of the cup, Moody
Russell (1694–1761) of Barnstable, Massachusetts, was the appraiser of her silverware. He
was a nephew of Edward Winslow (1669–1753)
to whom he was apprenticed. The Rev. John

279. MOODY RUSSELL. H. 3 in.

Russell, his grandfather, of Hadley, long con-
cealed the regicides Goffe and Whalley at his
house where they died, and their bodies were
buried in his grounds, near the foundations of
the house; Eleazer Russell (1663–91), his uncle,
was a silversmith of Boston; his sister Abigail
married Nathaniel Otis and their son Major
Jonathan Otis (1723–91) an ardent patriot, was
a silversmith who, at the capture of Newport
by the British in 1778, moved to Middletown,

Connecticut, where he was active in aiding those made destitute by the war. Moody Russell made beakers for the Barnstable and Truro churches ; in the First Parish Sandwich, Massachusetts, is a pair of beakers, also made by him — the gift in 1719 of Shearjashub Bourne who resided on the Marshpee plantation and carried on a lucrative trade with the Indians.

# TOBACCO SNUFF AND NUTMEG BOXES

A CENTURY has brought about a change since Cowper wrote:

"Pernicious weed! whose scent the fair annoys,
Unfriendly to society's chief joys:
Thy worst effect is banishing for hours
The sex whose presence civilizes ours."

Sir Ralph Lane, appointed governor of Virginia by Sir Walter Raleigh in 1585, abandoned the Province in 1586 and returned to England with Sir Francis Drake taking with him tobacco and pipes. He appears to have been responsible for the smoking habit which became popular in England and rapidly spread throughout Europe. Charles Lamb said: "For thy sake, tobacco, I would do anything but die." Silver boxes for holding tobacco were made in England by the middle of the seventeenth century.

An oval box (Illus. 280) made by John Coney (1655-1722) of Boston, with a loose lid engraved with the arms of Jeffries, belongs to Mr. William A. Jeffries; it is inscribed: "Donum RG 1701."

Mr. Jackson tells us that when the habit of taking snuff followed that of smoking, the article was first made in long, hard dried rolls, called "carottes", which were rubbed on a grater; in the last quarter of the seventeenth century

280. JOHN CONEY. L. 3⅞ in.

it was sold grated.   In the reign of Queen Anne the habit of taking snuff became general among all classes and snuff boxes of great variety were fashionable.

Goldsmith in "Retaliation" says of Sir Joshua Reynolds :

" When they talk'd of their Raphaels, Correggios, and stuff, He shifted his trumpet and only took snuff."

Owned by the Misses Loring is a gold snuff box (Illus. 281) made by Jacob Hurd (1702–58) of Boston, engraved with the Dummer arms and bequeathed by William Dummer in his will of June 28, 1756 to his nephew William Powell. Lieutenant-Governor William Dummer was acting chief-magistrate for the greater part of his term (1716–29) while Governor Samuel Shute was absent: one of the principal events of his incumbency of the office was the introduction by Dr. Zabdiel Boylston of inoculation for smallpox. In "Old Landmarks of Boston" Mr. Samuel Adams Drake says: "This terrible distemper which had scourged Boston with great violence at different times was arrested

281. JACOB HURD. L. 2⅝ in.

by this simple expedient, which the Western world owes to a woman. Lady Mary Wortley Montagu accompanied her husband to the

Porte, where he was ambassador, in 1716.
While there she witnessed the custom among the
Turks of 'engrafting' for smallpox.  She at
once exerted her extraordinary epistolary powers
to procure the introduction of this great boon
into England and by great exertions happily
succeeded."  William Dummer was the donor
in 1726 of a flagon made by John Edwards
(1670–1746) to the First Church, Boston; of a
flagon, made by William Cowell junior (1713–61)
of Boston, to the Hollis Street Church and of
two cups, made by John Edwards, to the Byfield
Parish Church at Newbury, Massachusetts.
There may still be seen his farm and house as
well as Dummer Academy which he founded.
Jeremiah Dummer the silversmith was his father.

282. WILLIAM WHITTEMORE.  L. 2¼ in.

A silver snuff box (Illus. 282) inscribed : " S. Smith" was made by William Whittemore (1710–70) of Portsmouth in New Hampshire, whose mother was a sister of Sir William Pepperell.  He was the maker of three beakers given by his grandfather William Pepperell to the First Congregational Church, Kittery, Maine; of a beaker belonging to the Congregational Church, Newington, New

Hampshire, the gift of John Downing; and of a chalice in St. John's Church at Portsmouth given by Captain Christopher Rymes.

A snuff box (Illus. 283) with the London date-letter for 1819–20, belonging to Mr. George E. Brown, has in relief on the hinged cover a tavern scene after Teniers. It was given by the Duke of Sussex, son of George III, to Robert Ball Hughes

283. LONDON, 1819–20. L. 3⅜ in.

the sculptor who, before coming to the United States in 1829, had received for his busts of royalty and nobility, all the honors the Royal Academy could bestow. His statue of Alexander Hamilton — the first work executed in marble in the United States — for the Merchants Exchange at New York was unfortunately destroyed by fire in 1835. His model of an equestrian statue of Washington for the city of Philadelphia was unanimously accepted but the financial panic of 1837 prevented its erection in bronze; the original clay model in perfect preservation still exists.

Nutmeg boxes were small enough to be carried

in the pocket so that one might season the food when travelling. They did not come into fashion in England before the eighteenth century.

Aaron Hill wrote these lines on a window in Scotland:

"Tender-handed stroke a nettle,
     And it stings you for your pains;
Grasp it like a man of mettle,
     And it soft as silk remains.

'Tis the same with common natures:
     Use 'em kindly, they rebel;
But be rough as nutmeg-graters,
     And the rogues obey you well."

A cylindrical nutmeg box (Illus. 284) with a loose cover encloses a cylindrical grater which

284. H. 3¼ in.
JOHN COBURN.

must be removed to grate the nutmeg on to the food or drink; it has been presented to the Museum of Fine Arts, at Boston, by the Misses Rogers who are descendants of the maker, John Coburn (1725–1803) of Boston.

Owned by Mr. George S. Palmer is a small box (Illus. 285) circular in form, with a flat back and a hinged cover. On the back is inscribed: "The Rev.ᵈ G. W. to M. D." and on the front: "Rev.ᵈ George Whitefield, Ob.ᵗ 30 Sept. 1770 Ætatis 56." It belonged to Rev. George Whitefield, the celebrated preacher and

the founder of the Calvinistic
Methodists, who thrilled his
vast audiences by his eloquence
and powerful rich voice; he
died at Newburyport, Massachusetts, and his body was in-
terred before the pulpit of the
Presbyterian Church there.

285. COLONIAL.
H. 1½ in.

A nutmeg box (Illus. 286) belonging to Mr. J. D. H. Luce,
with the date-letter for 1792–93 and the maker's
mark RB, is oval in shape. When the top lid
is raised a grater, fixed to the box, is disclosed;
the powder, caught in the box below, was

286. LONDON, 1792–93.   L. 2⅛ in.

emptied by opening the bottom lid which is
hinged at the narrow part of the oval, to prevent opening the wrong lid by mistake.

## SUGAR–BOXES BOWLS TONGS

"VERY little sugar was used in England before the latter part of the seventeenth century. One of the earliest references to it in Great Britain is in a record of the shipment of 100,000 pounds to London from Venice in 1319; the same year the Chamberlin of Scotland purchased a quantity of sugar at the rate of 1s.9½d. per pound, which, having regard to the purchasing power of money in those days, was a very high price. About the end of the fifteenth century, the art of making loaf sugar was invented, but throughout Europe sugar continued to be a very costly luxury down to nearly the end of the seventeenth century, when the increasing consumption of tea and coffee brought it into the list of food staples." (c. j. j.)

Confiture boxes for sweetmeats were made in England at the time of Charles II and were regarded as necessary articles in the houses of persons of rank. In early New England wills they are referred to as sugar-boxes. An oval box (Illus. 287) made by John Coney (1655-1722) of Boston, with a convex body slightly everted at the rim, is embossed with twelve plain oval lobes divided by flutings terminating

in conventional leaves; it rests on four voluted
scrolled feet. The hinged cover, embossed and
chased, has a border of sixteen circular bosses;
on a matted ground are oak leaves radiating
from the centre where is affixed an applied
ring in the form of a convoluted snake. A plain

287. JOHN CONEY. L. 8½ in.

hasp pierced and serrated is hinged to the
moulded rim of the cover and is fastened to a
projecting staple on the body. It is inscribed:
"The gift of Grandmother Norton to Anna
Quincy born 1719." Rev. John Norton died
in 1716 and his widow went to live with her
daughter Elizabeth who married John Quincy:
the box was given to their daughter Anna
Quincy and has descended to her great-great-

granddaughter Mrs. Joseph R. Churchill who
has presented it to the Museum of Fine Arts at
Boston, as a memorial to her mother.

Small hemispherical bowls without covers
and vessels of the caudle cup form were probably
used in England when sugar was first placed
upon the table; and in the Colonies the porringer
was doubtless used for such purposes.   The next

type of the English
sugar bowl (Illus.
288) has a hemi-
spherical body
which rests upon
a moulded circular
foot; the saucer-
shaped cover with
the reel-shaped
handle-foot is simi-
lar to that of the
paten-cover of a
chalice.   It bears
the London date-

288. LONDON, 1728–29.   H. 3½ in.

letter for 1728–29 with the maker's mark for
John Gammon; and belongs to Judge A. T.
Clearwater.

A similar sugar bowl (Illus. 289) made by
John Coburn (1725–1803) of Boston, is decorated
with an engraved border of acanthus leaves
around the handle-foot.   The initials $_{I\ E}^{\quad S}$ are
those of Isaac and Elizabeth (Storer) Smith who
were married in 1746.   Elizabeth Storer was the

daughter of Eben-
ezer and Mary (Ed-
wards) Storer and
the granddaughter
of John Edwards
the silversmith. It
is called a sugar
dish in the inven-
tory of the estate
of Isaac Smith; it
is owned by the
Misses Cruft, his
descendants, who
also possess a por-
trait of Elizabeth
Smith by Smibert.

289. JOHN COBURN. H. 4 in.

John Burt (1691–1745) of Boston made a
similar sugar bowl (Illus. 290) with a cover that

290. JOHN BURT. H. 4 in.

2 D

has a very decided
shoulder; it has
been given to the
Museum of Fine
Arts at Boston, by
Miss M. H. Hinck-
ley a descendant
of Ebenezer and
Lucy (Davenport)
Turell who were
married in 1735
and whose initials
T
E L are upon it.

Rev. Ebenezer Turell in 1759 gave to the church
of Christ in Medford, of which he was pastor,
an unusually large tankard pounced with the
initials $\begin{smallmatrix} & C & \\ N & & E \end{smallmatrix}$ which cannot be traced to any of
the Turell family. As these same initials are
on a plate in King's Chapel wrought by the same
maker, Jeremiah Dummer, and referred to in the
will of Edward Mills junior as having belonged
to his grandfather Nathaniel Cary (and his wife
Elizabeth), it seems not unlikely that the Turell
tankard may be that bequeathed by Edward Mills
to his friend Jacob Wendell; the estate was
insolvent and the tankard may have been purchased by Ebenezer Turell. The very early
turned chair with a wedge-shaped seat known at
Harvard University as the "President's Chair"
has been sung by
Oliver Wendell
Holmes in "Parson
Turell's Legacy";
an illustration of
this chair is in
Irving Whitall
Lyon's "Colonial
Furniture of New
England," 1891.

291. JOSIAH AUSTIN.  H. 4½ in.

Owned by Mr.
Norman W. Cabot
is a sugar bowl
(Illus. 291) made
by Josiah Austin

(1719–80) of Charlestown, with a body of similar form supported on three feet; the saucer-
shaped cover with
a pierced finial
is surmounted by
three lions.

A sugar bowl
(Illus. 292) oc-
tagonal in section,
made by Jacob
Hurd (1702–58) of
Boston, belongs to
Miss Mary Weld
Allen.

A plain sugar
bowl of the in-
verted pear-shaped variety was made contem-
poraneously with tea and coffee pots of similar
form. A sugar bowl (Illus. 293) of this type,
made by Paul Revere (1735–1818) of Boston,
embossed in the rococo style with festoons of
fruit and flowers, has a centre panel enclosing the
Chandler arms; it is inscribed: "B. Greene to
L. Chandler." Benjamin Greene (1712–76) and
his brother Rufus Greene (1707–77) were silversmiths of Boston. Gardiner Greene, a wealthy
merchant of Boston and son of Benjamin Greene,
married Elizabeth Copley the daughter of John
Singleton Copley and sister of John Copley
who became Baron Lyndhurst and thrice lord
chancellor of England. Lucretia Chandler, the
sister-in-law of Benjamin Greene, was the

292. JACOB HURD. H. 4¼ in.

daughter of Judge John Chandler, the "honest tory" of Worcester, whose wife Hannah Gardiner was a descendant of Lion Gardiner of Gardiner's Island; the seven Gardiner sisters were famed for their beauty.

293. PAUL REVERE. H. 6¼ in.

The sugar bowl was given to Lucretia Chandler upon her marriage in 1761 to Colonel John Murray a tory who fled to the Provinces at the time of the Revolution ; upon his death his daughter Lucretia Murray returned and made her home with Mrs. Goodhue the daughter of Colonel Abijah Willard a tory who had also fled to the Provinces ; Lucretia Murray gave it to Joseph Willard, a descendant of Major Simon Willard of Colonial fame and an ancestor in the direct line of two presidents of Harvard College — Rev. Samuel Willard (1700–07) and Rev. Joseph Willard (1781–1804). The sugar bowl belongs to Miss Susanna Willard, a descendant.

Pierced sugar bowls fitted with colored glass linings were made in England in the second half of the eighteenth century; they were frequently vase-shaped with a high cover and often basket-shaped with a hinged handle. In the last quarter of the eighteenth century the English silversmiths made a sugar bowl of the basket shape but not pierced, which often formed part of a tea service. Belonging to Mrs. Alfred Winsor is an example of this type (Illus. 294) made by Paul Revere. The bowl is canoe-shaped with wide concave flutes radiating from the base which rests on a high spreading concave foot.

An example of a vase-shaped sugar bowl is that of the tea service (Illus. 251) made by Paul Revere.

Sugar tongs do not appear to have been made until the early part of the eighteenth century and are

294. PAUL REVERE.    H. 4⅝ in.

of a variety of forms. Some are like scissors with shell-shaped terminals; and others in bird form with long beaks to grasp the lump of sugar, were made in England from about 1750 to 1780.

A pair of scissor tongs (Illus. 295) given to the Museum of Fine Arts, Boston, by the Misses Rogers, was made by John Ball who wrought

in 1762 a beaker given by Captain James Eager and Lieutenant William Hollo-way to the First Church and Society at Northborough, Massachusetts ; also, five beakers in 1761 the gift of Mr. Joseph Brooks to the First Congregational Church at Lincoln, Massachusetts.

By far the largest number are bow-shaped with limbs like long-stemmed spoons, connected by an arch which has been so hammered that the limbs are flexible and spring open when the pres-sure is removed. A pair (Illus. 296) owned by the writer have acorn tips and are decorated with bright-

295. JOHN BALL.
L. 4¾ in.

cut engraving. They were made by John Hancock the son of John Hancock and Susanna Chickering, the granddaughter of Rev. Zechariah Symmes junior; the latter's sister Mary was the wife of Thomas Savage, the grandfather of the silversmith. John Hancock married in 1760 Martha Sparhawk; her grandfather was a brother of Rev. John Spar-

hawk, pastor of the church at Bristol in Rhode Island, to which he gave a beaker made by Knight Leverett (1703–53) of Boston. Nathaniel Sparhawk, his son, became the husband of Elizabeth Pepperell the daughter of Sir William Pepperell; their son, William, assumed the name of Pepperell and succeeded to the baronetcy.

From 1750 to 1790 the limbs were pierced and chased in various designs.

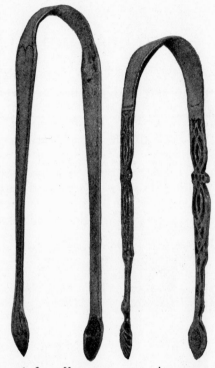

296. JOHN HANCOCK.
L. 6⅛ in.

297. AMERICAN.
L. 5½ in.

Without a maker's mark is the pair of tongs (Illus. 297) of this type, belonging to the writer.

In the late Georgian period the fiddle pattern prevailed in the United States.

## PITCHERS AND SAUCE BOATS

PITCHERS are invariably called jugs in England. When tea was first introduced into England it was not customary to use cream with it and not until the eighteenth century did small pitchers for this purpose come into fashion.

Cream pitchers with pear-shaped bodies, not unlike those of the bellied mugs, were made in England at the beginning of the reign of George II. Of this type is the small plain pitcher (Illus. 298) perhaps made by Josiah Austin (1719–80) of Charlestown, with a low circular foot; the open spout is applied over a V-shaped cut at the lip. It is owned by Mr. and Mrs. Henry W. Cunningham.

One of the most popular cream pitchers made in

298. JOSIAH AUSTIN? H. 3¼ in.

England was that
with a pear-shaped
body supported on
three applied scroll
feet. Of this de-
scription is the
pitcher (Illus. 299)
with a similar lip
and spout, owned
by Mrs. Nehemiah
Perry and made
perhaps by Tobias
Stoutenburgh, a
freeman of New
York in 1731.

299. TOBIAS STOUTENBURGH? H. 5 in.

The most com-
mon form of this
type of pitcher had an undulating lip, a much
everted spout and a double scrolled handle. The
pitcher (Illus. 300) made by Andrew Killeck,
with the London date-letter for 1746–47, belongs
to Miss Alice Hayes. In England this type was
very popular between the years 1735 and 1760
but continued to be made for a longer period. A
plain Colonial pitcher (Illus. 301) of this variety,
with the initials HC for Hannah Chauncey, is
owned by the Misses Parsons. It was made by
William Swan (1715–74) of Worcester, Massachusetts, who made the two-handled cup with
a cover now in the Essex Institute at Salem,
which is inscribed: "The Gift of the Province of the Massachusetts Bay to Benjamin

Pickman Esq.ʳ 1749." It was given to him in recognition of his financial aid at the time of the Louisburg expedition.

The pitcher (Illus. 302) made by Paul Revere (1735–1818) of Boston, is of the inverted pear-shaped variety which in England followed the

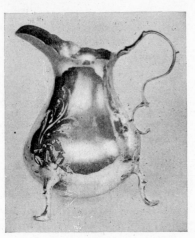

type with three feet; the high circular foot is gadrooned. The entwined initials SDS are those of Stillman and Deborah (Ellis) Smith who were married in 1762; it belongs to Miss Lucy W. Valentine, a descendant.

Belonging to Mr. Marsden J. Perry is a helmet-shaped pitcher (Illus. 303)

300. LONDON, 1746–47. H. 3⅝ in.

made by Joseph Richardson, with the London date-letter for 1750–51. It is decorated in the rococo style: similar pitchers made earlier in the century had three feet.

Cream pitchers in the shape of a cow with the tail looped to form the handle and in the middle of the back a small hinged cover with a bee in relief, were made in England during the reign of George II; the cream was poured out

through the mouth of the cow.  English examples are not common but modern reproductions, principally of Dutch make, are doubtless
familiar objects to many readers.

In the last decade of the eighteenth century,
a pitcher with a well-everted lip and a looped
handle had a coni-
cal body with a
circular foot rest-
ing on a square
plinth.  Of this
type is the pitcher
belonging to the
tea service (Illus.
251) made by Paul
Revere. The bodies
were wrought out
of sheet silver and
varied in shape, as
did the plinths.

Another type of
pitcher (Illus. 304)
made by James
Howell of Phila-

301. WILLIAM SWAN.  H. 3⅝ in.

delphia about 1810, was common at the end of
the eighteenth century.  The bottom is flat and
oval; the everted spout and lip is strengthened by
a beaded band and the handle is square-shaped.
Engraved upon the side is the initial C for
Coffin.  It belonged to Lucretia (Coffin) Mott
the famous preacher of the Quaker tenets —
obedience to the inward light and an adherence

302. PAUL REVERE. H. 5⅛ in.

to principles of peace — who was active in organizing the American Antislavery Society in Philadelphia in 1833. As a delegate to the World's Antislavery Convention at London in 1840 she was excluded from a seat, a majority denying the right of women to take part in public assemblies; she was a strong advocate of woman's rights. A maxim of hers: "Truth for authority, not authority for truth" is worthy of remembrance. The pitcher is now owned by a descendant, Mrs. Lucretia Mott (Hallowell) Churchill.

Large pitchers made in the late eighteenth and early nineteenth century often had

303. LONDON, 1750–51. H. 3⅝ in.

covers and were probably used for cider or punch. Joseph Moulton 2d (1740–1818) of Newburyport made the pitcher (Illus. 305) shaped and hooped like a barrel; a hinged strainer covers the spout. Upon one side is inscribed: "To Mr. Isaac Harris for his intrepid and successful exertions on the roof of the Old South Church when on fire, December 29ᵗʰ 1810 the Society present this token of their gratitude. Boston, January 29ᵗʰ, 1811." A representation of the fire is engraved upon the other side and in front are the initials IH. Isaac Harris is said to have ascended

304. JAMES HOWELL. H. 5 in.

the steeple and extinguished the flames; he had worked as an apprentice in the mast yard at Hartt's Naval Yard and had a share in the building of the *Constitution*. It was he and Samuel Bentley who first hoisted the stars and stripes over "Old Ironsides"; this was done contrary to orders while Commodore Nicholson, who had intended to reserve the honor to himself, was breakfasting. He put new masts in the famous frigate in 1812 and to him is attributed

305. JOSEPH MOULTON 2D.   H. 10½ in.

the important improvement of making masts
in sections.  The pitcher was presented to the
Museum of Fine Arts, Boston, by Mrs. Edward
Wyman, a descendant.

Sauce boats were made in England as early
as the first half of the eighteenth century.

Mr. Jackson thinks that they probably received the name from their resemblance to the hull of an oldfashioned boat.    English sauce boats sometimes had spouts at both ends with one or two handles in the middle — a form quite commonly seen in chinaware.    The more usual form had an everted spout at one end, the handle opposite and the body supported on three feet.

306. LONDON, 1736–37.    H. 3½ in.

Of this type is a sauce boat (Illus. 306) belonging to Dr. Samuel A. Green, with the London date-letter for 1736–37, which was made by Robert Brown.    A late inscription is: "From Mrs. Anna Winslow to her Nephew Joshua Green 1802."

Owned by Miss Margaret C. Wyman is one of a pair of sauce boats (Illus. 307) made by John Burt (1691–1745) of Boston.    The initials

AS
1750  are those of Ann Simpson who married
Nathaniel Glover September 27, 1750.

A sauce boat (Illus. 308) made by Benjamin
Burt (1729–1805) of Boston has a row of

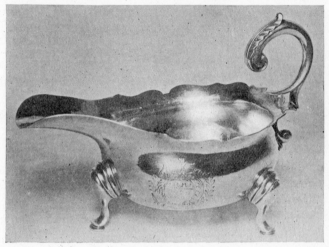

307. JOHN BURT.  H. 3½ in.

punched beads surrounding the lip for the pur-
pose of strengthening as well as decorating it.
In a circular panel are the entwined initials
NRP for Nathan and Rebecca Peirce who were
married in 1770.  It belongs to Miss Alice C.
Allyn, a descendant.

A sauce boat (Illus. 309) with the London
date-letter for 1785–86 and the maker's mark
TR, is engraved with the Hancock arms: it

308. Benjamin Burt. H. 4¾ in.

309. London, 1785–86. H. 3 in.

belonged to John Hancock and was bought at the sale of his effects by an ancestor of Mrs. Samuel Johnson, the present owner.

Small tureens made at a later date were used for sauce or gravy and, in all probability, for serving soup to one or two persons.

# PUNCH BOWLS

AMONG the numerous forms of drinking vessels in use in England from the thirteenth to the sixteenth century, that most highly esteemed by all classes was the common Mazer bowl. It was usually of maple wood highly polished, with silver mounts often wonderfully engraved and frequently gilt; sometimes it was fitted with a foot and stem. They varied in diameter from five to nine inches; and in height from one and a half to three and a quarter inches.

Silver bowls for mixing punch first appeared in England during the reign of Charles II. An early punch bowl in the collection of the late Mr. J. Pierpont Morgan bears the London date-letter for 1685–86. It has eight scallops cut into the rim to hold the stems of glasses which were placed with the feet outward. At that period a punch bowl came into fashion in England called a Monteith; this had a removable notched rim which held the glasses, and was so named from a "fantastical Scot called Monteigh" who wore a coat with a similar notched border.

The punch bowl (Illus. 310) belonging to Dartmouth College is fitted with a removable rim of this sort. It is inscribed: "His Excellency

310. DANIEL HENCHMAN. D. 10¾ in.

John Wentworth Esq$^r$. Governor of the Province of New Hampshire, And those Friends who accompanied him to Dartmouth College the first Commencement 1771. In Testimony of their Gratitude and good Wishes, Present this to the Rev$^d$ Eleazer Wheelock, D.D. President And to his Successors in that Office."

Sir John Wentworth, created a baronet in 1795, gave its charter to Dartmouth College; and Rev. Eleazer Wheelock was its founder and first president. The bowl was made by Daniel Henchman (1730–75) of Boston but the inscription was engraved by his brother-in-law Nathaniel Hurd whose initials are in the scroll below.

A plain bowl (Illus. 311) engraved on one side with the Dawes arms is inscribed on the opposite side: "The gift of the Field Officers and Captains of the Regiment of the Town of Boston to Thomas Dawes Esqr. for his past services as Adjutant to said Regiment Sept. 13, 1763." Thomas Dawes, an ardent patriot in the Revolution, was the architect who designed and built the Brattle Street Church in 1773; he was also the builder of the State House on Beacon Hill. The tories nicknamed him "Jonathan Smoothing-plane." He was a deacon of

311. William Homes. D. 9¾ in.

the Old South Church to which he bequeathed in 1809 a plain cylindrical flagon made by Joseph Moulton 2d (1740–1818) of Newburyport in Massachusetts. Thomas Dawes bequeathed the bowl to his grandson Thomas Dawes from whom it descended to Ambrose Dawes whose widow has fittingly presented it to the Museum of Fine Arts at Boston.   It was made by William Homes (1717–83) of Boston, known as the "honest goldsmith," whose mother was Mary Franklin sister of Benjamin Franklin; his wife was Rebecca Dawes an aunt of Thomas Dawes. William Homes was a member of the Old South Church in 1748 and held many public offices; 1st sergeant of the Artillery Company in 1752, 4th sergeant 1754, lieutenant 1761, captain 1765; he was clerk of the market in 1753; warden 1764; fireward 1764–70; purchaser of grain 1766–69.   His son

312. PAUL REVERE.  D. 11 in.

312. PAUL REVERE. H. 5½ in.

William Homes (1742–1825) was also a silver-smith and succeeded to the business.

Probably of greater historic interest than any other piece of Colonial silver is the plain bowl (Illus. 312) made by Paul Revere (1735–1818) of Boston which was ordered by the fifteen Sons of Liberty whose names are inscribed around the rim: John Marston, Ichabod Jones, John Homer, Will^m Bowes, Peter Boyer, Benj^a Cobb, Caleb Hopkins, Nath^l Barber, John White, Will^m Mackay, Dan^l Malcom, Benj^n Goodwin, John Welsh, Fortescue Vernon, Dan^l Parker.

This bowl is of the same shape as the punch bowl of Chinese porcelain in the British Museum, on which are painted portraits of John Wilkes and Lord Mansfield.

On one side of the bowl is the inscription:
"To the Memory of the glorious NINETY-
TWO : Members of the Hon.<sup>bl</sup> House of Representatives of the Massachusetts-Bay, who,
undaunted by the insolent Menaces of Villains
in Power, from a strict Regard to Conscience,
and the LIBERTIES of their Constituents, on
the 30<sup>th</sup> of June 1768, voted NOT TO RESCIND."

"The Illustrious NINETY-TWO recalls the defiance to the King given by the Massachusetts
House of Representatives in 1768. It was at
the time when the Ministry, forgetful of the
lessons taught by the Stamp Act, were again
attempting repressive measures against self
government in the colonies.

"The House of Representatives of Massachusetts early in 1768 had sent to London a
most vigorous protest against the policy of
the Ministry and one month later forwarded
a circular letter to the Assemblies of the sister
colonies, advising them of this measure and
suggesting some form of united action against
the policy of Parliament. The news of this
circular letter excited great indignation among
the Ministry, and the House of Representatives
of Massachusetts was peremptorily ordered
to rescind the letter. This they flatly refused
to do by a vote of ninety-two to seventeen.
This bold defiance awakened great joy throughout the Colonies. 'The Illustrious Ninety-
two' were glorified in song and toasted at all
political gatherings. The numerals 'ninety-two'

became a numerical symbol which appeared in public decorations, a political symbol which left no doubt as to the partisanship of the owner.

"The crude emblematical design on the opposite side testifies eloquently to the enthusiasm aroused in these Sons of Liberty by the splendid struggle John Wilkes was then making in England in defence of Constitutional Government. The bowl was made at the time when Wilkes was lying in the King's Bench prison, whither he had been sent shortly after his election to Parliament as a Representative from Middlesex. Gifts and congratulatory letters were showered upon him from all parts of England and America. Among them was one from the Sons of Liberty in Boston, in which Wilkes was informed: 'The friends of liberty, Wilkes, peace and good order assembled at the Whig Tavern to the number of Forty five, and upwards — took the first opportunity to congratulate his country, the British Colonies and himself, on his happy return to the land worthy of such an inhabitant.'

"The letter besought Wilkes to use his efforts in behalf of the Colonies, and humbly entreated that a reply be sent addressed to John Marston at the Whig Tavern. As Marston's name leads the list of owners, the bowl was probably kept at his long-time famous Tavern the 'Bunch of Grapes' in King Street (State), which in these times of excitement had gained the appellation 'Whig Tavern,' owing to its being the gathering place of the Sons of Liberty.

"The inscription, 'No. 45,' was the symbol adopted by the supporters of Wilkes and was derived from the 45th issue of his paper, the *North Briton*, in which appeared the especial attack upon the Royal policy which brought down the Royal wrath. The torn parchment, 'Generall Warrants,' is symbolic of the illegal warrant instigated by the King in 1763, which had permitted Wilkes to be arrested, his house to be searched and private papers stolen. The flags labelled 'Magna Charta' and 'Bill of Rights' were the emblems of Wilkes's fight for Constitutional Government." (R. T. H. H.)

Encircling the body of the bowl just above the moulded base is the following inscription: "This BOWL Commemorative of Events prior to the American Revolution, was purchased of the Associates whose names are inscribed upon its surface, by W^M MACKAY, one of their number, from whom upon his decease in Jan^y 1801, it passed to W^M MACKAY, his Son, and upon the demise of the latter, in Feb^y 1832, it became the property of W^M MACKAY, his Grandson in direct line, a Resident of the City of New York. The Associates were citizens of Boston." On the bottom is inscribed: "At whose death in 1873 it passed into the hands of his Brother Rob^t C. Mackay of Boston." "And Robert C. Mackay on March 11, 1902 trans- ferred it to Marian Lincoln Perry of Providence R. I. a great-great-granddaughter of John Mars- ton one of the fifteen Associates."

# JEWISH SYNAGOGUE SILVER

THE oldest Jewish synagogue in the country is that at Newport, Rhode Island, which was founded in 1713. As early as 1677 Hebrews had begun to settle on the island, coming from Spain, Portugal and Holland. Rabbi Isaac Touro was the first preacher and came from Holland. His son Judah Touro was born in Newport in 1775 and as a young man emigrated to New Orleans; in the war of 1812 he volunteered his services, enlisted under General Andrew Jackson and was severely wounded. Judah Touro was a wealthy merchant and a great philanthropist; he contributed quite as freely to Christian as to Hebrew charities. Amos Lawrence an equally philanthropic merchant of Boston promised $10,000 toward the completion of Bunker Hill monument provided as much more was raised; Judah Touro immediately sent his check of like amount. When the dedication of the monument took place June 17, 1843 in the presence of President Tyler with Daniel Webster as orator, these benefactors were commemorated in the following verse:

"Amos and Judah — venerated names,
Patriarch and prophet press their equal claims
    Like generous coursers, running neck and neck,
Each aids the work by giving it a check.
    Christian and Jew, they carry out one plan,
For though of different faith, each is in heart the same."

313. MYER MYERS.
H. 14 in.

In the Jewish synagogue at Newport are eight ornaments, known as Crowns of the Law; they are used as crowns for the wooden rollers, " ez hayyim," around which is rolled the Pentateuch which must be written on a scroll of parchment — the skin of a clean animal, whether beast or fowl.  One pair (Illus. 313) having crowns and bells is decorated with chased acanthus leaves, open flowers, strap ornaments and beading; and was made by Myer Myers a freeman of New York in 1746 and president of the New York Silver Smiths' Society in 1776. Another similar pair (Illus. 314) by the same maker is differently decorated, the bodies being engraved and

punched with flowers and
foliage; the gilt bells are
suspended from brackets;
they are engraved on the
stems Hays and Myers
from whom perhaps they
were a gift. A third pair
(Illus. 315) is hexagonal in
shape, some of the bells
being in arches, and six
others attached to chains;
the tops are open and em-
bossed with flowers; the
names Hays and Myers
are engraved upon the
stems of these also. The
remaining pair (Illus. 316)
of different shape is chased
with flowers and foliage on
the upper parts; the gilt
bells are suspended from
brackets. The pointer
(Illus. 317) is fluted diago-
nally, a human hand form-
ing the pointer.

314. MYER MYERS.
H. 14 in.

In the synagogue are
five bronze chandeliers; two given in 1760 by
Isaac Pollock and Napthali Hart Myers; two
in 1765 by Jacob Rodreques Reveira and his
son Abraham, and the fifth by Aaron Lopez
in 1770. The synagogue was dedicated in
1763.

In the oldest synagogue in London — the
Spanish and Portuguese Synagogue — founded
in the seventeenth century, the present building

315. Hays and Myers?
H. 14 in.

316. American.    H. 14 in.

dating from 1701, are several pairs of old silver Crowns of the Law, the earliest having been made in London in 1712–13.

317. AMERICAN. L. 12 in.

Belonging to the First Congregational Church and Society at Northborough, Massachusetts, is an inverted bell-shaped beaker without a maker's mark. It is inscribed: "The gift of M.ʳ Judah Monis Hebrew Professor of Harvard College to the Second Church in Westborough for the Use of the Communion Table Nov.ʳ 12ᵗʰ A : D : 1760." The donor was professor of Hebrew from 1722 to 1761; he was baptized by Nathaniel Appleton March 27, 1722 as the records of the First Church at Cambridge show: "Mr. Judah Monis, a jew by birth and education being converted to the Christian Faith owned yᵉ Covenant and was Baptised and Declared a Member in full Communion with the Church of Christ, after a prayer and Discourse made by Mr. Coleman from John 5, 46, and a Discourse of his own from Psal. 116, 10 answering the common objections of the Jews against Christ's being already come and giving confession of his faith in the Close. Sang part of the 110 Psalm. Which solemnity was performed in the College Hall. Soli Deo Gloria." Judah Monis was a brother-in-law of Rev. John Martyn, pastor of the church at Northborough.

# ROMAN CATHOLIC CHURCH SILVER

IF it were possible to make an examination of the silver which belongs to the Catholic churches of the country doubtless many interesting and valuable vessels would be discovered. The illustration of an urn which was presented by the Catholics of Boston to Charles Bulfinch, may be seen under that heading.

In St. Mary's Roman Catholic Church at Lancaster, Pennsylvania, founded in 1742, is an Italian silver-gilt ciborium (Illus. 318) which is the oldest piece of silver in any church in the country; it dates from about 1500 but has been restored in recent years. The high plain cover is surmounted by a cross; the plain body is enclosed in an open frame composed of vine and corn extending half way up the body; the stem has a large ornamental knop with diamond-shaped projections; the lower part of the stem and the base are enriched with Gothic ornament.

A ciborium of early nineteenth century American make is in St. Joseph's Roman Catholic Church at Philadelphia, Pennsylvania. The shallow bowl, decorated with foliage, is supported by a slender stem which rests on a moulded base. The domed cover is surmounted by a plain cross.

The large silver-gilt ciborium (Illus. 319) is German of about 1725. The conical bowl is embossed, or decorated in repoussé, with cherub faces and plain bosses and scrolls, leaving the lip plain; the cover is in two sections, the upper is fluted and the lower, decorated with large scrolls, has a fluted edge; a plain cross surmounts the cover. The stem is ornamented with scrolls, acanthus leaves

318. Italian, 1500.  H. 14 in.

and fluting. The eight panels on the top of the base are enriched with figures of the Holy Virgin and an ecclesiastic, as well as the Sacred Heart,

2 F

alternating with scrolls. The octofoil border is covered with plain bosses and scrolls on a matted ground. In a heart affixed to the base is inscribed: "Charlotte De Furstenberg Stulingen Chamoinesse De Munsterbilen 1725." As will be observed from this inscription, the ciborium was originally presented by Charlotte von Fürstenberg-Stülingen to the chapter of canonesses at Münsterbilsen in Limburg of which she was a member. It has been deposited in the museum of Georgetown Roman Catholic University in the District of Columbia.

Some old silver vessels (Illus. 320) from Jesuit

319. German, 1725.    H. 16 in.

missions in Maryland may also be seen in that
museum.    The plain old English chalice (No. 1)
of 1640–41 came from Newtown in Maryland.
The taller plain chalice (No. 2) has the Dublin
date-letter for 1814.    The pair of small silver-
gilt vase-shaped cruets (Nos. 3 and 5) with

320. ROMAN CATHOLIC CHURCH SILVER.

covers and scrolled handles, decorated with
reeds and vines, is of French make of about 1810.
A silver ostensorium (No. 4) with the top in the
form of a glory surmounted by a cross is probably French of about 1700 and came from the
old Maryland mission of St. Thomas.    A plain
silver chalice (No. 6) of the eighteenth century,
on a baluster stem, was used by the Rev. Samuel

Barber on the Eastern Shore of Maryland; it was given to the museum by Rev. Joseph Foley. The last chalice (No. 7) has a bell-shaped body supported by a stem to which three cherub heads are applied; the base is hexafoil in outline and engraved with a crucifix and a border of foliage. It was probably made late in the seventeenth century. This belonged to Rev. Father McAleer who died in 1881; it was presented to the Jesuit fathers by his niece Mrs. James McSherry.

# OTHER OBJECTS

AN object of very great interest is the historic inkstand (Illus. 321) in Independence Hall made by Philip Syng (1703–89) of Philadelphia in 1752 by order of the Assembly of Pennsylvania at a cost of £25.16.0. It was used by Isaac Norris and successive speakers until 1775, when it was relinquished to the Con-

321. PHILIP SYNG. L. 10¼ in.

tinental Congress: upon the signing of the
Declaration of Independence it was used by
every signer as he affixed his name. When
Washington presided over the convention which
framed the Constitution of the United States,
he too dipped his pen into this ink-pot. Transferred to Harrisburg, it was used by the Pennsylvania legislature until 1849 when it appears
to have been lost sight of : after many years'
search it was discovered in the possession of Mr.
Smull, former clerk of the house, in whose custody
it had been placed at that time. In 1875 the
inkstand was restored to Independence Hall on
June 7 — a day memorable in our annals.
On that day ninety-nine years previous, in 1776,
Richard Henry Lee offered his famous resolution : "That these United Colonies are, and of
right ought to be, free and independent States ;
that they are absolved from all allegiance to
the British crown ; and that all political connection between them and the State of Great
Britain is, and ought to be, totally dissolved."

Independence Hall also cherishes another
object of great historic interest — the "liberty
bell." Originally brought from England in 1752,
it became cracked and was recast the following
year, in Philadelphia, by Pass and Stow with
these prophetic words surrounding the upper
part : "Proclaim liberty throughout all the
land unto all the inhabitants thereof."

Small sauce pans with wooden handles, for
mulling wine and other beverages, were fre-

quently used in the first half of the seventeenth
century. Larger stew pans of the same form,
or cylindrical in body, were made as early as the
time of Charles II for serving the boiled or
stewed viands when placed upon the table, after
preparation in the kitchen. A large stew pan

322. JOHN CONEY. H. 4 in.

(Illus. 322) made by John Coney (1655–1722) of
Boston, engraved with the Dummer crest, is inscribed: "William Powell." It belongs to Mr.
Paul M. Hamlen, a descendant. William Powell
was the husband of Anne Dummer the daughter
of Jeremiah Dummer (1645–1718). A portrait,
by Copley, of Anne Dummer is in the possession
of Miss Annette P. Rogers, a descendant.

Siphons made in different sizes are frequently found. The small one (Illus. 323) belonging to Mrs. L. B. Taft was probably placed over the lip of a porringer serving the same purpose as a spout cup. Owned by Mr. Lawrence Park is a larger siphon, used for filling bottles, which bears the mark of Thomas Hamersly a freeman of New York in 1756: it belonged to Benjamin Bussey (1757–1842) a silversmith of Dedham,

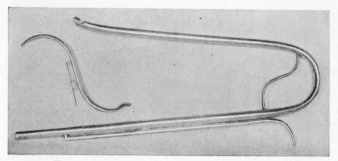

323. THOMAS HAMERSLY. L. 13¾ in. AMERICAN. L. 4¼ in.

Massachusetts, who became a "soldier in the Revolutionary army and was at the capture of Burgoyne." Benjamin Bussey was a benefactor of Harvard University; the grounds of the Arnold Arboretum are a portion of the gift.

Decanter stands were used when the fashion prevailed in England of removing the table-cloth for dessert; the decanters filled with wine were placed in the stands and sent "coasting" round the table in front of the guests who filled their glasses and passed the decanter. The name "coaster" was thus applied to them. A coaster (Illus. 324) one of a pair belonging to the writer, made by Edward Lowe with the London date-letter for 1772–73, is pierced, a form of decoration fashionable in England late in the eighteenth century, when all sorts of objects were thus made.

English bread baskets of oval form became popular from about 1740 and were produced in

324. LONDON, 1772–73. D. 4¾ in.

large quantities throughout the century. They were deemed a necessity on a well-appointed table, so much so, that recourse was had to the expedient of exchanging or melting older plate. There was hardly a house in England, if it boasted of any plate at all, without a silver bread basket. They doubtless served for fruit and cake, and in our country such baskets appear to have been used principally for the latter purpose. Many were wrought in pierced designs.

An effect somewhat similar to that of pierced work was obtained in the latter half of the

eighteenth century by making the frames of
baskets of silver wire and fixing on the wire
ornamental hammered work formed as floral
branches.    Similar   work   was   wrought   in
France   at   the   same   period.   A   wire-work

325. LONDON, 1767–63.   L. 13¾ in.

basket (Illus. 325) of this description, with the
London date-letter for 1767–68, was wrought
by the unknown maker of the four sauce tureens in Holburn Museum at Bath, England.
The oval base is embossed with flutings alternating with rows of beading which radiate
spirally from the centre; sprays of roses and

leaves, bunches of grapes and wheat-ears are attached to the wires; the edge is beaded and the swinging handle is arch-shaped. The basket belonged to Judge Theodore Atkinson who was born at Newcastle, New Hampshire, in 1697. He was the son of Colonel Theodore Atkinson and became secretary of the Colony in 1741; chief justice in 1754; and major-general of militia in 1769: but the Revolution deprived him of all these offices. He saw active service in the French and Indian wars and was collector of the port at Portsmouth. The basket belongs to Miss Alice A. Appleton, a descendant.

Knee and shoe buckles were made by the New England silversmiths in the eighteenth century. On the title page is the illustration of one of a pair of shoe buckles belonging to the writer. The frame, made of bronze, is overlaid on the front with silver; at the top and bottom are medallion portraits of Washington. At his death, all sorts of objects commemorative of Washington were made.

To form any adequate idea of the various objects wrought in silver the reader must be referred to such books as Mr. C. J. Jackson's "History of English Plate" and to the various volumes by Mr. E. Alfred Jones which contain illustrations or references to important and unique examples. In the luxurious reign of Charles II (1660–85) that "Merry Monarch" expended enormous sums on the apartments of his mistresses. A magnificent bedstead and many extravagant ornaments of silver were provided for Nell Gwyn. Tables and frames for looking-glasses were also overlaid with plates of silver. Fire-dogs, or andirons, massive wine cisterns, sconces and chandeliers were made for the rich and noble who could afford them. Because of the extravagant and ostentatious use of silver during the last quarter of the seventeenth century in England that period is referred to as the "silver age." A remarkable piece of silver furniture is the large and richly decorated throne and footstool of Peter the Great in St. George's hall in the Winter Palace, Petrograd, made by a London silversmith in 1713–14.

The Colonial silversmiths without doubt could have made many objects which they did not. They confined themselves to the ordinary requirements of their customers, making such vessels as are herein illustrated, but doubtless many other articles wrought by them have long since gone into the melting pot.

# INDEX TO SILVERSMITHS

445

# GENERAL INDEX

# The Fascinating Story of Spoons

O F ALL the articles and utensils that are used in the modern household there is none which can be traced to earlier beginnings than the spoon.

Besides having a fascinating history, a spoon is one of the loveliest, most graceful pieces used on the table.

Going back to its origins the first reference made to spoons is in the Bible, where Moses was commanded to make gold spoons for the Tabernacle.

During medieval times spoons were made of silver, horn or wood. Even though England is so closely associated with lovely silver designs, it was on the continent that silver spoons were used first . . . probably Italy.

After the silver spoons became popular in England, about the time of the Tudor and Stuart reigns, it became fashionable to give apostle spoons as Christening gifts. They were called apostle spoons because of the figure of an apostle at the end of the spoons. A complete set of these was very valuable, and were owned only by the wealthy families. This gave rise to the saying of "being born with a silver spoon in his mouth."

As is always true, the moment spoons became fashionable in the homes of the rich, they were copied in less expensive materials for people of limited means. Pewter and alchemy were two materials used extensively. Alchemy is somewhat like brass.

When New England was settled by the early colonists, they naturally brought their spoons with them, and the early American sliversmiths patterned their designs closely after the English spoons. It is easy to determine when American silver was made because it fol-

Apostle Spoon, in the Metropolitan Museum of Art.

lowed closely upon the styles set in England which was hall-marked or dated.

The rat-tail spoon came in the last part of the seventeenth century. They were called by this name because of the ridge, shaped like a rat's tail, which ran down the center from the tip of the handle to the beginning of the bowl. The bowl of the spoon was then perfectly oval. It was not until the time of our grandparents that the bowls of spoons became egg-shaped.

Modern silversmiths have the facilities for designing silver which is more nearly perfect in line and detail than the old craftsmen ever dreamed of, yet there is a naive charm in the irregularities of the early hand-wrought pieces. They have an individuality and distinction that has been lost to a certain extent in the age of mass production.